Charleston Conference Proceedings 2007

Charleston Conference Proceedings 2007

Edited by Beth R. Bernhardt, Tim Daniels, and Kim Steinle

Katina Strauch, Series Editor

LIBRARIES
U N L I M I T E D
A Member of the Greenwood Publishing Group

Westport, Connecticut • London

Library of Congress Cataloging-in-Publication Data

Charleston Conference (27th : 2007 : Charleston, S.C.) Charleston Conference proceedings, 2007 / Katina Strauch, series editor ; edited by Beth R. Bernhardt, Tim Daniels, and Kim Steinle.
p. cm.
Includes bibliographical references and index.
ISBN 978-1-59158-731-6 (alk. paper)
1. Library science—Congresses. 2. Library science—United States—Congresses. 3. Collection management (Libraries)—Congresses. 4. Electronic information resources—Management—Congresses. 5. Libraries and electronic publishing—Congresses. 6. Serials librarianship—Congresses. I. Strauch, Katina P., 1946– II. Bernhardt, Beth R. III. Daniels, Tim, 1963– IV. Steinle, Kim. V. Title.
Z672.5.C53 2008   2008028683
020—dc22

British Library Cataloguing in Publication Data is available.

Library of Congress Catalog Number: 2008028683
ISBN: 978-1-59158-731-6

First published in 2008

Libraries Unlimited, 88 Post Road West, Westport, CT 06881
A Member of the Greenwood Publishing Group, Inc.
www.lu.com

Printed in the United States of America

The paper used in this book complies with the Permanent Paper Standard issued by the National Information Standards Organization (Z39.48-1984).

10 9 8 7 6 5 4 3 2 1

Collection Development

Contents

E-Books

Journals

Technical Services and Cataloging

Miscellaneous

The 2007 (27th) Charleston Conference—Issues in Book and Serial Acquisition: What Tangled Webs We Weave—was held November 7–10, 2007, in Charleston, South Carolina. The weather was perfect, Charleston is fun to visit, and more than 1,000 librarians, publishers, vendors, aggregators, consultants, and others attended to discuss the serious business of content in the twenty-first-century library environment.

This volume represents just some of the 175 papers, issues, and discussions that occurred during the 27th Charleston Conference. The monograph is divided into five categories encompassing collection development, e-books, serials and e-journals, technical services workflow and cataloging, and miscellaneous subjects. The keynote address was by Clifford Lynch, Executive Director of the Coalition for Networked Information. Dr. Lynch spoke about the emergence of a variety of text and data mining technologies that are being used on large textual corpora of scholarly material and the implications of these new technologies on licensing agreements, delivery platforms, and editorial and authoring practices. He also considered implications of the linkages and interpenetration of content intended primarily for machine processing and texts targeted for human readers.

A paper by Deborah Wiley, Senior Vice President, Corporate Communications, John Wiley & Sons, followed Clifford Lynch's presentation. Deborah's 200-year-old company has managed to remain current in today's environment. Deborah pointed toward scenario planning as a necessary resource to navigate our emerging environments. Next, Greg Tananbaum's panel brought together several of scholarly communications' forward thinkers to gaze into the crystal ball of the future.

Friday's sessions began with a look at media publishing giants on the part of a seasoned lawyer, Bill Hannay, and was followed by an open access panel/debate/discussion run by Scott Plutchak, Director, Lister Hill Library of the Health Sciences, University of Alabama at Birmingham, and Rick Anderson, Associate Director for Scholarly Resources and Collections, University of Utah, both well known in open access circles.

Jane Burke, Vice President and General Manager, Serials Solutions, urged the audience and the library community to abandon silos and format-driven tools for integrated approaches to content. Ann Okerson's (Associate University Librarian, Yale University) panel urged librarians to meet not only traditional but also new, even unimagined, needs.

Saturday morning's sessions were designed to share perspectives on innovations in our environment. JoAnn Sparks, Director, Memorial Sloan Kettering Cancer Institute Library, spoke of structured serendipity as an old and new principle of content management. Next, Robert McDonald (Director, Strategic Data Alliances, San Diego Supercomputer Center, UC San Diego), and Elisabeth Leonard (President, Library Solutions) spoke about planning for change, innovation, and innovation theory.

Many of the papers in this monograph were presented during concurrent sessions, panels, or luncheons. One is struck in looking over the papers and reading about many of the plenary sessions by how much our community of librarians, publishers, and vendors is engaging in real "out of the box" thinking as we grapple to find our way in the expanding electronic world that libraries have become while still respecting our print resources.

We would like to extend our thanks to Beth Bernhardt, Tim Daniels, and Kim Steinle, who have edited this volume with love and care. The staff at Greenwood Publishing and Libraries Unlimited have also provided invaluable assistance and expertise and, we might add, patience! Thank you!

The 28th annual Charleston Conference will be held November 5–8, 2008, in Charleston. The theme is "The Best of Times/The Worst of Times." We invite you to come to historic Charleston this November for camaraderie, discussions, debates, and a little fun. Visit our Web site http://www.katina.info/conference.

See you soon!

Cordially,

Katina Strauch

Founder, Charleston Conference

Bruce Strauch

Owner, The Charleston Information Group, LLC

MSC 98, The Citadel, Charleston, SC 29409 USA

August 11, 2008

The Charleston Conference continues to be a major event for information exchange among librarians, vendors, and publishers. Now in its twenty-seventh year, the Conference continues to grow in popularity and interest. This year's Conference attendance was the largest ever. Conference attendees continue to remark on the informative and thought-provoking sessions. The Conference provides a collegial atmosphere in which librarians, publishers, and vendors talk freely and directly about issues facing their libraries and information providers. All this interaction occurs in the wonderful city of Charleston, South Carolina. This is the fourth year that Beth R. Bernhardt has put together the proceedings from the Conference and the third year for Tim Daniels and Kimberly Steinle. We are pleased to share some of the learning experiences that we, and other attendees, had at the conference.

The theme of the 2007 Charleston Conference was "What Tangled Webs We Weave." Although not all presenters prepared written versions of their remarks, enough did so that we are able to include an overview of such subjects as open access journals, electronic resources, and usage statistics. Topics also include issues related to collection development, e-books, and technical services workflows. The unique nature of the Charleston Conference gives librarians, publishers, and library vendors the opportunity to examine these and other points of interest holistically.

Katina Strauch, founder of the conference, is an inspiration to us. Her enthusiasm for the conference and the proceedings is motivating. We hope you, the reader, find the papers as informative as we do and that they encourage the continuation of the ongoing dialogue among librarians, vendors, and publishers that can only enhance the learning and research experience for the ultimate user.

Co-Editors of the 27th Charleston Conference proceedings

Beth R Bernhardt

Beth R. Bernhardt, Electronic Journals / Document Delivery Librarian, University of North Carolina at Greensboro

Tim Daniels, *PINES Program Manager, Georgia Public Library Service*

Kimberly Steinle, *Library Relations Manager, Duke University Press*

W hen you think of the Charleston Conference, you think of collection development. Collection development librarians find themselves looking for ways to evaluate resources accurately. Key topics essential to collection development were presented including different tools and ways to analyze, using consultants for collection assessment and transforming an academic business collection.

Collection Development

BOON OR BUST? INFLUENCES OF ONLINE VENDOR TOOLS ON LIBRARY ACQUISITIONS AND COLLECTION DEVELOPMENT

Jessica Bowdoin, Collection Development Librarian, George Mason University, Fairfax, Virginia

Lisa Sheets Barricella, Acquisitions Librarian, East Carolina University, Greenville, North Carolina

This paper presents the librarians' remarks from a panel consisting of both librarians and vendors which addressed the advantages and disadvantages of online vendor tools for library acquisitions and collection development.

Our discussions will include only some of the advantages and disadvantages of online vendor tools, based upon our own experience both due to the vendors' systems that we use and our libraries' workflows and implementations of these tools. Additionally, remember that not all advantages and disadvantages apply to all vendors or all libraries.

In collection development, one of our biggest concerns is the consolidation of business to one main vendor. Though this practice has many, many advantages, it can negatively impact the strength of libraries' collections, especially if selectors only order items available from one vendor.

Why will selectors order only from one vendor? It might be encouraged or required by the institution. The library might have access to one online vendor tool for selectors. Selectors may find it easier to spend their money and make their selections from the available titles in the online system. Regardless of the reason, a vendor database will have only a subset of all items published on a topic or in a discipline for any given year. For example, a vendor may only treat or cover 80 to 85 percent of physics books published in 2007, so if the selector only orders from that vendor, he or she will miss seeing the other 15 to 20 percent of physics books published in this year.

To avoid this disadvantage, some libraries establish relationships with multiple vendors to narrow the gap of missed titles and see a larger subset of the published materials in a given subject area. For example, a library establishes relationships with six vendors. Between all six vendors, the selector now sees 95 percent of the titles published in a discipline. Increased access to more of the literature is a good thing, but it comes at several expenses.

The costs include that it can be challenging to learn to navigate many different systems, for both selectors and acquisitions staff. In this scenario, people must learn multiple systems, each similar and different. The library probably will have to implement multiple workflows for each vendor. Library staff will have to check multiple places to determine if an item is already on order. Libraries will not be able to take fullest advantage of vendor services such as de-duping of duplicate orders.

If Technical Services imports from vendor systems, libraries must also implement custom settings to import records from each different system into their Integrated Library System. This setup, though it does save time in the long-run, can be time-consuming and difficult initially.

Each vendor system has different administrative tools and different levels of local controls for such things as turning on/updating link resolvers, creating user accounts, and setting permissions.

Many vendor systems only show list prices, not anticipated net prices or expected discounts, so libraries usually have to encumber funds at the list prices and wait until receipt of items to update records to reflect the actual net prices. This process can have a big impact on the managing and spending of funds.

Some vendor systems allow customer-entered records that are not verified or normalized by the vendor. These records can cause confusion among selectors, as information may be inaccurate, duplicated elsewhere in the vendor's database, or create false expectations of availability.

Along with unverified records, incomplete vendor records can be problematic. Examples of these records include volumes in a series where all volumes could have almost an identical record with the exception of the ISBN. This situation can create confusion with the selector and Acquisitions staff regarding the specific volume that should be ordered.

Finally, one disadvantage of some vendor tools can be the cost for access and use of the tool.

To highlight advantages, we will consider a case study of Joyner Library at East Carolina University. Joyner Library is in its second year of using our major book vendor's online ordering system as the exclusive way to place firm orders for monographic materials with that vendor. In fiscal year 2005–2006 we tested the vendor's online ordering system while still continuing to mail them some paper purchase orders. Prior to that, we sent all our purchase orders in paper format to the vendor via the U.S. Postal Service (USPS). All orders are finalized and submitted to the vendor by staff in the Acquisitions Department, but title selections are generated by librarian subject liaisons. From an Acquisitions perspective, the use of the online vendor system has proven to provide us with many advantages. Not only have we saved on postage and printing costs, but we are enjoying many additional benefits as well. In no particular order, here are some of the advantages.

An important advantage is the immediate notification of problems with the order and the ability to resolve questions about nonstandard orders such as duplicates and nonreturnable titles. Previously we were made aware of these issues by getting a query slip via USPS mail, or a call or e-mail from our customer service representative. Now, at the time of submitting an order electronically, we are immediately presented with an exceptions report, if applicable, and can communicate our decision to continue or cancel the order for a title via the online vendor system.

An advantage of particular interest to librarian subject selectors is the ability to view added information about the title, which can help drive purchasing decisions. From the online ordering system selectors can view such things as *Choice Reviews,* images of the table of contents and book jacket, and information about how many other libraries got the title as an approval book or placed a firm order for it.

Speed is the most notable advantage. The speed at which we are getting books in the building has greatly increased. Keep in mind that we previously mailed paper purchase orders, and therefore we had to add on the time for the purchase order to reach the vendor and for them to rekey the order information into their system. With online ordering, it is not unusual for our vendor to indicate that they have shipped the book three days after we have ordered it.

With shipping methods being fairly fast, we have had occasions where we have ordered a title on Monday, and it is in the building on Friday—and I am talking about normal orders, not rush orders. This also allows us to spend money quickly and encumber our funds later into the fiscal year than ever before. We no longer have to worry about whether an invoice for a last-minute order will arrive before the end of the fiscal year. We can print invoices directly from the vendor's online ordering system and send them to our Accounts Payable office within a couple of days of placing the order.

A reduction in the chance for human error leading to the receipt of the wrong title is another advantage. Admittedly we never had a problem with this, but the fact that all our orders used to be rekeyed from a paper purchase order into the vendor ordering system created the possibility that a mistake could be made during data entry. Online ordering eliminates the possibility of errors during rekeying.

Ease of sharing title notifications has been enjoyed by both Acquisitions staff members and librarian subject selectors. In the past, new title notifications came in paper format and had to be sorted and sent to subject selectors by a member of the Acquisitions Department. The weekly sorting of the notification slips was time-consuming, and we could only send a title notification to one selector even if the notification would have been pertinent to several of them. With the online ordering system, each librarian subject selector now has access to view notification slips that they would never have received in paper format. Not only does this help them catch new titles in interdisciplinary subjects, but they can also e-mail the notifications to other selectors or to their teaching faculty contacts.

Most helpful has been the ability to see stock-level information and the status of a title. At any point, we can search a title in the vendor's online ordering system and see if it has been selected, ordered, shipped, etc. Further, stock-level information helps librarian subject selectors decide whether to order a title right away or if they can wait. A selector might earmark a book with normal stock levels for purchase later in the fiscal year if funds allow, but a book with low stock level might get chosen immediately to ensure the library obtains a copy.

Another advantage to using a vendor's online ordering system is how easy it can be to cancel a title. If the status of a title shows as ordered but not yet shipped, oftentimes there is a way to cancel the order with the click of one button.

The ability to download order records, which are created as a result of using our vendor's online ordering system, has been advantageous as well. Every day, an Acquisitions staff member imports these records into our Integrated Library System and uses them to automate the process of creating purchase orders. In addition, we have saved the time that staff previously spent on searching and downloading records from OCLC. This also reduces the time it takes for a record to appear in our catalog indicating that a particular title is on order.

A benefit that some libraries have taken advantage of is to use the Open URL feature common to many online vendor ordering systems. Open URL allows a user to search the vendor database and their library catalog simultaneously. This searching feature saves time by eliminating separate preorder searching. This setup can also work in a consortia setting by allowing the user to see how many copies are available by other member libraries.

As an Acquisitions manager, it has been helpful to be able to print additional copies of invoices and statements directly from the online ordering system without having to request that the vendor send the duplicates via USPS mail. If we have lost paperwork, want to reconcile our monthly statement early, or simply cannot wait for an invoice to arrive with a shipment of books, we can go into the online ordering system and print copies ourselves any time we want.

A final advantage to highlight is the reporting features. The variety and usefulness of the reports available from within the vendor's online ordering system has been very helpful. From open-order reports, to expenditure reports, to approval plan activity reports, we have a lot of information available to us. We can create, view, and save all the reports in a variety of formats, such as HTML, PDF, and Excel, and the ability to access the data ourselves has helped us provide statistics to library administrators.

These eleven advantages are by no means an exhaustive list, and no doubt some important ones might have been left off. The eleven are the ones that Joyner Library's Acquisitions Department and librarian subject liaisons have found most beneficial and have made using the vendor's online ordering system worthwhile.

These comments were followed by comments from four vendors, who also discussed advantages and disadvantages of online vendor tools from their perspectives. Vendor participants included representatives from Coutts, Blackwell's, YBP, and OCLC Selection Service.

BEYOND EXCEL AND ACCESS FOR DUMMIES: CREATIVE USE OF WEB-AUTHORING TOOLS TO MAKE LIBRARY DATA ACCESSIBLE FOR A BROADER AUDIENCE

Susanne Clement, Head of Collection Development, University of Kansas, Lawrence, Kansas

As part of communication with both internal and external constituencies, libraries impart a tremendous amount of data. We collect and disseminate data about the number of items we have in our collections, the number of transactions conducted in libraries—anything from amount spent on collections to the number of items circulating; the number of interlibrary loan transactions; the number of patrons asking for reference assistance, etc. Much of this data is pretty simple—both to collect and to disseminate and generally consists of a single number for each category.

However, not all library data is that easy to disseminate and most library data resides within databases. Some library data is much more complex, and in order to understand all the complexities of the data, a certain amount of manipulation is necessary to discover scope and connections. For instance, how do you communicate the complexities of having to cancel journal titles and which titles can or cannot be cancelled? How do you communicate which print titles may or may not have online counterparts and that not all online access is equal? A simple spreadsheet can communicate some of this information, but if the user is not adept at using the spreadsheet's SORT features, the information is often confusing or overwhelming.

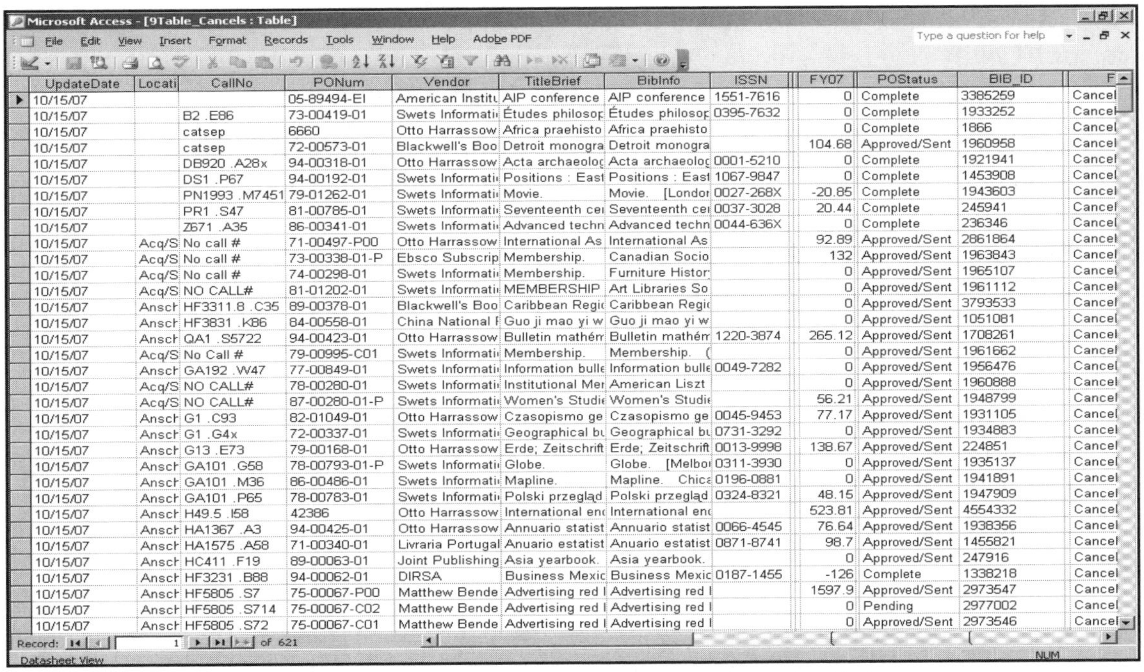

UpdateDate	Locati	CallNo	PONum	Vendor	TitleBrief	BibInfo	ISSN	FY07	POStatus	BIB_ID	F
10/15/07			05-89494-EI	American Institu	AIP conference	AIP conference	1551-7616	0	Complete	3385259	Cancel
10/15/07		B2 .E86	73-00419-01	Swets Informati	Études philosop	Études philosop	0395-7632	0	Complete	1933252	Cancel
10/15/07		catsep	6660	Otto Harrassow	Africa praehisto	Africa praehisto		0	Complete	1866	Cancel
10/15/07		catsep	72-00573-01	Blackwell's Boo	Detroit monogra	Detroit monogra		104.68	Approved/Sent	1960958	Cancel
10/15/07		DB920 .A28x	94-00318-01	Otto Harrassow	Acta archaeolog	Acta archaeolog	0001-5210	0	Complete	1921941	Cancel
10/15/07		DS1 .P67	94-00192-01	Swets Informati	Positions : East	Positions : East	1067-9847	0	Complete	1453908	Cancel
10/15/07		PN1993 .M7451	79-01262-01	Swets Informati	Movie.	Movie. [London	0027-268X	-20.85	Complete	1943603	Cancel
10/15/07		PR1 .S47	81-00785-01	Swets Informati	Seventeenth ce	Seventeenth ce	0037-3028	20.44	Complete	245941	Cancel
10/15/07		Z671 .A35	86-00341-01	Swets Informati	Advanced techn	Advanced techn	0044-636X	0	Complete	236346	Cancel
10/15/07	Acq/S	No call #	71-00497-P00	Otto Harrassow	International As	International As		92.89	Approved/Sent	2861864	Cancel
10/15/07	Acq/S	No call #	73-00338-01-P	Ebsco Subscrip	Membership.	Canadian Socio		132	Approved/Sent	1963843	Cancel
10/15/07	Acq/S	No call #	74-00298-01	Swets Informati	Membership.	Furniture Histor		0	Approved/Sent	1965107	Cancel
10/15/07	Acq/S	NO CALL#	81-01202-01	Swets Informati	MEMBERSHIP	Art Libraries So		0	Approved/Sent	1961112	Cancel
10/15/07	Ansch	HF3311.8 .C35	89-00378-01	Blackwell's Boo	Caribbean Regi	Caribbean Regi		0	Approved/Sent	3793533	Cancel
10/15/07	Ansch	HF3831 .K86	84-00558-01	China National I	Guo ji mao yi w	Guo ji mao yi w		0	Approved/Sent	1051081	Cancel
10/15/07	Ansch	QA1 .S5722	94-00423-01	Otto Harrassow	Bulletin mathém	Bulletin mathém	1220-3874	265.12	Approved/Sent	1708261	Cancel
10/15/07	Acq/S	No Call #	79-00995-C01	Swets Informati	Membership.	Membership. (		0	Approved/Sent	1961662	Cancel
10/15/07	Ansch	GA192 .W47	77-00849-01	Swets Informati	Information bulle	Information bulle	0049-7282	0	Approved/Sent	1956476	Cancel
10/15/07	Acq/S	NO CALL#	78-00280-01	Swets Informati	Institutional Me	American Liszt		0	Approved/Sent	1960888	Cancel
10/15/07	Acq/S	NO CALL#	87-00280-01-P	Swets Informati	Women's Studi	Women's Studi		56.21	Approved/Sent	1948799	Cancel
10/15/07	Ansch	G1 .C93	82-01049-01	Otto Harrassow	Czasopismo ge	Czasopismo ge	0045-9453	77.17	Approved/Sent	1931105	Cancel
10/15/07	Ansch	G1 .G4x	72-00337-01	Swets Informati	Geographical bu	Geographical bu	0731-3292	0	Approved/Sent	1934883	Cancel
10/15/07	Ansch	G13 .E73	79-00168-01	Otto Harrassow	Erde; Zeitschrift	Erde; Zeitschrift	0013-9998	138.67	Approved/Sent	224851	Cancel
10/15/07	Ansch	GA101 .G58	78-00793-01-P	Swets Informati	Globe.	Globe. [Melbo	0311-3930	0	Approved/Sent	1935137	Cancel
10/15/07	Ansch	GA101 .M36	86-00486-01	Swets Informati	Mapline.	Mapline. Chica	0196-0881	0	Approved/Sent	1941891	Cancel
10/15/07	Ansch	GA101 .P65	78-00783-01	Swets Informati	Polski przegląd	Polski przegląd	0324-8321	48.15	Approved/Sent	1947909	Cancel
10/15/07	Ansch	H49.5 .I58	42386	Otto Harrassow	International en	International en		523.81	Approved/Sent	4554332	Cancel
10/15/07	Ansch	HA1367 .A3	94-00425-01	Otto Harrassow	Annuario statist	Annuario statist	0066-4545	76.64	Approved/Sent	1938356	Cancel
10/15/07	Ansch	HA1575 .A58	71-00340-01	Livraria Portugal	Anuario estatist	Anuario estatist	0871-8741	98.7	Approved/Sent	1455821	Cancel
10/15/07	Ansch	HC411 .F19	89-00063-01	Joint Publishing	Asia yearbook.	Asia yearbook.		0	Approved/Sent	247916	Cancel
10/15/07	Ansch	HF3231 .B88	94-00062-01	DIRSA	Business Mexic	Business Mexic	0187-1455	-126	Complete	1338218	Cancel
10/15/07	Ansch	HF5805 .S7	75-00067-P00	Matthew Bende	Advertising red I	Advertising red I		1597.9	Approved/Sent	2973547	Cancel
10/15/07	Ansch	HF5805 .S714	75-00067-C02	Matthew Bende	Advertising red I	Advertising red I		0	Pending	2977002	Cancel
10/15/07	Ansch	HF5805 .S72	75-00067-C01	Matthew Bende	Advertising red I	Advertising red I		0	Approved/Sent	2973546	Cancel

Figure 1. Access report of journals considered for cancellation.

Most librarians are able to create and use simple spreadsheets—such as those created in Microsoft Excel—and many are very adept at creating and utilizing more advanced spreadsheets. Creating and using databases—such as Microsoft Access—tends to be more complicated. The information contained in a database is extensive and contains much more information than our users will ever need to know. Most are able to use readymade reports, but few of us have sufficient experience in running queries and creating reports to take full advantage of all the data elements within the database. We can generate reports that extract certain data fields, thus making it easier for users. But again, it may require multiple reports, and it does not allow any flexibility in the way the data is displayed.

Use of Data: Examples from the Business World

Who has not purchased something via the Internet? Generally, we like the convenience of buying goods online but only if it is easy to navigate the Web site. Can anyone imagine having to run a query before being able to pull up a list of merchandise fitting certain parameters? Libraries can learn a lot from business and how they use web authoring tools to communicate what data, or merchandise, is available. Web authoring tools can be used to represent complex library data, but this paper will not demonstrate how to do the programming; rather it demonstrates the benefits of having somebody on your staff, either hired or trained, to use these tools well.[1]

Though most companies use some kind of inventory database system to tract their products, nobody can imagine a company such as the toy store F.A.O. Schwarz (http://www.fao.com/home.jsp) posting their products directly from their inventory database through either an Excel or Access interface. It is not beyond reason to assume that the F.A.O. Schwarz product database is fairly similar in its structure to the Access database displayed in Figure 1 listing library journals.

In its public interface, F.A.O. Schwarz has used a web authoring tool, ColdFusion, that allows users to almost seamlessly and intuitively extract related information from the product database.[2] ColdFusion is an Adobe product that many web designers consider quite easy to learn and use and which works very well with both Excel and Access.

The F.A.O. Schwarz Web site provides many ways of interacting with the products—from building your own toys to searching within various toy collections. Even toys on sale have been separated from the main collection through its outlet feature and, once there, a different kind of organization is available. All product information is pulled from the central database—the web authoring tool makes it possible to organize content in multiple ways.

eBags (http://www.ebags.com/) is another example of how a company is using ColdFusion to represent complex data pulled from a central database. Again, it is all about choice and assistance in how to narrow these choices in an easy to understand manner: broad category, designer and brand, characteristics, size, color, etc.[3] Many other companies and organizations use ColdFusion to display their data, including AT&T Wireless, Bank of America, Crayola, Foot Locker, The Limited, New York Giants, Peace Corps, Pepsi, PGA of America, Pottery Barn, Simon & Schuster, and Sprint.[4]

Learning from Businesses

Library data is often collected and presented in databases and spreadsheets and distributed to library staff as files linked from the library's Web site or stored on shared servers. However, when analyzing the data requires more than an elementary knowledge of Access or Excel, many users may be unable to take full advantage of the data. Just like businesses, libraries also have a need to present data in easy-to-use formats—both internally and externally. Using ColdFusion to access and display up-to-date library information through the library's

Web site can make complicated information more accessible and easy to use. At the University of Kansas (KU) Libraries, we have found that ColdFusion has greatly enhanced our ability to interact with and interpret data in a meaningful way with few or no additional skills required. At KU, ColdFusion has been used to present information for a recent serials review (external use), for annex selection review (external), and lost book reports (internal), as well as other smaller internal projects such as publisher title list evaluations.

Serials Review

During the last round of the Libraries' serials review (FY07), ColdFusion was used to display the combined list of journal titles that had been selected by librarians and faculty within various fund disciplines for cancellation. Since much research is multidisciplinary, it is not possible to assume that titles in support of a single discipline are only used by that discipline. Just as F.A.O. Schwarz and eBags provided many different ways to look at their various products, so we wanted to provide as much flexibility as possible in the way the titles could be reviewed.

The source data is in the main Voyager controlled database where all bibliographic information is contained. ColdFusion lists the data elements in the order needed for each of the display options. Without the use of ColdFusion each of the configurations would require its own table and report, but with ColdFusion it was possible to extract the various data elements from the main Voyager database queries so the titles could be displayed by call number, broad subjects, and fund/discipline in addition to title.[5]

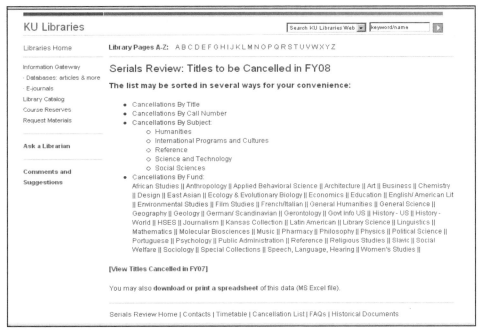

Figure 2. Serials review Web site displaying various options for displaying data.

Annex Selection

At KU, we have also used ColdFusion to facilitate faculty online review of titles selected to go to the Library Annex, an off-site high-density storage facility. ColdFusion has been used to take a Voyager report and display titles that have not circulated—thus being slated for transfer to the Library Annex. A main criterion for online review was to make the listings reasonably easy to use, but more importantly to make it easy for faculty to make recommendations to keep titles in the central campus browsable collections. Depending on the type of material being reviewed, we changed the information that displays on the screen. So, for instance, when we reviewed material from the Art Library, format and language were also included. By clicking on the call number, a shortened bibliographic record appears together with a comment box. Faculty can then easily indicate in the box why something should not go to the Annex, then click the button and return to the titles just selected—not to the beginning of the list. We discovered that minor additional coding was necessary to return to the last record selected. Otherwise it would return to the beginning of the list—quite infuriating when the title lists are very long.

As administrators of the site, we collect the records that have messages attached to them and can thus act on any title requested by faculty to stay in the browsable collections. Should we have questions about a recommendation, the log-in procedure allows us to identify the person who made the recommendation and to be in touch with that person. We have used this format for almost two years and have not had any complaints about its usability.

Lost Book Reports

Another very useful adaptation of ColdFusion technology is used for internal review of Voyager-generated lost book reports. A number of years ago, the library changed its method of declaring books lost. The system now automatically declares any book lost once it is more than twenty days overdue. This change has worked well for circulation but has had a negative impact on other units. Before the change, lost book reports were generated a couple of times a year, and bibliographers used these for the purpose of replacing significant titles. However, with the change the automatic report is no longer useful—not only is it significantly longer (hundreds of titles) but, as the majority of initially declared lost titles will eventually be returned, bibliographers would have to look through very lengthy reports to distinguish between late titles and those actually lost.

Running the Voyager-generated report through ColdFusion has, however, changed the usability of the lost book report. We are now able to distinguish easily between Voyager-generated lost title and what is coded as a library applied lost title only after the patron has informed the library that the book is definitely lost. As the original report also collects other data—such as patron group and location—the ColdFusion generated report allows for that level of specificity should that be useful. For example, we are now able to easily see which call numbers have the most lost books and what patron group is most responsible for that loss, from which library locations, etc. No surprises here—undergraduates tend to lose literature titles the most. Faculty, however, are not immune either, and on a couple of occasions when a faculty member has complained that only undergraduates lose books, we now have readily available and easy-to-interpret data to show otherwise.

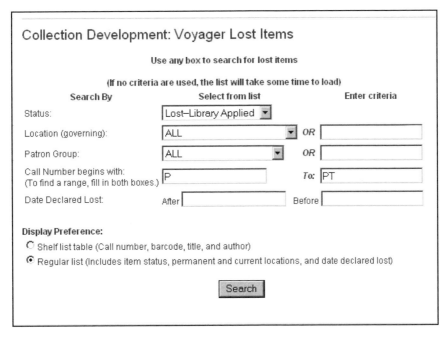

Figure 3. Searchable lost books report.

Conclusion: Why Use These Tools and Who Should Be Doing It?

So what are some of the features of ColdFusion that allow for these very easy-to-use displays, and how is it different from tools such a Dreamweaver? It is possible to use Dreamweaver to write ColdFusion pages, just as you could use a tool like Windows Notepad. However, it would be more labor intensive. You can use several other scripting languages such as ASP, JSP, etc. with Dreamweaver, or it can be used to create simple static pages.

The components (from ColdFusion documentation) are:

- Application server: the program that parses (reads and interprets) and processes supplied instructions

- CFML: tag-based language similar to HTML that uses special tags and functions, allowing the user to enhance standard HTML files with database commands, conditional operators, and high-level formatting functions, and rapidly produce easy-to-maintain web applications

- Administrator: used to configure and maintain the ColdFusion application server. It is a Web-based application that you can access using any Web browser, from any computer with an Internet connection.

However, more importantly, why should libraries try to emulate businesses in the way they display information, and who should be doing this work?[6] Assessment is increasingly important for libraries, and if we want to distribute our data broadly, we will make it easier for both internal and external users if we make the data easy to manipulate and use. It is very time-consuming to train staff to use library data effectively, and if Excel and Access are not used frequently, most of us forget how to use these tools well. Adding or training one person to manipulate the data and make it accessible for a broad audience is, in the long run, much more cost effective. Further more, it ensures that the right data is being used—any changes to the data is done only once and centrally. It may take some time to train a current staff member to become proficient in using web authoring tools, but once you have such a person on board the benefits are immeasurable.

Notes

1. Special thanks go to Monica Claassen-Wilson, KU Libraries Collection Development Program Assistant, for envisioning what the web authoring tool can accomplish and for learning how to use it effectively. All the ColdFusion enabled reports that we use are her creations.

2. http://www.fao.com/home.jsp (accessed November 1, 2007, and January 1, 2008).

3. http://www.ebags.com/ (accessed November 1, 2007, and January 1, 2008).

4. Information obtained from ColdFusion Web site http://www.adobe.com/products/coldfusion/customers/ (accessed several times during October 2007 and on January 1, 2008).

5. Alternate access is not a distinct search feature, but it is an important data element that has been present in all the display options.

6. I want to thank the audience attending my presentation at the 2007 Charleston Conference for their questions and input as it helped fine-tune some of these conclusions.

REVIEW OF THE ILL ANALYSES OF THE WORLDCAT COLLECTION ANALYSIS TOOL AS A RESOURCE TO GUIDE STRATEGIC COLLECTION DECISIONS

Hilary Davis, Collection Manager for Physical Sciences, Engineering & Data Analysis, North Carolina State University, Raleigh, North Carolina

Annette Day, Associate Head, Collection Management, North Carolina State University, Raleigh, North Carolina

Introduction and Context

Here we provide an evaluation of one of the recent enhancements of the WorldCat Collection Analysis (WCA) service, the ILL Analyses module, introduced in April 2007. In our evaluation of the ILL Analyses from WCA, we focus on this particular module as a resource (among many) that may help to guide strategic collections decisions. We also compare and contrast the ILL Analyses from WCA with our local ILL (interlibrary loan) data.

We have investigated ILL data from the WCA as a piece of the entire range of data sources that we use to make collections decisions that are attuned to the diversity and depth of our users' needs. It should be made evident that ILL data from any source should be considered only in context with other information that collection managers/collection developers use, such as subject knowledge, knowledge of resources in the field, knowledge of programmatic and research areas, circulation data, faculty and student feedback, accreditation needs, and so on.

At the NCSU Libraries, we try to consider all relevant sources of data (quantitative and qualitative) so that we can make the best-informed decisions about building our collections. We have been using the main WCA service for a variety of projects including peer comparisons, filling in gaps, isolating unique collections for potential digitization efforts, and developing our special collections. The ILL Analyses module includes approximately 95 percent of our ILL transactions as captured by OCLC, and, therefore, can be considered robust enough to use as another source to guide collections decisions.

As context for our investigation into the ILL Analyses in WCA, some details about North Carolina State University and our library are necessary. As part of our overall mission, our library supports over 31,000 students and 8,000 faculty members in areas focusing on engineering, science/technology, mathematics, and veterinary medicine. NCSU is ranked third in industry-sponsored research spending compared to all public universities (without a medical school focused on human medicine) and recently our university has been ramping up support for biomedicine and human medicine programs and research. This major growth trend is something we have had anecdotal knowledge of, but we needed evidence to justify increased spending focus and funding requests. The NCSU Libraries is also a member of the Association of Research Libraries and a member of the Triangle Research Libraries Network (TRLN), our local consortium including University of North Carolina—Chapel Hill, Duke University, North Carolina Central University, and North Carolina State University. All of these elements will come into play as we review the ILL data from WCA.

Evaluation Questions

So with context and rationale in place, we pose a series of questions for our evaluation. First, we wanted to know if the ILL Analyses from WCA could help us identify subject areas where there is a clear need for resources that are not already part of our collection. If we identified an area with a demonstrated need, we wanted to know if the need for resources in that subject is format-specific, that is, for serials, books, or other formats. We also wanted to know if the ILL Analyses could actually tell us exactly which books and serials are in highest demand and how many requests are coming from our users for those resources. Along those same lines, we wanted to know if what we are lacking in our collection is older content or newer content. With regard to our local library consortium, TRLN, we wanted to know how much of our users' ILL requests are being filled by TRLN. Cooperative collection development is practiced by TRLN, so if much of our material needs could be filled efficiently within our consortium, this may impact our decisions on whether we needed to fill those gaps in our local collection.

In the rest of this paper, we will move through each of those questions and show you to what extent the ILL Analyses in WCA were able to address our needs. Our findings are represented graphically, but the point should be made that these graphs are not the actual output of the WCA Analyses module. We have taken the data generated from the WCA reports and created these graphs ourselves.

Results

Right away we saw that our suspicions about the increasing demand for health- and human medicine–related subjects were verified. Figure 1 demonstrates the number of requests across 3.5 years of data provided by the ILL Analyses in WCA spanning mid-2003 through mid-2007. The subject in the most demand is Health Professions and Public Health with over 20,000 requests in a 3.5 year period—that is nearly 17 requests per day. It should be noted that the subjects listed in the figures that follow are based on the OCLC Conspectus of subjects, which is, itself, based on multiple classification schemes. For example, the Health Professions and Public Health subject division is mapped primarily to National Library of Medicine classification and secondarily to Library of Congress Subject Headings. The bottom line is that these are the subject divisions provided by WCA, and in application of the tool, users have no control over how the subjects are defined. One can, however, use the OCLC Conspectus to review call number mapping.

While we can determine the scale of need for subjects, frequency of need is also relevant. To help prioritize where to focus our collection decisions, we may need to concentrate on those with higher frequencies as we may not be overly concerned right away about items requested one time over 3.5 years. Figure 2 shows the requests made by our users by three levels of frequency—number of items requested two to five times during the 3.5-year period, number of items requested six to ten times, and number of items requested more than 10 times. The majority of requests are those that fall in the need category of two to five requests over the 3.5-year period. Again, Health Professions and Public Health stands out has having the most items that are requested six to ten times and more than 10 times.

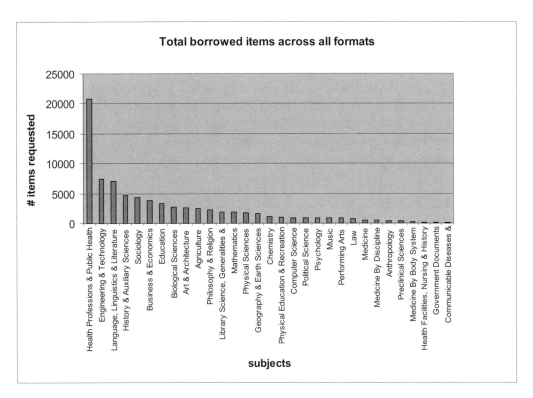

Figure 1. Number of requests across 3.5 years of data provided by the ILL Analyses in WCA spanning mid-2003 through mid-2007.

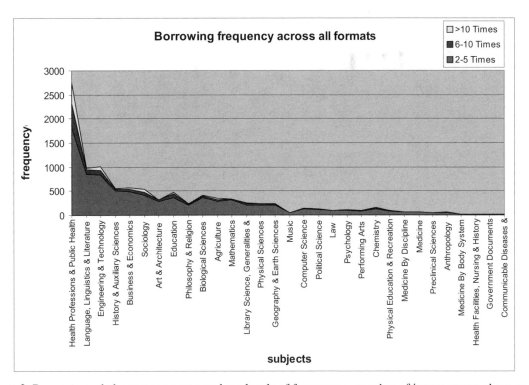

Figure 2. Requests made by our users across three levels of frequency—number of items requested two to five times during the 3.5-year period, number of items requested six to ten times, and number of items requested more than 10 times.

Using the data from the ILL Analyses, we were also able to determine if any of the requests were anomalies or if the pattern of need was consistent from year to year. In nearly all of the top ten most requested subjects, the need is increasing; however the demand is still greatest in Health Professions and Public Health. We know that the research needs of our faculty and students are increasing and diversifying across the board and in Health Professions and Public Health in particular, we are seeing greater needs in areas that were not as prevalent in the past. This increasing demand across all subjects may also be compounded by the fact that the information world is simply getting larger coupled with increasing awareness and use of relevant search tools and ILL services by our users.

Now that we know that there are some subjects that have a clearly demonstrated need—namely, Health Professions and Public Health, we wanted to know if the need for resources in that subject is format-specific, that is, for serials, books, or other formats. The ILL Analyses from WCA indicates that serials are in highest demand for Health Professions and Public Health with 95 percent of requests being for serials, and only 3 percent for books, and 2 percent for all other formats (Figure 3). Across the rest of the top ten most requested subjects, the trend of more serials requests for the sciences, more book requests for the humanities, and a split for the social sciences is in line with other evidence that we have about our users' needs.

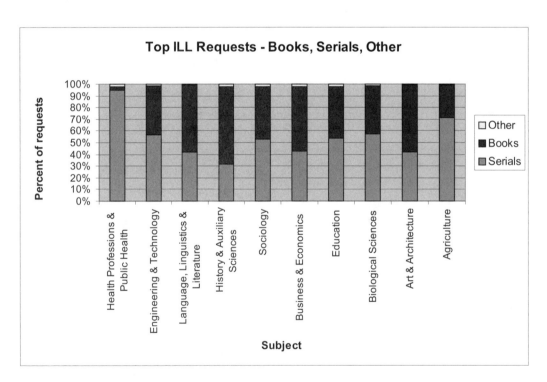

Figure 3. Top ten most requested subjects based on format.

From another perspective, we wanted to see if there was any relationship between the publication date/age of requested materials and the format. Figure 4 shows that for all requests within the past 3.5 years, we can see a pretty clear indication that more recently published books are in highest demand (for all subjects), while demand for recent serials is low in comparison. In fact, the greatest need for serials is for those that were published in the 1970s to 1990s.

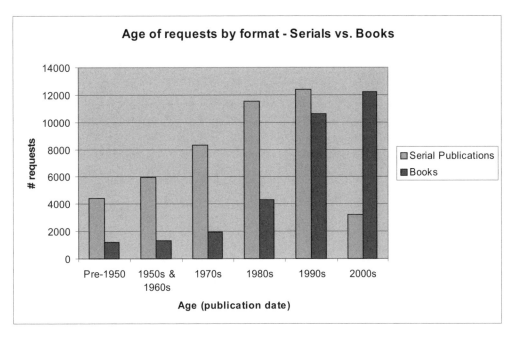

Figure 4. Age of requests based on format.

Likewise, the ILL Analyses data from WCA allows us to focus on any subject and see for which age of material the need is greatest. For Health Professions and Public Health, in the past 3.5 years, there is a clear indication that the greatest needs are for serials that were published in the 1980s and 1990s.

We also wanted to know if the ILL Analyses could actually tell us exactly which books and serials are in highest demand and how many requests are coming from our users for those resources. For serials, we can get at the actual number of requests, beyond just the request frequency categories. For example, we were able to determine that for the journal *Spine,* there were 122 requests over the past 3.5 years—an average of 34 requests a year.

For books, however, the WCA does not allow one to get at the exact number of requests. We were limited to those broad categories of request frequencies. This is a limitation if a library is trying to decide which books to acquire and they are all requested greater than ten times—one cannot tell which were requested only eleven times from those that may have been requested one hundred times.

Stepping back a bit and thinking about our consortium and the cooperative collection development opportunities, we also wanted to know how many of our users' ILL requests were being filled by TRLN. Figure 5 shows the top ten lending libraries, and the top four are from the TRLN consortium (representing about 49 percent of our ILL requests). This is what we would expect, as TRLN should be our lender of first choice with low or no ILL fees and a guaranteed turn around time of 48 hours. Also TRLN member institutions have a program of cooperative collection development providing complementary collections to NCSU in social sciences and humanities areas.

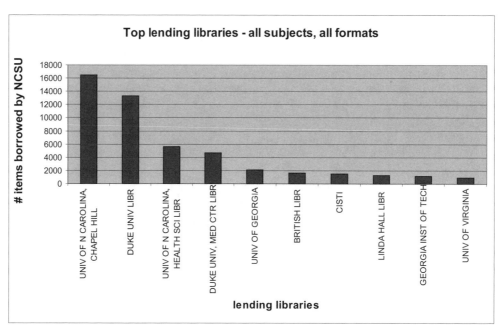

Figure 5. Top ten lending libraries across all subjects and all formats.

Using the ILL Analyses, we can also see the same data for any specific subject. For example, for requests in Health Professions and Public Health, of the top ten lending libraries, the top four are from the TRLN consortium (representing just over 60 percent of our ILL requests for this subject). Again we would expect this as TRLN should be our lender of first choice. This poses interesting questions about how we might develop our collections to fill the needs in this subject area. How do we balance growing our collection locally with the consortial benefits of being a TRLN member? Should we concentrate our efforts in filling in the 40 percent of materials not obtained via TRLN?

On the flipside, the ILL Analyses module allows us to look at our activity as a lender. We found that for the subject that we borrow in the most heavily, we also lend the greatest amount of content—Health Professions and Public Health. We loan about 42 percent of what we borrow in the subject. Because of the very broad nature of the Conspectus headings, interpretation of this data is a little difficult, but most likely, we have a specialized collection in the subject area amongst our history of science, toxicology and psychology collections, which might explain this data. The other trend to note is that across all of the top ten most requested subjects and the top loaned subjects, our borrowing nearly always exceeds our lending activity—and that is explained by the fact that the bulk of our research collection is relatively young with much of our aggressive collection building taking place only within the past fifteen years.

Summary

A huge benefit of the ILL Analyses from WCA is that we can get a big picture overview of our ILL borrowing and lending patterns. The ILL Analyses component enabled us to see trends in both our borrowing and lending patterns and where the demands on our collections were placed. We were able to identify subject areas in demand, formats requested, and publication dates of requested materials, and we were able to get title lists of those in-demand materials.

Specifically, we saw that Health Professions and Public Health was the most requested discipline by far.

As we would expect, the formats requested varied across disciplines. In health professions and Public Health, 95 percent of all requests were for serials. In fact, in all science disciplines serials dominated as the format most in demand. In humanities, the scenario was flipped with books being the format most requested. This is what we would expect to see with those formats being the main method of scholarly communication in those disciplines.

Regarding publication dates of serials requested, we saw that for all subjects, articles published in the 1970s through 1990s were most highly requested. Focusing solely on Health Professions and Public Health, requests were concentrated on the 1980s through 1990s. Knowing the history of collection building at NCSU, this data did not come as a surprise as it was not until in the last 15 years or so that NCSU Libraries has had the funding to build a truly deep research collection and that building has been mostly forward moving rather than retrospective.

As for publication dates of books, we saw that those requested were mainly for more currently published works, materials from the1990s through to the current year. Again, thinking about the history of and changes in collection building at the NCSU Libraries, this was not unexpected. The NCSU Libraries, like most university libraries, has seen its monograph budget put under pressure by increasing high prices of serials, and as a result, our purchasing power for books has diminished.

We were also able to compile specific title lists to help us identify highly demanded materials. As a result of this information, we have purchased all the books in the Health Professions and Public Health areas that were requested two or more times, and we are investigating purchasing several of the serials most in demand.

In terms of our consortium, we found out that 49 percent of our needs across all subjects are being met by our consortium partners and that 60 percent of our needs specifically in Health Professions and Public Health are being met by our consortium partners.

Interpretation and Discussion

How does the ILL Analyses compare with our local ILL statistics? We can obtain ILL data locally, but there are some differences between what we can get locally and what we can get from the WCA. Both our local data and the WCA can provide us with ILL activity reports with titles over a specific time period. At the NCSU Libraries, we have a data-savvy ILL librarian who is able to take the data from our ILL system and provide monthly activity reports for librarians. It should be noted that these reports require some data manipulation from our ILL librarian and that the data is not automatically generated from the ILL system. Likewise, the WCA is also able to give us activity reports, but those are over a broader time span with the minimum time period being a year. Therefore, while the WCA reports provide a larger overview of activity, obtaining prioritized title data from the WCA can be time-consuming and difficult. Our local data gives us a useful level of granularity indicating the college or department the requestor is from and whether he or she is a faculty member, grad student, staff member, and so on. This level of granularity is not available from the WCA.

Another limitation/difficulty we encountered with the WCA was the ability to retrieve ILL data based on a specific call number range. With our local data, we can ask our ILL librarian to tell us the ILL activity in a specific call number range, but with the WCA, we had to use those broad Conspectus headings. For example, if we wanted to grow our collections to support a new programmatic area such as alternative medicine and we wanted to investigate the ILL activity in this area, it would be very difficult to do using the WCA. We are not able to isolate or combine the specific call number ranges that characterize alternative medicine. However, the WCA does have the advantage of being able to very easily provide a big picture overview of our ILL activity over a broad time period. This is not easy to get with our local data. While we have that precise granular data, pulling back from that detailed level to create a broad overview would require much data manipulation and would be time-consuming.

Ideally, both sets of data are needed, as they complement each other well. This combined approach enabled us to see the complete picture of our ILL activity and pointed us to some useful interpretations for our collections. The WCA was able to provide us with a snapshot of where there may be gaps in our collections, which we were then able to use the more granular local data to flesh out. Using that local data, we could identify specific departments needing materials, and we could then discuss with them their needs and demands on our collections.

Our investigation into the ILL Analyses module in WCA provided some meaningful data for collections at the NCSU Libraries. It is clear that we need to strengthen our collections in the Health Professions and Public Health areas to support the research at NCSU in these areas. It is clear that our serials collections in these areas need to be strengthened as well. The publication dates of the serials requested imply that backfile purchases are necessary to fill gaps. We have used the ILL data to identify which publishers were most highly represented based on the journals that were requested and have mapped that data to publication dates to help determine which backfile packages are available to fill our collection gaps.

An interesting question that the data raised was: how do we balance building our collections locally with being part of the TRLN consortium? Do we concentrate on filling in collection gaps that are not available through TRLN or do we concentrate on strengthening our collections locally regardless of whether that material is available to us through TRLN? Another possible consortial advantage would be to collaborate with TRLN to leverage our joint purchasing power that might provide access to the in-demand materials that would benefit patrons of all the TRLN libraries.

All of these findings are in keeping with our local knowledge of campus activities and what we know about the historical growth of our collections at the NCSU Libraries. Having the data and the impactful graphs completes the picture and makes it much easier to explain to campus administrators an increased spending focus on a specific subject area or to justify increased library budget requests.

Data Interpretation

Regarding data interpretation, it is important not to look at the data alone but to make sure it makes sense for what you know historically and currently about your collection and also the programmatic and research activities on your campus.

One of the first things that we had to bear in mind was that this data may show us false gaps. For example, a book that was requested via ILL does not automatically mean that we do not hold it in the collection but that we may not have enough copies to meet the demand. We found this to be the case when we examined the title lists generated by the analysis for some subjects. This is useful information to have, and we can approach meeting the demand in several ways in consultation with our patrons—whether that means purchasing additional copies, buying an online version when possible, or perhaps putting the book on reserve if the demand is being generated by a specific class.

We also needed to think about how our patrons use ILL. It is quite possible that we have not captured all the gaps in our collections from this analysis as some of our constituents do not use ILL. They may use their own network of colleagues at different institutions to fax or e-mail them an article they need. Or they may in some cases choose to purchase the article themselves from a publisher's Web site as they are either unaware that the library can get them the article or they perceive the process as too time-consuming when they need the article immediately. So there may well be a section of need that we do not see in the data.

As was previously mentioned, it is important to understand your collections to make sense of the data so as to be aware of any anomalous results that may arise. The NCSU Libraries have a fairly young research collection, and it is only in the past fifteen years or so that the library has been funded to develop a strong and rich research collection with a dedicated collection management department. Therefore, the gaps we saw in our collections that pertained to serials from the 1970s to the 1990s makes sense in the light of this historical context.

Finally, we also interpreted the results in the light of the information landscape in which we work. We are seeing serials and e-resources really take a large bite out of budgets. As a result, monograph collections are beginning to feel that squeeze. Additionally, as publishers' print runs get smaller and smaller, collection managers often find that if a book is not purchased within a few months of its publication, it becomes out of print and is harder to find and more expensive to purchase. This could explain why the demand for monographs was for those more recently published.

Conclusions

We found the tool to be extremely useful for providing a big picture overview of our ILL activity over a broad time period. We were able to use that overview data to generate impactful graphs that helped us describe collection needs to administrators and thereby help them understand the justification for concentrating funding on a specific area or increased budget requests for library resources.

When used in conjunction with our local ILL data, we were able to generate a fuller picture of our ILL activity and where there may be gaps in our collections. The broadness of the WCA ILL data helped us see where there were issues with the collections, and the local data gave us more information to better understand that demand on our resources.

As we have mentioned throughout this article, some local manipulation of the data from the WCA ILL Analyses module was needed to create the graphs/charts and title lists. As a result, we feel that there is a learning curve associated with using this tool and pulling out, manipulating, and interpreting the data. At the NCSU Libraries, we are encouraged to use data sources such as the WCA and are given the time to work with the tools and develop the skills to use them effectively. In other libraries, we know that this is just not possible with too many pressures and demands on librarians' time. Therefore, some possible enhancements to the tool that might make it more usable and applicable would be to make the output more complex and flexible. Currently there are some basic graphs and charts that can be output from the tool, but they do not describe the data in as much detail or as clearly as the ones we generated ourselves using the source data from the WCA. Output more along the lines of our graphs may make the tool more appealing. Alternatively, perhaps OCLC could offer this tool via a service model whereby OCLC would run the analysis and work with libraries to produce output tailored to their needs.

TRANSFORMING AN ACADEMIC BUSINESS COLLECTION TO CREATE A COLLABORATIVE LEARNING ENVIRONMENT

Tomalee Doan, Associate Professor of Library Science, Purdue University, West Lafayette, Indiana

Marianne Ryan, Associate Dean for Learning, Purdue University, West Lafayette, Indiana

Abstract

At Purdue University's Management & Economics Library, a total library redesign project is in progress which encompasses revamping physical spaces, collection rightsizing, developing Web tools, organizational restructuring, and building partnerships with key internal and external stakeholders. This presentation will explore our process and address collection management issues incurred when moving from a primarily print collection to delivery of information in an electronic format. It will suggest approaches for developing critical relationships with library administrators to support the expensive shift to electronic resources and ongoing maintenance costs. It will also discuss the value realized by primary customers as well as by the additional benefactors of this format transition.

In today's academic library, change is the norm. In many respects, collections, spaces, and services bear little resemblance to what they were just a few years ago. For today's academic library to be viable, it must be willing to reposition itself in order to meet the ever-changing needs and expectations of a user group that is changing as well. Hard questions must be asked and responded to: Do you know your users' information and spatial needs to learn, discover, and create? Do you know what support libraries can offer to meet those needs? Do you know what it takes to accomplish those goals? While not easy to accomplish, this must be done—and done within and in response to the unique environment within which a library exists. At Purdue University, the Libraries have embarked on a transformational agenda, taking into account the dominant contexts that define it.

With more than 39,000 students at the largest campus in a multi-campus system, Purdue is a land-grant institution with the traditional emphases in the sciences, engineering, agriculture, business, hospitality, tourism, and management. The university is highly decentralized, with services, technology, and the Libraries operating in a distributed environment. This is the campus context.

The context of Purdue Libraries reflects that of the university. With an archives and special collections department plus a dozen subject-oriented libraries—down from twenty-eight in the 1970s—its highly decentralized framework brings a range of additional, complex challenges to the equation. Coupled with the decentralized campus computing, this structure results in distributed services and fragmented student spaces. The independent nature of each of the libraries, however, affords some latitude, flexibility, and freedom in devising an agenda to meet the needs of the respective individual and specialized user groups.

Librarians today have come to view change as the means to accomplishing significant goals, recognizing that if our organizations do not keep pace with user needs and acknowledging we have information competitors, we will be deemed unnecessary. At Purdue, an important factor that guides our organization's decisions is the Libraries Strategic Plan, which was developed internally for 2006–2011. The plan articulates the value and meaning for what we strive to achieve in our organization, our community, and beyond. We organize our work to enable the greatest possible success in what we do. This guides our decision making and actions to transform collections, space, and programmatic initiatives to create a new vision for the learning environment our users are demanding.

The key goals of the campus strategic plan are Learning, Discovery, Engagement, and Infrastructure. These elements are mirrored in the Libraries own plan, specifically as Information Literacy, Interdisciplinary Research, Enhancing Quality of Life, and Alignment. The challenge facing the Libraries is to successfully leverage institutional characteristics to reposition themselves to enhance the learning, discovery, engagement, and alignment aspects of their environment. This demands identifying and creating opportunities, building and capitalizing on relationships, and collaborating and partnering extensively; this had to be done within the evolving context for change. Simultaneously, the change itself had to be managed effectively.

The changing context of the Purdue Libraries extends beyond the changing needs of its customers. In the Libraries, a new organizational structure was unveiled almost in concert with implementation of the new strategic plan. Key administrative positions were established and filled at this time, including two associate deans, and changes in the middle management of the Libraries occurred as well. A critical element in managing the change that was needed in the individual libraries was to forge and foster the critical relationship between middle management and the associate deans. Only by doing this could the essential support be given to understand user needs and support the quick adjustments that were needed in the collection and learning contexts. In one of the campus libraries, these essential components came together to help transform an academic business collection into a collaborative learning environment.

In 2006, the Libraries forged a partnership with the Krannert School of Management to repurpose the physical space of one floor of the Management & Economics Library (MEL) to enable the School to relocate its undergraduate academic services and career counseling unit. A recommendation from a task force report done in spring 2005 and confirmed by the LibQual survey results of students and faculty conducted in fall of the same year indicated that the physical space of the main floor of MEL was inadequate, the library's business and economics collection was underutilized, and the Libraries' Web site was difficult to navigate. Addressing the challenges of space, collections, and increased user access to library resources required planning and action steps that would eventually produce the desired results—for example, a redefined business information center focused on the user experience allowing for enhancing discovery and learning, which would also accommodate the School of Management's new academic advising center. Aligning the Libraries' infrastructure by better utilizing space and maximizing facilities is one of the Libraries strategic objectives.

All organizations have assets. The platform for library assets rests in the services it provides to its customers. In the case of the MEL, these assets were hidden when a new library head joined the staff in spring 2006. The first order of business was to survey the environment, both internally within the library and externally in the School of Management and the Department of Agricultural Economics. It was important to define and assess the library's core customers, determine the perception and value of services being provided to those constituents, assess the capabilities of the library staff to support the services necessary to meet the demands of that group, and finally determine the readiness of the library's culture and current staff to make the necessary transformation toward becoming a collaborative learning environment. The overall challenge and opportunity was to figure out what MEL was doing, and doing well, and then to actively pursue new technologies to enhance the delivery of information resources allowing for the essential transformation of the entire library space and student experience. The need to do this and do it quickly was necessary to prepare for the library and management school's planned renovation.

So how quick is quick? Amazingly, libraries can create change as fast as they choose to do so. After an initial assessment of the internal and external environment, two key issues that were challenging MEL were identified. First, stakeholder perceptions of the libraries value within the departments had eroded. Second, the management and economics collection was viewed as outdated and underutilized in serving the research and curricular needs of the users. Within the first six months, attempts were made to meet with every department chair and to attend or be invited to departmental meetings to talk with faculty and meet with directors of all administrative units. By far, the most significant and meaningful development was the interactions established with the Dean of the Krannert School of Management and its three Associate Deans. Communicating and building positive relationships with the School's administration proved to be the most important strategic initiative undertaken by MEL. Significant results immediately became apparent. All Deans within the School of Management became advocates for the library, and the primary "word-of-mouth marketing" became the advertising mechanism for conveying MEL's vision and the value it could add to the School's success. The message disseminated was how the library could enhance what users were already doing—only helping them do it better! The Deans suggested key stakeholders to meet with, which created excellent opportunities to innovate and develop the services needed to support the learning and research environment that faculty and students were demanding. The library became involved in several of the management school's events, such as MBA case competitions, and became a member of the School's Information Access Council. These opportunities created the necessary exposure of our services, and the library began to seamlessly integrate into the life of this community.

While effectively building partnerships and determining needs with other units and departments within the School of Management, an ongoing collection analysis was conducted using the integrated library systems circulation data, WorldCat, and the WorldCat Collection Analysis tool. Krannert School of Management had two subject areas, economics and statistics, which had historical significance and strong alignment with current programs and research. Therefore, no de-selection of materials within those two areas occurred during the collection analysis. During the first four months under the new library head, the following collection projects were completed with the team effort of the MEL staff:

- Approximately 15,000 monograph titles that had not circulated in twelve years were withdrawn from the collection.

- Second copies of items held in MEL were either withdrawn or sent to a storage facility depending on usage statistics.

- If MEL held a title that was available elsewhere on campus, it was withdrawn (unless usage stats warranted sending to the Libraries storage facility).

- The approval plan was cancelled for monographs.

With strong support from the Libraries Administration and the School of Management for the collection analysis efforts, a compact storage facility was built in the basement of the management school and completed in 2007. To establish the vision and repurpose the space for the opportunity to build the learning spaces within MEL, collection parameters were set for all remaining MEL materials. All items, regardless of format, were evaluated. Items that had circulated twenty-five times or more stayed in MEL; items that circulated less often than that but had value to the curriculum and research efforts of the primary users were sent to the new compact storage facility, and a 24/7 twice-daily delivery service was created. All remaining items that had little or no usage were sent to the Libraries general storage facility.

Meanwhile, electronic back file journal sets were being purchased by the Libraries. All print volumes of the titles housed at MEL were withdrawn. All other print serials that were available electronically were tagged in the catalog, and a color label was placed on the spine of the volume and sent to the new compact storage facility. Now, if a user requests a print bound volume through the catalog form for a title with the color label indicating it is available electronically, the user is notified through e-mail and shown how to retrieve the article electronically through the e-journal finder application on the newly revamped MEL Web site. This provides an excellent opportunity for users to learn additional information literacy and search skills.

None of the collection analysis work, shifting of materials, and physical space changes could be made without restructuring the current staffing model and revising job responsibilities at MEL. With support from Libraries Administration, two new faculty positions were created, focused on establishing new instructional initiatives and implementing technology tools to enhance information delivery in the rapidly changing print-to-electronic collection shift. Additional graduate students were hired to staff the reference services desk, allowing library faculty to focus on additional outreach opportunities to faculty. All paraprofessional staff duties were evaluated; tasks that were considered nonessential to MEL's primary focus of directly impacting customer's needs were eliminated. These organizational changes produced unprecedented opportunities to provide better service to faculty and students: creating new tools to access information resources, such as the MyMEL toolbar and a new redesign of the library Web site; additional instructional efforts; increased partnerships between the library and faculty to assist in course content development; targeted collection building; and changing the libraries physical infrastructure by reducing the print collection to create more student collaborative space. Together, these changes resulted in a significant increase in student traffic throughout the library, as well as increased reference and instruction transactions.

The vision of the Purdue University Libraries is to achieve preeminence as an innovative and creative research library in meeting the ongoing challenges of the Information Age. Innovation means "renewal," and it is vital to an organization's success. It is about taking what is already there and making it better, as quickly as possible, to enhance the customer's experience. The Management & Economics Library will continue to focus on innovative services to provide an optimal learning and discovery experience in a collaborative setting. Meanwhile, the process to effect successful change that was undertaken by the library's staff may be modeled by other campus libraries to achieve similar transformative results.

ONE FOR ALL: A JOINT VENTURE TO EXPAND THE SUNY SYSTEM COLLECTION SUNY SHARED MONOGRAPH COLLECTION PILOT PROJECT

Kate Latal, Head of Acquisitions, University at Albany, Albany, New York

Caryl Ward, Head of Acquisitions, Binghamton University, Binghamton, New York

Abstract

Cooperative collection development—what does it really mean for Technical Services operations? The State University of New York stretches across sixty-four campuses that include colleges of arts and sciences and health sciences, university research centers, community colleges, and specialized colleges. To increase access to print resources for SUNY, a pilot project was instituted in 2006 to coordinate purchasing one copy of each monograph published by eight selected university presses. After much discussion, the Technical Services staff at Albany, Binghamton, Buffalo, and Stony Brook rolled up their sleeves and started adding the books to their local catalogs.

Introduction

We are now nearing the end of the second year of the SUNY Shared pilot project. Representatives from two of these libraries will discuss its challenges, pitfalls, and triumphs. We will share information about the history and goals of the project, each library's unique experience in planning for and implementation from the Technical Services viewpoint, and our recommendations for others who may decide to plan a similar project.

We would like to recognize Min-Huei Lu, Head of Acquisitions at Stony Brook, and Dave Nuzzo, Associate Director of CTS at the University of Buffalo, who contributed to this presentation.

SUNY is a large state system with sixty-four campuses in urban, suburban, and rural settings, from Long Island through the boroughs of New York City, up to the Canadian border and over to Western New York. Each campus has its own governance and culture. SUNY includes four University Centers, which are doctoral degree–granting institutions; thirteen 4-year colleges of arts and sciences including Purchase and Geneseo; forty-two community and technical institutions including Fashion Institute of Technology and the Maritime College; the statutory colleges such as Labor Relations at Cornell, Environmental Sciences at Syracuse, and Ceramics at Alfred; and Upstate and Downstate Medical. SUNY has expanded to include more than 418,000 students enrolled in 6,688 programs of study and over 18 million volumes in our libraries. We have a common library system (ALEPH) shared by all except the statutory sites, a Union Catalog and individual OPACs at each campus. We also have a very active professional group, SUNYLA (SUNY Librarians Association), which includes members and delegates from each campus and which sponsors a meeting at a different campus each year. As a result, SUNY librarians have many opportunities for professional interaction, and there is a strong spirit of collegiality.

History and Overview

SCAC and SUNY CONNECT: http://www.sunyconnect.suny.edu/sunyergy/28collacc.htm

The SUNY Council for Access and Collections was created by the SUNY Council of Library Directors in December 2003. The Council was created to plan for continuing access to specific e-journal packages, to coordinate cooperative purchases for the entire state university system, and to ensure maximum access at minimum cost for shared resources. This group is known as SCAC.

Initial membership was defined to include collection development and access services librarians from the University Center and Health Sciences Center libraries, and also Carey Hatch, who works in the Office of Library & Information Services (OLIS) as an ex-officio member.

At the first SCAC meeting, the attendees worked to "clarify goals and expectations." The overarching theme that emerged from that meeting was an understanding that the members of SCAC would work toward the concept of a unified collection.

SUNY*Connect* is the name of a joint initiative of the SUNY Provost's OLIS and the SUNY campus libraries to share collections and services across the state system.

The assessment and selection of one integrated library management system in October 1999 is an accomplishment that was directed by SUNY*Connect*. The goal was to move all SUNY libraries to one common platform. The ExLibris' ALEPH system was implemented SUNY-wide over several years. Although this one ILS was adopted SUNY-wide, the system is not run on just one server. Some of the libraries are on shared servers, and some libraries manage their own server. Another noteworthy second accomplishment is the creation of a Union Catalog. It brings the holdings of all SUNY libraries together so they can be viewed and utilized as a single OPAC. This is not meant to replace the local OPAC but to provide enhanced access to collections at other libraries through "one-stop shopping."

SUNY Shared Collection Pilot Project

Between March 2004 and April 2005, SCAC met nine times and worked on a number of cooperative, collaborative projects toward the goal of one library, one collection. SCAC was concerned about shrinking monographs collections—both local campus collections and the aggregate, system-wide collection. The Council discussed models that could first be applied among the council member libraries and then extended to the other SUNY libraries. They had discussed ways to expand the breadth of monographs available to the SUNY users by coordinating purchases and improving methods of resource sharing and material delivery.

SCAC wanted to develop a shared monographs collection, but they could not agree where to begin. SCAC needed to figure out what piece of this huge idea of purchasing books together they could focus on that would make an impact on the entire SUNY system for not a lot of money. A targeted analysis of the university press coverage at selected libraries provided SCAC with some numbers that they could relate to and provided the hook to build the project.

David Nuzzo from Buffalo reviewed all 2004 titles published by the University Press of Chicago, Cambridge University Press, Yale University Press, and Cornell University Press. He examined the collections at the University of Buffalo, Buffalo State College, the University at Albany, Binghamton University, and Fredonia. He wanted to assess the validity of the belief that the SUNY system as a whole is not building a comprehensive collection of major university press titles.

The total output of titles from all four presses for 2004 was determined to be 1,576 titles.

Dave discovered that 446 titles, or 28.3 percent, were not held by any of the libraries, while 704 titles, or 44.7 percent, were held by two or more sites. He also noted that 27 percent of the titles published by these presses could be found in only one of the libraries studied. A significant portion of the output of each press was not purchased by any of the schools.

This study illustrated the growing homogenization of the SUNY campus collections and the need to broaden the scope of the entire SUNY collection.

SCAC also concluded that the data collected demonstrated the need to expand the selections for these four university presses. They became interested in getting at least one copy of every relevant title into the SUNY system. After further consideration, it became clear that including Oxford University Press and Cambridge University Press was cost prohibitive for the pilot program. For example, purchasing all the Cambridge titles in 2004 would have cost $83,717.

Implementation

A subgroup of SCAC members (Austin Booth from Buffalo and Susan Currie and Ed Shephard from Binghamton) worked on a proposal for a shared monographs collection. They presented their initial proposal at a meeting in September 2005—that the four University Centers pool enough funds together to purchase a monograph collection in print. The four University Center libraries are Binghamton University Libraries, Stony Brook University Libraries, the University at Albany Libraries, and the University at Buffalo Libraries.

The original proposal designated Binghamton and Buffalo as the depositories for the pilot project. At some point, this changed, and it was decided that all four libraries would house books—two libraries one year and the other two libraries the following year. Albany was not supposed to be a housing library during the first year, but Buffalo decided that they were not able to participate at that time because they were in the process of migrating to the ALEPH system.

In December 2005, the University Center Library Directors approved the pilot project with a funding commitment of no more than $15,000 per library. SCAC contracted with Yankee Book Peddler, Inc. (now YBP) to supply the books. All four university centers contributed an equal amount in order to purchase nearly a complete run of the eight university presses for publication year 2006. Additionally, SCAC included plans to monitor the availability of electronic versions of the titles acquired in print in order to consider purchasing e-book versions together in the future.

The profile that was set up with YBP was limited to buying the majority of the output of eight university presses: Cornell University Press, Duke University Press, Harvard University Press, University of Chicago Press, University of Michigan Press, University of Minnesota Press, University of Washington Press, and Yale University Press. The presses were selected based on Dave Nuzzo's study and on interlibrary loan borrowing data.

Titles from four of the presses would be housed at Binghamton and Buffalo, and four would be housed at Albany and Stony Brook. It was believed that dividing the presses in this way would make it easier to remember which presses where housed where. This was not only for the benefit of the staff running the pilot project but also for the selectors who may not want to duplicate titles.

SCAC discussed the possibility of expanding the list of presses in the future, if the project continued. The final details of the profile were worked out by conference call in March 2006.

So the libraries went about implementing this pilot project.

Although the SUNY Shared project was envisioned by SCAC, and parameters such as the profile were set by SCAC, it was left to individual campuses to carry out processing details involving many library departments. At each campus, staff from Acquisitions, Cataloging, ILL/Circ, and Systems had to agree on MARC tags and locations and policies. Local decision making was surprisingly time-consuming. It involved discussions on how to document the cost of the books and track vendor payments, where to house the books (integrated or sequestered?), what the loan period for the Shared books should be (same as for the rest of the campus collection or same as for ILL?).

Technical Services implementation varied at each of the four sites, although we faced similar issues. We each had to devise a workflow to officially receive the books and to track the invoices. We had to determine the best method for getting MARC records into our system (remember, even though we are all on the Ex Libris ALEPH system, we have distinct OPACS) and for the whole copy cataloging process, and we had to figure out a workflow for getting the other sites' holdings into our catalogs.

As an example of local choice, Albany and Binghamton opted to include simple bookplates. We felt it was important to clearly identify the books as part of the Shared collection as it is expected they will circulate widely among our sixty-four campuses. We wanted to prevent the books from being returned to the wrong site and to ensure that the Circulation staff process loans appropriately. Because the Shared books processed at Binghamton are housed at the off site storage facility, it is essential to prevent the books from going back into the general collection. The book sides are stamped SUNY Shared, and the code SUNYBIN appears on the spine label so they do not go back to the stacks.

Discussion about whether or not to add records for these titles in Worldcat brought up a great deal of apprehension. One thing that concerned many of the SCAC members was who would "take credit" for these books. Who would count them toward their collection statistics? Would we create a new OCLC entity just for this pilot project? Any Worldcat record must tell other libraries which library owns the book in case they want to borrow it through interlibrary loan.

Counting the addition of volumes is of course political. Libraries live and die based on collection count statistics. So the concern about this issue is important.

Kate: So here is an example of the finished OPAC record for a book housed at Stony Brook in the Albany catalog. To my knowledge, this is the first time we have added records for materials housed at a separate library in our local OPAC.

Author	Amenta, Edwin, 1957–
Title	Professor baseball : searching for redemption and the perfect lineup on the softball diamonds of Central Park / Edwin Amenta.
Year	c2007.
Library Has	SUNY Shared Collection. Stony Brook copy available via Interlibrary Loan. Click ILL request link in full record view.
Availability	Click All Items to check current status
Location	University Library/at Stony Brook:GV881.A47 2007

Albany

Kate: Mary Casserly, our Assistant Director for Collections and User Services, was chairing SCAC at the time this project was developed. She kept me in the loop and invited me to attend several SCAC meetings. She also brought this pilot project to the attention of the bibliographers in December 2005. That gave them time to think about whether or not they wanted to adjust their existing approval plan profile or change their firm ordering plans for these eight presses.

I decided to tell the staff within the department about this project as early as possible as a "heads up." I kept key staff informed as the planning process moved along. The person who was responsible for unpacking the shipments asked some good questions: How many books will be coming? Will they come all at once? How will I know that the books are the books for this project? Will there be a list in the box? How will I know if we are going to keep all of the books?

One thing that we were determined to do was to make the Acquisitions process as easy as possible. Since we did not have to convey an order to a vendor for these titles, we did not have to follow the same workflow that we use for generating "perfect" firm orders.

We asked YBP to provide packing list records that were free of charge in order to add the titles to the Acquisitions/Serials module of our ILS. In this way we could document and track the cost of each title and not have to worry about downloading the correct record. We decided to leave the true cataloging up to the Cataloging Services Department. This took some work on both YBP's part and our Systems staff person's part to get the records just the way we wanted them. We created a budget for each publisher, so we could track the amount spent on each publisher if we needed to, so we wanted to map the publishers to the budgets. We also asked YBP to make sure that the shipments could be identified easily by adding SUNY Shared Collection to the address label.

So, when the books arrived a staff person from Acquisitions unpacked the box of books and then told me and our Systems staff person how many books were supplied. Then our Systems staff person would sign on to YBP's site, locate the latest file, compare the number of records in the file to the number of books in the shipment, and then bring over the file. Then she would load the records into our Acquisitions database.

We received the books and paid the invoice through our system to track the expenditures. Since we were housing books paid for with other peoples' money, we wanted to be able to extract information about the books later on. The books were property stamped, given bookplates, and sent on to cataloging.

We did not end up making any adjustments to our major approval plan or our firm ordering to eliminate duplicates. The staff seemed very concerned about this.

They did not understand why we would want to duplicate many of the titles we did. Since firm order funds are always in such high demand, I expect that we will consider changing our local collection policies in order to decrease the level of duplication if this project is continued.

Communicating details about the pilot project took time. The unnamed committee at Albany wrote an announcement that was sent out to our library-wide listserve. As soon as it was sent out, I received questions about how to find and borrow the books housed at the other libraries. We were not ready to include this information in the first announcement. A follow-up message was needed and is needed, but we have not sent out any other announcements.

Stony Brook

Min-Huei Lu, Head of Acquisitions at Stony Brook, is working with us on this project. Stony Brook housed the same publishers that were housed at Albany during the second year of the pilot. They started to receive books at the beginning of 2007.

Stony Brook added records for the titles housed in their library first. After Buffalo cataloged the titles held elsewhere, they provided a file that Stony Brook used to load records into their OPAC. Stony Brook received some titles that they did not think should come on the plan—a few reprints and some titles by presses that are distributed by one of the eight university presses. For example, they received a copy of the title *First English Dictionary, 1604: Robert Cawdrey's Table Alphabeticall* (ISBN#1851243852), published by Bodleian Library in 2007. It is a reprint of the 1604 edition with a new introduction and notes and is distributed by the University of Chicago Press. Since the "reprint" was published more than twenty-five years after the first edition, it did, strictly speaking, fit the profile. Nothing is perfect. Min-Huei believes that this book should have been excluded and not treated against our profile.

When the books arrived at Stony Brook, they processed payment for them in their Acquisitions system. They created one separate fund code for all of the SUNY Shared Collection books. Stony Brook does not have a different lending period or rules in place for the SUNY Shared titles. They circulate as any other books do, for six weeks. They had problems with how to handle titles that are part of a series or a reference title that would normally prohibit the title from circulating. They also had to remember not to put the copy from SUNY Shared Collection on reserve since these titles need to be available all the time.

Although all of the records have been loaded into their OPAC, Stony Brook is still discussing how they should look. They have two teams that work on the look of the OPAC: the OPAC team and the technical services team. The OPAC team includes a programmer, representatives from circulation, the branch libraries, and reference. If the technical services team makes a suggestion to change the look of the OPAC, this does not affect others; the technical services team just implements it without consulting the OPAC team. But if it affects other areas, they send a recommendation letter to get the approval from the OPAC team before the technical services programmer changes anything.

Stony Brook did not advertise the pilot project within the library or on the campus. It only shared information about this project informally at meetings. The selectors were told about the project. Most of the staff did not know about the project until January 2007 when they started to receive shipments.

At Albany, we decided to house the books for this collection in only two of our three libraries. One staff member did the bulk of the cataloging. We had to create new collection codes for the books housed in our library and the other center libraries in order to have them display properly in our OPAC. These are also used to gather circulation statistics.

We added a "logical base" to ALEPH in order to be able to limit a search in the OPAC to the SUNY Shared Collection titles.

The person who cataloged the majority of the SUNY Shared books for our library also added the records for the books housed at the other libraries this past summer. Later on it was mentioned that he probably should have involved other catalogers in the project. His primary responsibility was not cataloging, and other staff could have helped him with this project.

Binghamton

Caryl: At Binghamton, we started processing the material in earnest in January 2007—several months after the 2006 imprints actually began arriving from YBP. It took us that long to nail down the details! Once the logistics were in place, a member of the classified staff with extensive copy cataloging and approval receipt experience processed them. This work did not replace her other responsibilities, but it did complement what she already did. This staff member truly enjoyed being part of the project and had the presence of mind to ask questions when she came across unusual situations (more about this later). We processed 494 books for the four University Presses for 2006, and over 80 percent of them were second copies—that is, Binghamton already owned the title, so we did not have to bring another record in from OCLC. Because this is a pilot project, it had little or no impact on local selection. Should this project continue, we would expect bibliographers to consider what will be coming in the door via the project when making their selections for our own collection. We set up a fund structure for SUNY Shared and created a purchase order for each title and processed the invoice as usual (we were working from a prepaid deposit account). We also opted to sequester our books in our storage area. If one of our patrons wishes to borrow the book, it is requested via the normal ILL process. This involved ongoing dialogue between Acquisitions, Access Services, Systems, and Cataloging (which is a separate unit in Binghamton's Technical Services; most copy cataloging is done in Acquisitions). We have only recently begun to add the records for the books received at the other three sites.

Buffalo

At Buffalo, they are receiving the 2007 imprints from the same four presses that Binghamton received in 2006. The workflow differs markedly from the other sites. Records are downloaded individually from OCLC but are not linked to order information. Buffalo chose not to create a fund structure, order records, or invoices. Rather than add their receipts and then move on to those of the other sites, they are working on their books and the other sites' holdings simultaneously. Buffalo's Shared books are intershelved in their large collection, and specific collection codes are utilized in order to easily identify and retrieve material.

Caryl: This is an example of a book that was already owned by Binghamton when a second copy was received via the Shared project. (This was one of the first books we processed, and I got to know this title very well!) The Shared copy comes up first in the OPAC display. Although we didn't want it to, we couldn't spend the time to figure out how to reverse the holdings. As you can see, the Shared copy has a link under PLACE A REQUEST that leads to Illiad—remember that all patrons must request via ILL, even our local users.

Handley, Paul M.,	Book		2006	
		The king never smiles :a biography of Thailands Bhumibol Adulyadej /		**Location/Request:** Main LibraryStacksDS586.H36 2006REGULAR LOAN SUNY Shared CollectionDS586.H36 2006PLACE A REQUEST **Library (Owned/Out):** Main Library(1/ 0) SUNY Shared Collection(1/ 0)

Patrons can search all "SUNY SHARED" books in our online catalog using keywords. The OPAC records for books that are held at our sister institutions, that is, those we have access to but do not have on site, do not include a call number. This is so staff can distinguish between Binghamton and Albany, Buffalo, and Stony Brook books and so our patrons don't go on a wild goose chase in our stacks for the books.

Local Problems and Surprises

Kate: It was surprising how much time it took to involve all of the necessary people in the planning stages of this project.

Everything we do behind the scenes in the Acquisitions system at Albany ends up being visible to the public in ALEPH. Our order records are visible in the OPAC instantly. As soon as something is in the OPAC, we need to be prepared for someone requesting to RUSH it.

We relied on Systems staff quite a bit to help create the loader and to load the packing list records for us.

Sharing data between sites is not always easy. Stony Brook had difficulty loading the file of records into its local system. It took time to figure out the problem and resolve it.

Sometimes books end up in the wrong place. I recently discovered that one was housed in the third library, and it is being moved.

Caryl: I was astonished at how much back-and-forth there was between my colleagues in other units. So many decisions had so much interdepartmental impact. We received some unusual material: a sketch pad with an art book; a foreign language workbook; a dual-language work—English and Arabic—which required consultation with our Arabic cataloger, something that was not difficult but certainly out of our normal workflow for copy cataloging. We also realized that when order records for the Shared butted against the order record for Binghamton's copy, the prices were often markedly different because the Shared profile specified cloth, not paper.

Assessment, Evaluation and the Future of the Project

Caryl: Criteria for the project's evaluation will include ILL data and on-site circulation statistics. Kate will discuss that in a moment. Reviewing usage is important: we did establish the collection as a research-level collection (which sometimes means some of the titles are not used heavily). The project will continue, but SCAC will be looking at e-book packages. So Kate and I may be back at Charleston the year after next to report on that stage of the project! We both agree that in any cooperative project, it is essential to continue to share information at all levels.

Kate: The assessment criteria used to judge the success of this pilot project were not fully developed into clear, measurable pieces of information at the beginning of the pilot. Here are some of the questions from project documents that SCAC planned to use in evaluating the pilot:

- Impact on SUNY collection: Has redundancy been reduced? Have gaps been filled?

- Impact on local collections: Have participating campuses' purchases of university presses included in the project been reduced? Have any changes in acquisitions practices affected vendor discounts?

- How has this project affected the circulation and interlibrary loan of university press monographs?

- Does this project improve access to university press materials for patrons throughout the participating campuses? Are there ways in which local access was hampered?

This may be a problem later on since we may not be able to collect statistics that someone wants at the end of the pilot if we did not set up our records to provide the desired statistics at the beginning of the pilot. Circulation statistics will of course be something to review, but how do we decide that adding these titles has added to the breadth of the collection. Just by sheer numbers? To check on how well this process worked in building the collection of the eight university presses covered, it would be helpful to check to see what percentage of the total output from the presses was purchased. The problem is finding staff time to check this. It is my opinion that we need to publicize this initiative more. More books might circulate, and people will know that we are still interested in building relevant print collections. The teaching faculty might be interested to hear about it. I believe that we can build support for this project if we share information about it with a wider audience.

Conclusion

Based on the interest from our colleagues, we believe that cooperative collection development will continue to flourish and that opportunities for collaboration will increase. All the face to face meetings, conference calls, and emails helped strengthen working relationships with other librarians and staff, and we all benefited from the networking opportunities that this project offered. Participating in SUNY Shared pilot project was an enjoyable effort and we look forward to the next phase.

Library Web Sites

Albany: http://library.albany.edu/

Binghamton: http://library.lib.binghamton.edu/

Buffalo: http://ublib.buffalo.edu/libraries/

Stony Brook: http://www.sunysb.edu/library/

THE HUMAN FACTOR: WHY USE A CONSULTANT IN COLLECTION ASSESSMENT?

Thomas W. Leonhardt, Director, Scarborough-Phillips Library, St. Edward's University, Austin, Texas

There are many reasons for using a consultant to assess or evaluate a library's collection, the general one being that an outside expert can get the ear and attention of administrators even when he is saying much the same thing that the library director and staff have been saying, perhaps for years. Consultants, whether formal or informal, are important for all of us in decision making, whether it be professional or personal advice we are seeking. And paid consultants are paid to give the advice that is desired and needed for a given purpose. Henry Wheeler Shaw's character, Josh Billings, summed it up thus: "When a man comes to me for advice, I find out the kind of advice he wants, and I give it to him."

In truth, a consultant does give the advice that he client wants, but sometimes, as we will discuss later, the advice, delivered in a report, has unintended consequences. This may be the result of the inexactitude of the instructions given to the consultant and the broad scope of the stated purpose of the evaluation or assessment—the devil is in the details.

Here are three reasons for hiring an outside consultant to evaluate a library collection. An outside consultant provides:

- expertise and experience that may not be present in the library;
- distance, objectivity, and neutrality; and
- a report that fulfils the contract—that is, it documents the stated purpose of the assessment and evaluation.

I have been using assessment and evaluation in tandem because of the distinction that Peggy Johnson (*Fundamentals of Collection Development and Management*, Chicago: ALA, 2004) draws:

"Evaluation seeks to examine or describe collections in their own terms or in relation to other collections and checking mechanisms, such as lists." (p. 269)

"The aim of assessment is to determine how well the collection supports the goals, needs, and mission of the library or parent organization." (p. 269)

"Both evaluation and assessment provide a better understanding of the collection and the user community." (p. 269)

Another thing that a collection development consultant ought to do is provide an overview of the whole collection development and management program at a library that includes the mission statement, the collection development policy and practices, local assessments (surveys, list checking, etc.), and staffing and its organization.

I am doing a reality check when I look at stated policies and goals to see if they are being followed. I look at the policy manual to see when it was last updated and look at what it covers.

In the literature on collection assessment, a physical examination of the stacks is mentioned, but in terms of a subject expert looking at a specific area of the collection. I do not claim to be a subject specialist but rather an academic librarian generalist with a book collector's mentality developed over a lifetime of association with books in libraries and bookstores and with an interest in too many areas to allow me to become an expert in any or a collector with a specific passion. I make no apologies, I have no regrets.

The ideal generalist, however, exists in limited numbers. Let me give you an example of the ideal collection evaluator and then tell you what I do and why it can cause problems once the report is filed.

> They [Shirley Hazzard and Jacques Barzun] had been asked by the head librarian of the New York Society Library to help him weed out superfluous and out-of-date volumes. "There we were," Hazzard told me, raising her arm, "books stacked this high, and I thought, We're really in for it. We'll never get through these. Then Jacques reached into a pile, glanced at the title—it didn't matter which book it was—and said, 'This one's been superseded by another; this one is still valid; this one can stay until someone or somebody finishes his new study,' and in a couple of hours we were done. It was a very impressive performance, because, you know, he wasn't performing at all. It's just Jacques." —*AGE OF REASON* by Arthur Krystal, *New Yorker,* (0028792X), October 22, 2007, Vol. 83, Issue 32, p. 103

I would have to make a deal with the devil to have the universal scope of a Jacques Barzun, but I use a browsing technique that, while leaving the actual weeding and subject scrutiny to others, gets a good sense of the collection—its strengths, weakness, use, and condition.

Browsing, as it turns out, is something that humans and animals all do when looked at as a form of exploration and helps us deal with our daily lives that exist somewhere between boredom and overstimulation (see Marcia J. Bates, 2006, "What Is Browsing Really? A Model Drawing from Behavioural Science Research," *Information Research,* 12(4), paper 330; available at http://InformationR.net/ir/12-4/papers330.html).

Here is how Bates defines browsing:

> Browsing is the activity of engaging in a series of glimpses, each of which exposes the browser to objects of potential interest: depending on interest, the browser may or may not examine more closely one of more of the (physically represented) objects; this examination, depending on interest, may or may not lead the browser to (physically or conceptually) acquire the object. (p. 14)

In my terms, as I browse the stacks, I take in the general condition and spacing of the books on the shelves. I look for wear and tear, at the dates on the call numbers, and at the length of a series. I look for duplicate or multiple copies and for broken sets. I pull books off the shelf at random or perhaps because I was drawn to the book. I look inside for condition and use and hope that there is a circulation slip inside the book, but even without one, some indication of use can be determined.

I look for standard authors, standard editions, and scope. I look for things that don't belong. For example, in a library far from Philadelphia, I spotted a history of Thomas Jefferson University. The book jumped out at me because I have a friend who went to medical school there. It had no business in that collection and suggested that it was a gift and that there might be other similar titles that should be culled.

A consultant, when looking at the adequacy of a collection, should meet with faculty and librarians and, when the university wants to expand its research mission, with administrators. For me, this is a reality check. Does the collection development policy, the library mission, the budget, and the library practices coincide with the opinions being offered? When they don't, this will be apparent in the consultant's report, and then those varying opinions need to be reconciled because nerves will be touched and discussion will ensue.

BUSINESS INTELLIGENCE: SEEKING CLARITY ON COMPANIES, SECTORS, AND ECONOMIES

Lawrence Maxted, Collection Development, Gannon University, Erie, Pennsylvania

Introduction

Effective business intelligence gathering requires the unending collection and analysis of a continuum of information. Collecting information about a single company in isolation gives an incomplete picture. To achieve a comprehensive result, information must be gathered beyond the target company on comparable and competing companies, the broader sector, and the overall economy. Business intelligence is more than just collecting numbers. It is an amalgamated understanding of numerical data and the narrative story behind the numbers.

Many types of information come into play in getting a more complete picture of a particular company. It is "more complete" and not "complete" because it is impossible to ever know everything that needs to be known about a company. Striving for an adequate level of business intelligence is the equivalent to shooting at a moving target. By the time a mass of information is gathered and digested, some of it has changed. The practitioner of business intelligence must therefore always accept that judgments will be made using a somewhat incomplete set of data.

Practitioners of business intelligence come in many forms. Business students need to carry out varying assignments that require the gathering and analysis of data. People in business need to gather information on competitors or potential customers. Job seekers need to find and research potential employers. Investors want to determine which stocks and other investments will make them money. All of these users and others are seeking business intelligence in one form or another.

Types of Business Intelligence

Business intelligence comes in two basic types: quantitative and narrative. Quantitative information represents the numbers or, as they are often called, metrics that measure a company, sector, or economy. Numbers can lie because they are not always accurate and can be misinterpreted, but generally they are the easiest part of the intelligence equation to collect and understand. Narrative information is much more ephemeral and open to widely different interpretations. A 2.8 percent general rate of inflation is a fairly definite figure, though what it means to the economy can be debated. A statement from the chairman of the Federal Reserve that inflation looks good next year is much harder to get a handle on. What does "good" mean? Is he trying to sound optimistic to mislead? Narrative information is important because it puts the numbers in context.

Sometimes understanding the narrative overshadows the numbers. During the dot.com frenzy of the late 1990s, valuations of companies connected to the Internet reached what many considered to be absurd levels. It was the narrative that propped up the boom, until the boom became a burst bubble. The numbers never justified the boom, but market sentiment overwhelmed the numbers for years. Also, numbers change. The price of oil was under $20 a barrel for much of 1998. Now it is approaching $100. The narrative explains what has happened.

A combination of increased demand from China and India, declining oil supplies, conflict in oil-producing regions, and speculation has driven up the price.

Figure 1 is a graphical representation of how quantitative and narrative information is important at all levels of collecting business intelligence.

	Company	Sector	Economy
narrative	YES	YES	YES
quantitative	YES	YES	YES

Figure 1. Types of information.

Understanding the implications of the narrative and numerical data together is what makes for effective business intelligence. One supports and verifies the other.

Economies

Individual national economies are growing into one global economy, but we're not there quite yet, so it is still accurate to talk about different economies with phrases like "the U.S. economy is slowing" or "the Chinese economy is sizzling." To support such narrative conclusions, data is collected on a myriad of topics by governments and private industry. Such numbers are termed "economic indicators." They are interpreted both to determine the health of a particular economy and to plan for the future. Governments, through agencies like the Federal Reserve, can take actions to influence future economic activity. Businesses attempt to make forecasts to determine the best strategies for dealing with changing economic conditions.

It is not possible to understand the circumstances of homebuilders like Pulte and Hovnanian or lenders like Countrywide and Washington Mutual or brokers like Bear Sterns and Merrill Lynch today without understanding the broader economy. Over the past several years, interest rates climbed, home prices declined, and defaults soared. These companies and their sectors are all being hammered by the same economic storm. An improving American economy would lift all these companies. The current round of interest rate reductions by the Federal Reserve are intended to do just that. Of course every action has a reaction. Cuts in the interest rate by the Federal Reserve gives the dollar a lower return compared to foreign currencies which then tends to make the dollar lose value. Commodities like oil and gold then tend to increase in value relative to the dollar. This bodes well for mining and energy companies.

Companies like Philip Morris and Coke can do well in a falling U.S. economy because people still smoke and drink soda no matter what is happening around them. Such companies are also tied to the secular trend of a growing global economy. These companies and others actually benefit when the value of the dollar falls because so much of what they sell is overseas. A cheaper dollar means that what they sell in the local currencies of Europe, Asia, and the rest of the world then gets translated into higher dollar earnings. With a lower dollar, all U.S. exporters find their products to be more competitive in foreign markets. The reverse is true for importers. Wal-Mart and other retailers may find the cost of their imports higher. They must then either absorb the costs or pass them onto customers with the expectation of losing some sales. It is a vicious circle.

One doesn't have to be an economist to understand the economic basis of business, but it is necessary to beware of what is happening in the general economy. *Guide to Economic Indicators: Making Sense of Economics,* 5th ed. (Bloomberg Press, 2007) goes into far more detail on what economic numbers mean than can be written here. News media outlets like the *Wall Street Journal,* CNBC, and PBS's *Nightly Business Report* keep close watch on what the Federal Reserve does and the varying job, inflation, and other reports that take the pulse of the economy. Lately, it would seem impossible not to come across reports of deterioration in home sales and increasing foreclosure rates.

Sectors

Sectors (industry groups) exist inside the overall economy. Each sector of the economy reacts differently to economic conditions. During times of high oil prices, the auto sector can become depressed as people have less desire to buy large cars that require more fuel. The casual dining and leisure travel sectors become depressed too because people may tend to skip eating out and not travel as much. On the other hand, the oil sector should see greater activity as the higher price of oil spurs the development of new oil finds. A minimal representation of the effects of higher oil prices on the oil sector is depicted graphically in Figure 2. Even this simple diagram shows how interconnected and nuanced everything can be in an economic system.

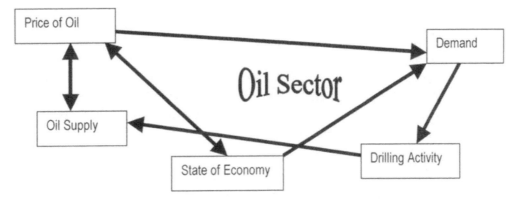

Figure 2. Effects of higher oil prices on the oil sector.

Companies within sectors will tend to perform together. There will be some companies that do better and others that do worse, but the sector will tend to control much of a company's prospects. The old saying that rising water raises all ships is very true here. The reverse is also true. Hence, in a time of job layoffs and a declining economy, most retailers will have problems selling merchandise. Perhaps a specialty retailer like a Game Stop will buck the trend, but the chances are that most will suffer similarly. When the price of oil is high and there is great demand for drilling, it would be hard for drilling companies like Transocean and Diamond Offshore to not do well.

Markets

Business intelligence gathering would not be complete without at least a passing nod to the concept of markets. Prices are not set arbitrarily in market economies (most of the world now). Rather, they are negotiated as a compromise between supply and demand. There are discontinuities in pricing that prevent perfect correlation, but over time prices do settle at equilibrium between the two. Many markets are informal with sellers offering goods at a price and adjusting them, as they perceive demand based on sales. Retail clothing stores begin discounting items when they find sales to be slight.

Formalized markets exist in the form of exchanges such as the New York Stock Exchange and the Chicago Mercantile Exchange. They are established places of trust where various parties can come together to buy and sell. Prices are publicly reported. The exchanges take care of the paper work. Exchanges permit the ready transfer of such assets from one party to another. This makes exchange traded assets more liquid. A more thorough treatment of financial markets is *Guide to Financial Markets,* by Marc Levinson, 4th ed. (Bloomberg Press, 2006).

Company Metrics

While the sector or sectors that a company is in will determine much of its success, different companies will react in different ways. Therefore, companies within a sector can be compared by their metrics (various quantitative measures of performance). There are many different metrics and their importance varies by sector or industry. The metrics are distilled from various corporate reports.

All U.S. public companies are required to report their financial condition by law periodically. The U.S. Securities and Exchange Commission (SEC) issued its Regulation FD (fair disclosure) in 2000. It mandates that all publicly traded companies must disclose material information to all investors at the same time. This ensures that individual investors have the same access to information as powerful fund managers or other supposed insiders. Public companies have gone out of their way to disseminate information in various ways. The Internet has become a preferred vehicle both because of its wide accessibility and the speed with which information can be conveyed. It is therefore possible for researchers almost anywhere to get hold of the latest information on a company almost instantaneously.

Privately held and foreign companies are another story. Privately held companies must disclose information to their investors or owners, but they do not fall under the same disclosure laws as public companies. Foreign companies that do not trade in the United States are held to the standards of their country of origin. European and many other countries have high reporting standards enforced by law comparable to the United States. Some countries do not. In these areas it is exceedingly difficult to find meaningful information.

Company metrics are derived from their financial statements. Reading financial statements requires some measure of accounting acumen. U.S. companies report their finances according to Generally Accepted Accounting Principles (GAAP). This set of principles allows comparison between companies because all companies using GAAP should be calculating their numbers on the same basis. Many books deal with the process of evaluating company financial information. *Guide to Analyzing Companies,* by Bob Vause, 4th ed. (Profile Books, 2005) covers most of the basics, as does *Business Ratios and Formulas: A Comprehensive Guide,* by Steven Bragg (Wiley, 2003). A gentler introduction is *Five Rules for Successful Stock Investing*, by Pat Dorsey (Wiley, 2004).

One better-known metric is the price-to-earnings (P/E) ratio. It represents the price of a company's common stock divided by its earnings per share. The P/E for Transocean at the close of the day of October 31, 2007, was 17.97. It should be noted that a metric like P/E that is tied to a company's stock price will be consequently volatile as stock prices can change rapidly during a trading day. In the case of Transocean, a reported dramatic increase in quarterly earnings and a rise in its stock price gave it a P/E of 13.8 by the next afternoon. Up-to-date metrics are readily available at various public Internet Web sites (see below). They also provide access to more detailed company financial reports such as income statements and filings with the SEC like 10-K reports (a legal version of a company's annual report to shareholders that is loaded with financial performance data).

http://finance.yahoo.com/

http://moneycentral.msn.com/investor/home.asp

Brokers like E*Trade provide some free data, too. More complete and historic metrics are available through various paid services like ValueLine and Morningstar as well as Standard & Poor's. It is important in choosing a service to make sure it includes the desired metrics in a convenient format on a timely basis. Timeliness cannot be overemphasized. The flow of business information is ceaseless. Historic data is just that—historic and must be treated as such.

Narrative Company Information

The narrative provides the story behind the numbers. News stories, company press releases, and company presentations provide the basis of the narrative for specific companies. Taken together with broader economy and sector views, these sources provide the details to complete the picture of a company.

As it may be imagined, timeliness is all-critical in gathering the narrative as with numerical data. Announcements of new business, earnings, lawsuits, financial problems, executive changes, mergers, or the like greatly affect a company's story. That is why its immediacy makes the Internet such a powerful business intelligence-gathering tool. Perhaps the most immediate source of information for companies is the quarterly earnings conference calls that most conduct. These are available live and are recorded. They are available to anyone with Internet access from the investor relations portion of most companies' Web sites. During conference calls, company officers provide up-to-the-minute data and insight into the company's current and future prospects. During these calls, companies take questions from brokerage analysts. The answers company officers give can go far in fleshing out their presentations and in addressing outsider concerns.

A company's Web site may provide more current information than any other source. Of course, companies do not like to report negative things, but they cannot lie by law (some still do—think Enron or WorldCom).

Third-party analysis is usually available to provide some color to a sector or company. Articles and discussion in the financial media often go beyond reporting events to interpreting them. Paid analysis is available from the major brokerages and sources like Morningstar, Standard & Poor's, and ValueLine. Much of this is focused on the investment outlook, but it all provides the background story necessary to understand the current state of a sector and company.

Transocean

To put this altogether, let us consider one company (everything here is from October 31, 2007, and numbers are stated in the past tense). Transocean, stock symbol RIG, is a company in the oil sector. More specifically, it is in the drilling part of the oil sector. Yahoo Finance provides the following profile:

> Transocean, Inc. provides offshore contract drilling services for oil and gas wells. It contracts drilling rigs, related equipment, and work crews primarily on day rate basis to drill oil and gas wells with a focus on deepwater and harsh environment drilling services. As of February 2, 2007, the company owned and operated 82 mobile off-shore and barge drilling units, including 33 high-specification semi submersibles and drill ships, 20 floaters, 25 jackup rigs, and 4 other rigs. The company also provides other integrated services. Transocean primarily operates in the Far East, India, U.S. Gulf of Mexico, United Kingdom, Nigeria, the Mediterranean and Middle East, Brazil, Norway, other West African countries, Australia, Canada, the Caspian Sea, and Venezuela. The company was founded in 1953 and is based in Houston, Texas.

Yahoo goes on to say that Transocean employs 10,700 full-time employees. It gives Transocean's address, a list of its top corporate officers, and its Web site: http://www.deep-water.com

Transocean's P/E ratio was shown as 17.97. There are dozens of other metrics. One problem in evaluating a company is to determine some type of benchmark. One way to do this is to compare companies to their peers (services are available that compute ratios for entire industry groups). Take profit margin for example: Transocean had a profit margin of 40.86 percent compared to another drilling company, Hercules Offshore, whose profit margin was 28.97 percent. A third drilling company, Parker Drilling, had a profit margin of 17.26 percent. We could take all of Transocean's metrics and run them against the other two, but are we comparing apples to apples or apples to oranges? This is where the narrative is important.

Transocean is a deep-water driller. Hercules Offshore is a shallow-water driller, primarily in the Gulf of Mexico. Parker Drilling drills in shallow water and also on land. This makes them different. More research would find that Transocean is the largest of the deep-water drillers. Further research would make the discovery that it is planning to merge with the second largest of the deep-water drillers—Global Santa Fe. The merger announced in the summer is a critical event to be taken into consideration for any analysis of the two companies or, for that matter, the entire drilling space. Articles or other information prepared before the announcement would therefore be somewhat obsolete. Timeliness is everything.

To add more perspective, it is necessary to learn more about the sector in general. Research finds that oil is becoming scarce except in deep water—as evidenced by industry reports and the price per barrel reaching new highs in the past twelve months. Demand is increasing. The global economy has seen the rise of China and India as economic powers. Both are oil importers, and both have the foreign exchange necessary to bid up the price of oil. Transocean and Global Santa Fe appear to be in a sweet spot.

On Transocean's recent conference call, management summed up their prospects by saying that they see strong demand for their services with increasing fees through 2008 and probably beyond. The company reported earnings of $973 million, or $3.24 per share for their third quarter of 2007, compared with $309 million, or 96 cents per share, in the year-ago quarter. Here, the narrative and the earnings, taken together with sector and broader economic indicators, begin to fill in the picture quite nicely.

To do a fuller analysis of Transocean, these summary conclusions need to be fleshed out with in-depth research on the company and comparisons to like and even unlike companies.

A rigorous understanding of the company's business model and the sector's prospects needs to be reached. Many questions will arise in analyzing Transocean. Will oil still be important in the future? If the price falls, will drilling continue at the current pace? How much deep-sea drilling will be required in the future? Are there personnel or technological issues? Is there geopolitical risk?

Summary

Achieving a useful level of business intelligence requires a relentless hunt for the facts in a multiplicity of timely information sources, coupled with endless analysis, because with every breaking dawn, the situation changes.

The Charleston Conference appears to be one of the best places to talk about e-books. This year several talks were given on e-books. One program looked at technical processing of e-books. Another program focused on a locally hosted e-book platform for a consortium.

E-BOOKS

WOULD YOU LIKE THOSE E-BOOKS SHELF-READY?

Heather D'Amour, Head of Technical Services and Digital Access, University of Calgary, Calgary Canada

Kathy Carter, Coordinator, Bibliographic Services, University of Alberta, Edmonton, Alberta, Canada

Jim Shetler, Vice President, Library Technical Services, YBP Library Services, Contoocook, New Hampshire

The Changing E-Book Environment

Until recently the "print" format has reigned supreme for monograph publications particularly in the academic environment. Libraries purchased books in quantities that were manageable for acquisitions and cataloguing. It is now possible to buy hundreds or thousands of e-books in various ways: publisher packages, aggregators, and individually through traditional books vendors. Management issues have arisen for libraries as this growth of e-books begins to realize its potential. For example, a library may purchase quadruple the number of e-books in one year in comparison to their print book acquisition.

Some of the resulting issues include:

- Technical Services or systems staff not having the resources to cope with the increasing influx of materials

- New skills or workflows may need to be researched and introduced (e.g., globally updating/editing large batch loads of records)

- Expectations that more can be done with less and that e-books will have different needs or permit more discovery or access electronically

- Various scenarios for discovery and access are being explored but aren't yet available

- Reliable management tools for libraries to catalogue, track, and keep statistics are needed

- Libraries are looking to their suppliers to provide catalogue records. At present, the catalogue is the most effective way for libraries to provide access to e-books, and usage jumps dramatically when cataloguing is provided.

As a result of these issues at the University of Calgary, we decided we needed to establish some principles and practices for MARC records with our e-book acquisitions.

Selection and Purchase

- MARC records are needed to capitalize on the Library's significant investment

- Address catalogue record issues during product review and purchasing

- Include Technical Services in vendor meetings

- Aim to purchase products that come complete with MARC records—as close to "shelf-ready" as possible

- Load individual e-book records into the Online Catalogue

- Provide the best access possible to users—broad access not niche access

- Recognize that quality metadata is required to work with integrated library systems (ILS), facilitate user access, and enable library processes such as collection assessment

Following from this, we must begin to ask our vendors and publishers specific questions like the following during meetings or demonstrations:

- What short or long term e-book publishing plans do they have (frontlist and backlist)?

- What plans were in place to address catalogue records (MARC, subject headings, and name authorities)?

- Would e-books be able to go "shelf-ready" with vendors who supplied "print" monograph records?

The results of these discussions were mixed. It is obviously an area that many of the publishers and vendors are exploring. What the discussions demonstrated was that publishers or their representatives may have little knowledge of MARC or the requirements of online catalogue systems. New technologies are being developed which libraries, vendors, and publishers all need to explore to see how they will work with their existing systems. At the same time, there is a need to continue to work in current environments and provide the best possible access to our users.

"Shelf-Ready"

What makes e-books "shelf-ready"? The simple answer is load-ready catalogue records. Libraries do not use records in isolation; they integrate them into an existing catalogue. This requires standard, consistent, and easy-to-manage records. Publishers who specialize in providing collections in microform have been doing this for years, providing high-quality catalogue records on cards and later in MARC format. Some book vendors have added cataloguing to their service for printed books, but for most publishers, the demand from libraries for e-book cataloguing is new and just one more challenge they face with the transition to digital format. Many vendors and publishers are responding with alacrity to this demand.

The University of Alberta has over 400,000 catalogued e-books. Most of the records were supplied by the publishers and vendors from whom the e-books were purchased.

In the past two to three years, we have reviewed, edited, loaded, unloaded, and reloaded records from dozens of suppliers. We have encountered great variety in record quality and delivery.

Standard Records

Producing standard records requires cataloguing expertise. Some suppliers hire cataloguers, and some outsource to an organization that has the expertise, such as OCLC or private companies.

- Librarians prefer full AACR (Anglo-American Cataloging Rules) records including Library of Congress (LC) Subject Headings, and LC or Dewey Decimal Classification (DDC), encoded in MARC21 format.

- Electronic reproductions, sets, and serials should be catalogued according to AACR and LC's rule interpretations.

- Authority-controlled headings are especially important. The introduction of nonstandard headings for names and subjects would create conflicts with authority records, impede access, and prevent collocation such as bringing together different editions and formats of the same work.

- Librarians find it useful to know the source of the records and what quality assurance measures are applied.

- Some vendors offer records at finer levels of granularity than are customary in library catalogues, for example, records for individual book chapters or literary works such as poems. These should be available in separate files for libraries that do not wish to load them.

Guidelines are available to assist vendors and publishers, most notably the PCC BIBCO *MARC Record Guide for Monograph Aggregator Vendors.* The National Library of Australia has produced *Guidelines for the Cataloguing of E-Book Resources for Contribution of Records to the Australian National Bibliographic Database.*

Consistency

Internal consistency within a collection is important because library staff do not have time to examine each record. They want to be confident that what they see in sample records will be true for all records in a collection.

Local and Consortial Data

Another consideration affecting record integration into library catalogues is local and consortial needs. Local data may include site-specific URLs, call numbers, fund numbers, notes, and location/holdings. Catalogues shared by a consortium may require different local data for each member. Further complicating matters, members may join or leave a consortium and may purchase e-book collections at different times and in different configurations from one another. The catalogue must show, accurately and simply, who has access to what.

Some local data can easily be added by the library using a program such as MARCEdit, which is sometimes preferable to requesting it from the e-book provider.

Easy to Manage Records

Even with good quality records, the process of loading them is more complex and time-consuming than one might expect, especially for collections that are growing and changing. Unfortunately many ILS have poor record management functionality, making loading, unloading, matching, and overlaying a real challenge. There is much that record providers can do to ease these processes.

- Unique and stable record numbers allow match and overlay of existing records with revised ones, deletion of records for e-books no longer available, and duplicate detection.

- Separate files for each purchasable collection enable libraries to load records that match the content they have purchased without having to merge or separate files.

- It seems obvious, but there must be a book for each record and a record for each book. Libraries are no longer "receiving" each e-book as it "arrives" as they might with print books—they need to be sure the records they load match the books they have bought.

- Libraries may process and load serial records differently from monographs, so serial records should be available in separate files.

- When revised records are provided, they should be available separately from new ones to facilitate overlay or deletion and reloading.

Other Considerations

URLs, preferably OpenURLs, provided in 856 fields should link directly to the book described, and be stable.

Ideally, records should be available as soon as the e-books are accessible. Delays dramatically reduce use of the e-books and therefore the value of the library's investment. Equally important is timely availability of new, updated, and deleted records.

What is on the horizon for e-book cataloguing? Proliferation of separate records for the same e-book available from different providers has prompted discussion of vendor-neutral records. These are records that can be used with any and all versions of an e-book because they do not include any mention of individual providers. Libraries embraced vendor-neutral records for e-journals some years ago when the same e-journal content became available from multiple providers.

Materials Vendor Perspective

The sale and distribution of e-books present significant challenges to the materials vendor in respect to technical services support. As the market evolved, it became readily apparent that customers expected the following:

- The mode of acquisition, and the resultant workflow, should be no different from that already established for print. In other words, customers want to acquire e-books by placing firm orders, by placing orders from notification slips produced by approval plans, or by receiving access automatically (analogous to automatic print book shipments from an approval plan).

- Customers expect the same level and quality of cataloging support as is currently supplied for print. This includes cataloging records that are delivered in response to an order in a vendor's system (an order confirmation record), a record used to facilitate/generate an order in the library's local system, and a record when orders are filled and invoiced.

- Customers expect that cataloging records for e-books contain URLs that provide site-specific access to content. In other words, the URL in each record should lead catalog users to the correct title and, for catalog users in the library's IP address range, direct, unfettered access to content.

Essentially, from a technical services perspective, very little will change. Ultimately, the customer's goal is to obtain cataloging records that accurately describe the e-book acquired and provide controlled access to the content. In addition, these records should also be able to convey all the embedded local data (order data, invoice data, etc.) that are now provided in cataloging records for print.

The Challenges

The evolution of e-book cataloging policy and practice is, in many respects, similar to the evolution that occurred in the cataloging of e-journals. Access to a given title can be obtained from multiple sources, such as an aggregator, directly from a publisher, or some other third party. The same is true for the cataloging records themselves, as multiple agencies are now creating and distributing e-book cataloging records. Given the multiple options, how best to describe and catalog any given resource? Is a separate-record approach preferable to a single-record approach? In addition, cataloging was (and is) performed as policy and practice evolve, with the result that the cataloging utilities are populated with multiple records for the same resource. Which one is appropriate? Even as standard practices evolve, will individual customers adhere to that practice? This presents a significant challenge to the materials vendor. How far do you go to in order to meet a customer's expectations? Are standards strictly adhered to, or is flexibility required?

Regardless of the approach to policy and practice, cataloging e-books places the same operational burden on the materials vendor as it does the customer. For print, materials vendors are able to access and capitalize on the same shared cataloging environment that is used, and built, by our customers. However, for e-books, the shared cataloging environment is not as robust, with the result that many cataloging records may have to be created originally or edited to the point that it may as well be original cataloging. Original cataloging is significantly more expensive, and labor intensive, than copy cataloging. How best to manage that cost and to recover the investment? What cost will the market bear?

Furthermore, for the foreseeable future, it appears that libraries will remain "OPAC-centric." As a result, MARC should remain, for the most part, a viable data structure for storing and distributing bibliographic data. However, current trends in the integrated library systems marketplace lead many to question whether or not the ILS will remain the library's primary resource discovery and management tool in the future. If not, what will replace it, and what data structure or structures will become the standard? Will materials vendors be required to support both during any period of transition?

Current Practice

Fortunately, there are guidelines that the materials vendor can follow in order to create and distribute cataloging records for customer's e-book purchases. The *MARC Record Guide for Monograph Aggregator Vendors* (prepared by the Program for Cooperative Cataloging in 2006) provides an excellent starting point. These guidelines provide background in guiding principles and best practices, definitions of categories of e-books, and specifying what bibliographic data is mandatory, mandatory if applicable, or optional.

In addition, in the current environment most e-books have an associated print equivalent. As a result, cataloging records for the print can be programmatically manipulated to create cataloging records that appropriately describe whatever version of the e-book is acquired by the customer. Furthermore, the format of URLs is often predictable, with easily identifiable strings of data that lend themselves to programmatic construction of URLs specifically tailored for a customer. However, as the number of books "born digital" that remain only digital increases the availability of cataloging data for the print equivalent will wane. Therefore, the need to create original records, by whatever means, will increase proportionally.

Conclusion

For all materials vendors, the technical services support for e-books presents many of the same challenges—and pitfalls—as exist for our customers. Perhaps the most significant challenge for all concerned is to resist the temptation to apply the practices that worked, and continue to work, in the print world to the evolving world of digital content. Attempting to impose policy, practice, and business models that worked for print may not work at all for e-books, with the result of unmet customer expectations and an operational nightmare. As always, communication and cooperation are key elements in ensuring that customer expectations are met. Fortunately, it does appear that the landscape is becoming more stable, but the future remains unwritten. Both the materials vendor and the customer have a responsibility to ensure that future becomes a viable, working legacy for whatever follows.

A LOCALLY HOSTED E-BOOK PLATFORM IN A CONSORTIAL ENVIRONMENT

Tony Horava, Collections and Information Resources Coordinator/Coordonnateur des Collections et Ressources d'Information, University of Ottawa/l'Universite d'Ottawa, Ottawa, Canada

As all of us struggle to deal with e-book acquisitions and delivery models, a consortium in Ontario, Canada, is moving into uncharted territory. This paper will summarize a presentation on e-book access and delivery in a consortial environment.

The Ontario Council of University Libraries (OCUL) is composed of twenty publicly funded universities in the province of Ontario. These range from very large (i.e., 60,000 students at the University of Toronto) to the very small (i.e., 1,000 students at the Royal Military College). The consortium currently has agreements for approximately 185 products, representing a wide variety of content—e-journals, e-books, reference sources, and specialized tools. Participation is voluntary, as there is no central funding for the acquisition of content. There is an Information Resources Committee, made up of collections representatives from each school, that discusses a wide range of content, licensing, vendor and strategic issues on a daily basis via a listserv.

There is a committee that focuses on e-book offers, as e-books are becoming more strategic in collection development thinking. It is the mandate of this group to examine any offers and negotiate with the vendors to obtain the best possible deal, thereby maximizing our consortial buying power. We have learned that there are many details and wrinkles to be ironed out for any e-book offer, and we ask the vendor to complete a template of questions regarding their offer. This captures all of the important information concerning content, licensing, pricing, platform, and technical issues. Providing this to our members helps them in understanding the offer and making an informed decision as to whether to participate. The process also allows us to educate the vendor as to what issues are important to us and to frame the negotiations in those terms.

OCUL works within the Scholars Portal environment, which is a service infrastructure providing for local loading of over 8,000 full-text scholarly journals; a front-end user interface (Illumina); a link resolver system (SFX); a citation management server (RefWorks); and a document delivery system (RACER—from VDX Fretwell Downing).

This is a highly innovative integration of content, services, and tools allowing researchers the ability to discover content and incorporate the results into their own workflow. A crucial missing element is an e-book delivery mechanism.

Recently the consortium obtained funding of $750,000 from the Ontario government for the acquisition and development of an e-book platform to be integrated into Scholars Portal. This is based on a three-year project plan (2007–2010) and involves the hiring of a project manager and the setting of milestones/deliverables for this exciting new service.

Developing an e-book delivery platform will address various challenges faced by our patrons. Currently our students and faculty need to use multiple systems to access e-books from a variety of sources in their home institutions. There is a myriad of different permissions and rights attached to e-book collections from publishers and vendors. There are library differences in cataloguing practices regarding e-books, for example, what is catalogued and what is not and the quality of MARC records which is assessed by each school. Promotion and teaching activities for e-books differ widely across the libraries, and therefore the profile of e-books can vary greatly. There is no federated tool that is seen as adequate for allowing searching across disparate e-book collections and individual titles. Most important, there is no integration of e-book content and discovery tools in Scholars Portal, thus diminishing the visibility of this valuable and expensive resource for patrons' research and information searching.

The overriding objective of the project is to provide a single retrieval and delivery platform for licensed e-books. We also intend to load out-of-copyright books that have been scanned in the context of the Open Archive/Open Content Alliance project. The system should be capable of housing about 50,000 licensed scholarly e-books as well as 50,000 out-of-copyright e-books. Rights for local loading and secure archiving will need to be negotiated with each vendor/publisher. This is intended to be an archive in perpetuity for housing and serving this content. It is not about content selection—this remains the domain of each school. The platform is intended to provide a unified access and delivery vehicle within Scholars Portal, and each school remains in charge of its own collection development and acquisition strategy. Thus the approach represents an important balance between collective action and local autonomy in relation to e-books.

There are various basic requirements for the platform: it needs to support the loading/archving/searching of e-books in a variety of formats: PDF, XML, HTML, OEB, etc. It needs to support intellectual property rights (DRM) and permissions management to ensure that publishers' concerns are met. It needs to support a large and growing collection and demonstrate scalability. It needs to support the loading of metadata for describing remotely housed collections, particularly for historical collections that would be problematic to load locally. This will ensure the discoverability of these collections within the search interface. Lastly, the platform needs to support a variety of operating systems to ensure maximum uptake and usage by university students and faculty from across the province.

There are other requirements that are intended to ensure equity of access and flexibility of application. The platform should support all major browsers without plug-ins. It should support access for persons with disabilities. It needs to allow local branding and allow patrons to save their own settings, for example, bookmarks or annotations. It should support durable links, OpenURL standards, and various authentication schemes. Lastly, it should support the incorporation of e-book data into local integrated library systems (ILS; e.g., XML and MARC records) and be able to integrate with course management systems such as WebCT and Blackboard.

There has been a working group mandated to lead the process of developing requirements for an RFP and evaluating the vendor proposals and to eventually make a recommendation to the consortium. A Request for Information to solicit interest was released in April 2007. Two respondents were invited to give presentations: MyiLibrary and e-brary. This experience helped crystallize various issues and requirements that were incorporated into an RFP that was issued in October 2007. The same two companies submitted proposals and were invited to give presentations on their systems. The deliberation and assessment stage has continued, and no decision had been made as of this presentation given at Charleston in early November 2007.

Assessing the bids has been a challenging process. There are many technical issues regarding the variety of e-book formats, the loading of data files, the handling of metadata, and the implementation of rights management systems. As we are moving into uncharted territory, it has been essential to ensure that the vendors understood our concept of local control over e-books and how we see the system being managed and developed over time. It has also been important to see this as a partnership approach with a vendor, so that the vendor's development plans for the front-end interface and the back-end software and hardware are understood and are compatible with the consortium's strategic goals. Along the way we have learned about the complexities of how e-books are created, stored, protected, searched, and used. It is self-evident that the e-book is at a much earlier stage of development than the e-journal, and that business models, licensing strategies, and access issues have not been standardized. This immaturity of the e-book publishing landscape has been a backdrop to our discussions and deliberations over vendor proposals. However, we believe that through this innovative project we can sensitize vendors and publishers to our needs and to the interests of the academic community in general.

It has also become clear that we are at an intersection between technology and strategic direction: we need to harness the appropriate technological solution to help us meet our strategic goals. Exposing students and faculty to a critical mass of e-book content in the Scholars Portal will bring a wealth of new research and discovery opportunities to the current and future generations of patrons in Ontario universities. It will allow them to search, compile, extract, store, and use this material within their workflow and research patterns. It will also help ensure that Scholars Portal can provide a wide range of scholarly content for the university community, to serve different resources for different needs, in relation to Web 2.0 concepts of exploring, collaborating, and using scholarly information in novel ways. We look forward to a decision in the near future that will guide us in this direction.

Journals continue to be a major focus of the Charleston Conference. Open access journals and their influence and usage were addressed. Other issues included weeding your periodical collection, Project TRANSFER, usage statistics, workflow changes, and collaborative collection development projects.

Journals

PROJECT TRANSFER: AN UPDATE OF THE UNITED KINGDOM SERIALS GROUP INITIATIVE TO IMPROVE THE PROCESS OF JOURNAL TRANSFERS BETWEEN PUBLISHERS

Nancy Buckley, Managing Director, Burgundy Information Services Ltd., Mollington, Oxfordshire, United Kingdom

Abstract

This paper will update the Charleston Conference on the United Kingdom Serials Group project called Project Transfer. The Transfer Working Group is currently creating best practice guidelines and standards for the movement of titles between publishers. The ultimate aim of the group is to create an industry code of practice similar to the excellent work that the Project COUNTER organisation has done for journal usage statistics.

In late 2005 the United Kingdom Serials Group (UKSG) organisation recognised the need for an improvement, and standardisation of the process of journal titles moving between publishers. UKSG sponsors the popular library list-serve Lis-E-Journals, where librarians can raise issues concerning their electronic journal holdings. More and more frequently, the mails posted were concerning access and ownership issues for those titles that had recently moved from one journal publisher to another or from a self-publishing arrangement to that of a commercial publishing house. Some of the subject headings on the list read as:

"Now You See It Now You Don't—Where Have the Backfiles and Archives of Contemporary Economic Policy and Economic Inquiry Gone?"

"Agricultural history—a lost journal?"

"Pediatrics—will this publisher ever get anything right?"

The UKSG agreed to fund the creation of a working group made up of publishers, intermediaries, and librarians in order to meet and discuss all of the issues encountered by the parties in the information chain. The first meeting occurred in late 2005 and highlighted the following main themes.

For librarians the issue of perpetual rights was seen to be a huge problem. When a title moves publisher, the librarian is unaware of the change until access is cut off because of a change of URL or access arrangement. A particular frustration is when the librarian loses both access to the newly published issues of the title as well as those back volumes that they have paid for in the past. Another key problem is when a title moves between two publishers who offer different pricing models: for example, a librarian may receive full access to a title via their consortia deal, but when a journal moves, they have to resort to rebuying a journal subscription if the title moves to a publisher that does not offer a similar consortia-collection model.

Publishers highlighted how upon receiving a journal they often did not receive the required amount of subscription information required in order to be able to ensure uninterrupted access to the journal for the newly transferred subscribers. Their call was for standards to ensure that a minimum amount of core information is supplied by the transferring publisher.

They also emphasized that many of the contract decisions and timings of journal transfers were due to the editorial board or owner society making decisions without understanding the consequences to their library customers.

After much discussion the Working Group condensed the issues into three key areas where we would like to see standards emerge:

The first was **Communication**—the Group considered who, what, when, and how parties within the info chain can learn about title transfers. Agents were identified as being key stakeholders in ensuring that this level of information was provided to its library customers, but agents in turn rely on timely information from publishers.

The second theme was **Legacy**—that is, how to track and record which volumes of a transferred journal are available, where they are hosted, and how to identify who has rights to them. All agreed that a central repository of such data would be extremely valuable to cope with these issues.

The third theme was **Packages and Price Models**—looking at how journal transfers are handled in the context of the big deal in terms of pricing, access rights and licensing.

In order to roll out the project to the information community, the Group decided to divide the work into phases, ensuring that the three themes above are considered. The first phase would be the Transfer Code of Conduct for publishers. The second phase monitoring and compliance of the Code, and the final phase would be the creation of a Transfer Web Service to try to deal specifically with the communication issues, centralizing the details of any journal transfer on a central, accessible Web site.

Phase One, the Transfer Code of Conduct, was launched in first draft in April 2007 at the UKSG Annual Conference. The Project was praised widely by the library and publisher community and quickly gained support from the following publishers:

BioOne—www.bioone.org (23 August 2007)

Co-Action Publishing—www.co-action.net (4 September 2007)

Haworth Press—www.haworthpress.com (23 May 2007)

Mary Ann Liebert Inc Publishers—www.liebertpub.com (15 May 2007)

Multilingual Matters—www.multilingual-matters.com (27 July 2007)

SAGE Publications—www.sagepub.co.uk (11 May 2007)

Symposium Journals—www.symposium-journals.co.uk (11 May 2007)

Taylor & Francis Publishers—www.tandf.co.uk/journals (10 May 2007)

The Code was written to help publishers to ensure that their journal content remains easily accessible by librarians and readers when it is the subject of a transfer between parties and to ensure that the transfer process occurs with minimum disruption.

The principles of the Code of Conduct should apply to both the transferring and receiving publisher. Publishers who agree to align their procedures with the Code and to apply them in practice when working with other, similarly aligned publishers will be considered "Transfer Compliant." The Code is concerned primarily with online content and not with print, except where the Code mandates that print subscription lists are communicated.

The Code is intended to be universally applied regardless of the nature of the publisher or whether a society is involved or if one publisher is acquired by another. It is recognized that such a Code of Conduct needs to evolve and develop in line with the marketplace it purports to serve.

However, in September 2007, the sign-up of publishers had slowed down, and feedback indicated that some sections of the publishing community were unhappy with the language and direction of the Code. The Publishing organisation Association of Learned and Professional Society Publishers (ALPSP) and Science, Technology and Medicine (STM) jointly wrote to Transfer to complain about the Code of Conduct, their main issues were as follows:

- [The Code did not] recognise the complexity of business models and approaches used by different publishers.

- All "mandatory" requirements should be removed.

- It should be less prescriptive in its description of how ongoing archival access is given but be consistent with customer contract arrangements.

- The prescribed transfer of the subscription lists is mentioned without respect to data protection or compensation.

- The requirement for Transferring Publishers to continue to give one month's access after Transfer is unnecessary if other factors within the Code are complied with.

- General comments were made regarding the nonexclusive transferral of publishing rights from one publisher to another.

But overall ALPSP and STM were very supportive of Transfer and its aims. Project Transfer needs industry buy-in in order to be successful, but the Code must still be strong enough to protect the library customers and their end-users. Therefore, to ensure industry buy-in the Working Group invited additional members to join the meetings: Springer, Wiley-Blackwell, OUP, and Elsevier joined exiting members from Sage, Nature, ALPSP, and CrossRef, as well as librarians and agents. The next steps for the Group were to redraft areas of the Code that were inconsistent or out of line with publisher processes.

At the time of writing this paper the third draft of the Code of Conduct has been completed, and is being circulated for discussion amongst the broader library and publishing community. It is hoped that the final versions can be publicised before Christmas 2007. The next section of this paper will discuss the key sections of the Code:

ROLES AND RESPONSIBILITIES (Phase 1): TRANSFERRING PUBLISHER

Key responsibilities:

*To ensure effective and rapid transfer of subscriber information to the Receiving Publisher and facilitate the continued access for subscribers to journal content

*To ensure effective and rapid transfer of journal content to the Receiving Publisher

1. Access to the title: Where perpetual access rights have been granted, the Transferring Publisher must ensure continuance of access to their customers (on a nonexclusive basis) even if the Transferring Publisher will cease to host the online version of the journal after the effective transfer date.

Transfer recommends that publishers follow the STM Guideline for STM Member Signatories which says that "Publishers with society journal contracts should always ensure that their customer licenses for electronic or online journal access do not exceed the scope of the license granted to them by the journal-owning societies." *(International Association of Scientific, Technical & Medical Publishers: "Ensuring quality customer access to online content when society journals change publishers").*

If the Receiving Publisher has received all of the content files but is unable to provide access on the effective transfer date, the Transferring Publisher shall continue to provide access until the Receiving Publisher has made the files available.

2. Digital content files—current and archive (Backfile/Legacy): With consideration to contract terms covering the journal transfer, the Transferring Publisher will make the digital files available to the Receiving Publisher within four weeks of signature of the contract or (with the express written permission of the Sponsoring Society if the Transferring Publisher is not the journal owner) four months prior to the effective transfer date, whichever is sooner.

3. Subscription lists: Subject to contract terms, the Transferring Publisher will make the subscription list of the journal available to the Receiving Publisher within four weeks of signature of the contract (or with the express written permission of the journal-owner if the Transferring Publisher is not the owner), four months prior to effective transfer date (whichever is sooner). Complying with appropriate data protection legislation, the list should include the following types of subscriber data:

- Personal/Membership subscriber details

- Institutional full price subscriber details (print, Online or print + online), specifying which subscribers have perpetual access rights

- Consortia subscribers—specifying which subscribers have perpetual access rights

- Lapsed subscribers

4. Journal URL: With consideration to contract terms covering the journal transfer and ownership rights, the Transferring Publisher will transfer any existing title-related journal domain name to the Receiving Publisher. If the journal title homepage URL is part of the Transferring Publisher's domain then the Transferring Publisher will provide a URL link to the Receiving Publisher or create a redirect for a minimum of 12 months after the effective date of transfer.

5. Communication: The Transferring Publisher will use best endeavours to communicate journal transfer information to its subscribers, eTOC subscribers, and relevant intermediaries as soon as possible after signature of the contract and ideally no less than 1 month before the effective date of transfer.

6. DOI name ownership: The Transferring Publisher will follow the CrossRef DOI Name Ownership Transfer Guidelines to enable the transfer of control of DOI names to the Receiving Publisher (http://www.crossref.org/02publishers/guidelines.html). The Transferring Publisher will give its consent to the change of DOI name ownership as soon as possible after signature of the contract.

ROLES AND RESPONSIBILITIES (Phase 1): RECEIVING PUBLISHER

Key responsibilities:

*To ensure that content is made available to subscribers as soon as this is no longer the responsibility of the Transferring Publisher

*To ensure that subscribers have uninterrupted access to the journal content

7. Access to the title: The Receiving Publisher will provide access to the journal from the effective transfer date. If the Receiving Publisher has received all digital content files but is unable to provide access from the effective transfer date, it must permit the Transferring Publisher to continue to make the files available on a nonexclusive basis until the files are made available.

8. Subscription lists: The Receiving Publisher will contact all existing subscribers as soon as possible on receipt of the subscription lists (point 3), and make arrangements with them for continued access to future issues, subject to subscription renewal.

9. DOI ownership: The Receiving Publisher will follow the CrossRef DOI Name Ownership Transfer Guidelines to transfer control of DOI names from the Receiving Publisher (http://www.crossref.org/02publishers/guidelines.html). The Receiving Publisher will request consent for the transfer from the Transferring Publisher as soon as possible after signature of the contract.

In addition to the redrafting of the Code the Working Group will also reestablish itself, under the auspices of UKSG, as a more formal international committee composed of librarians, publishers and agents. The Transfer Committee will:

• Develop guidelines for publishers on practical aspects of implementing the Code of Conduct

• Oversee implementation of a Transfer Alerting Service that will provide a central location for publishers to register basic details of transfers which will be available to libraries and other interested parties

• Oversee compliance with the Code, conduct periodic reviews of the effectiveness of the Code and receive complaints on non-compliance with the Code

• Consider future revisions to the Code of Conduct

The Working Group hopes that this version of the code will gain acceptance from other, larger publishers and will become an essential tool in the business of journal transfers. Indeed, if the Code is accepted for publishers, it could be used to encourage societies to update journal contracts, persuade stubborn societies to apply best practice and aid PR by using the Transfer logo to demonstrate compliancy and best practice. For Librarians, it will help to ensure consistent access to users and will improve renewal period and processes. Transfer would also encourage librarians to insist on Transfer compliancy in your publisher agreements and license terms.

From a personal perspective, I am proud to have initiated Project Transfer and have enjoyed chairing the Working Group. However, when leaving Blackwell to set up my company Burgundy, I no longer had as much time to dedicate to the Project, and in December 2007 handed over the Chair to Ed Pentz of CrossRef. Ed will be continuing the good work of Transfer and can be contacted at: epentz@crossref.org. See the Project Web site at: www.projecttransfer.org.

MANAGING CHANGES IN SERIALS WORKFLOW WHILE MIGRATING TO A NEW LIBRARY AUTOMATED SYSTEM: LESSONS FROM EXPERIENCE

Myrna Douglas, Serials Cataloguer, University of the West Indies, Mona Campus, Jamaica

Abstract

The purpose of this paper is to share the challenges in setting up a serials Technical Services Unit while migrating from one library automated system to another at the University of the West Indies (UWI), Mona Campus in Jamaica, West Indies. The paper examines the local requirements that played an important role in the selection of a new system. UWI Mona Library experience is reviewed and provides important lessons for other developing countries currently considering changes in Library Automated Systems, which affects serials technical services workflow. Such lessons concern maintaining a strong relationship between librarians and support staff and among staff in Periodicals, Technical Services, and Public Services, for a more effective management of serials workflow during the change process.

Highlighting management of the change process should benefit libraries not only in the Caribbean region and other developing countries but also libraries around the world that are intend to migrate from a legacy system to a new system.

Introduction

Since 1949, the University of the West Indies (UWI) enjoyed monopoly status in the provision of higher education services in the Caribbean region. The UWI has served the region from this position of dominance through its main campuses located on three different island states—Mona in Jamaica, St. Augustine in Trinidad and Tobago, and Cave Hill in Barbados, as well as over twenty-seven distance centers spread across sixteen Caribbean islands.[1] As a major of provider of human resource training in the region, UWI has been producing innovators with the creative skills and capacity to create new knowledge for the society at large. The Library plays a central role in UWI's position, being an important hub of the university which nurtures such individuals, by providing access to materials and information services for their development. With a mandate to provide central intellectual space in the university and to contribute to the economic, political, and social development of its clientele through information access, the library has a responsibility to ensure that it is on the cutting edge. It is the responsibility of each campus to provide library support to underpin the academic programs, not only for the main campus but also for its numerous distance centers (McLean 2006). Since the late 1990s, there has been an influx of providers of higher education services in the Caribbean, mainly from developed countries. This has resulted in the libraries of traditional higher education institutions in the Caribbean being faced with the urgent need to ensure their institutions remain on the competitive edge.

At UWI Mona, the Periodicals Section, like the rest of the library, is willing to play its part in reorganizing its operations, with a view to improving the level of efficiency in delivering the relevant materials and services to the rest of the institution. We are committed to repositioning ourselves to help the UWI to remain dominant in the Caribbean higher education marketplace. Late in 2006, the Library took steps to set up the Periodicals Technical Services

Unit, relocating the technical activities of serials to a physical space previously occupied by the Cataloguing Section. The head of the Periodicals Section was transferred to this Unit. She, along with her support staff, joined the Serials Cataloguer and a paraprofessional who has had the responsibility of centralizing cataloguing activities and the creation of serials holdings records since May of that year.

The Local Requirements

Choosing a system was not without its challenges. The implementation team consisted of representatives from all three main campuses, each having its own mandate and emphasis to select a system best suited to their local situation. The cost of acquiring and maintaining the subscription for the new system was to be borne by the three campuses with the larger campus, Mona, paying the larger portion. The economies and currencies of Barbados and Trinidad are stronger, and so the challenge for Mona is that we had to dig deeper into our budget to meet our financial obligations.

A challenge for us was the huge outlay of U.S. dollars required to acquire a system that was affordable to the three campuses. The rapid devaluation of the Jamaican currency continues to pose a challenge to our library's ability to purchase materials, equipment, and services from overseas, which is inevitable for developing countries. In addition to novelty and enhanced access, what we were looking for in a new system included:

1. The ability of the system to run on the latest version of Oracle, Linux, or Sun. The latest version of our legacy system, VTLS, had been around since August 1999. VTLS, Oracle, and H-UX software underwent upgrades—VTLS to version 94-99, Oracle to version 7, and HP-UX to version 10-11 (partly due to Y2K compliance of VTLS) (Kerr-Campbell, n.d., p. 11)

2. Enhanced client windows

3. The ability of the system to work with existing software like Peoplesoft (HRM) and Banner for invoicing purposes and for student accounts administration

4. The system's functionality to effectively track items sent to and returned from our Bindery; computerized tracking of our Bindery's intake and production (output) has resulted in improved turnaround time for our home bound serials

5. Finally, a system that would help us to remain competitive in the provision of the kind of services a modern library catalogue is capable of providing. This was part of the strategy in ensuring that our university remain competitive and dominant in the business of providing quality education and requisite access to such services for our Caribbean and global citizenship.

The Library is called upon to play its part in achieving the strategic objective of UWI: increased student centeredness by providing a more enhanced search interface for improved accessibility of materials and services. The blended learning approach to distance learning at UWI, and the intended reach of the planned UWI Open Campus will require the cooperation and connectivity of libraries on all campuses on different island states, by providing collaborative access to materials and resources.

More importantly, for serials, we were looking for a system that would help us streamline our operations, consolidate work activities, and centralize our technical processes, while effectively working together more closely with the Library's book Acquisitions and Cataloguing Sections. With increased acquisition of single titles of electronic serials and database serials, staff members could no longer pretend we could manage the increase workload while offering customer service. The increased responsibilities resulting from the serials acquisition process, liaising with departments, evaluating e-resources, setting up trials for them, marketing them, and resolving the queries of an increasing number of students sent to us by the Reference desk staff. To escape the additional workload, Serials staff were searching for a system which would twin the technical responsibilities with the nonpublic Technical Services groups—cataloguing or acquisitions. Exlibris' ALEPH was one such a system, which would allow us to clearly separate our circulations functions from our technical serials-acquisitions functions.

Choosing the Vendor

Early in 2006, a series of vendor demonstration sessions were held on each of the three campuses during which five vendors demonstrated their products, impressing upon us the capabilities and functionalities of each system. All levels of staff, librarians, clericals, paraprofessionals, and library attendants attended the demonstrations. Emphasis was, however, not placed on the inclusion of students and faculty in these sessions. Later, the feedback suggested that we could have benefited from the inclusion of the latter groups, as this would have heightened their awareness of the intended changes. As the primary end user, students and staff have a better idea of the type of systems they would like to see adopted as they understand the types of facilities and services they need.

In the end, ALEPH scored the highest on all our combined vendor evaluation criteria, and the decision was made collectively by all three campuses to migrate to ALEPH. The acquisition of ALEPH, which combined both the serials and acquisitions functions in one module, meant that the planned reorganization of separating serials technical work activities from that of serials circulations could finally become a reality.

Preparing for ALEPH at Mona

Once the vendor was chosen, the next big step was to provide staff training. In organizing the training, the challenges were many. The important questions for some of us involved were:

- *When* should the training begin?

- *What* samples should be used for the training?

- *How* should the training be organized?

- *Who* should participate in the training and in which unit(s) of the training?

Training began in mid to latter part of 2006, using the vendor's sample records. This was long before our first batch load of records were migrated and returned to us for batch testing. Among the lessons learned from this experience is that libraries stand to benefit more if they carefully consider and negotiate into the contract with the vendor for:

- Training to be conducted after the first or second batch loads of the library's records are delivered and

- Vendor training to be conducted using samples from the library's migrated batch records after batch testing is completed.

It may not be in the best interest of the library to organize initial training on vendor sample records since they may not offer the same degree of complication and challenges, missing out on the opportunity to tackle some of the very difficult problems that your own local records present. The benefits to be gained here, in the early stages, include occasioning the opportunity for staff to raise the *right* questions and solving problems which may come up concerning difficult serials records, among other things.

The initial vendor training sessions were conducted by teleconferencing, followed by two weeks of face-to-face training workshops. Training by teleconference involved a carefully selected group of staff, but the face-to-face training incorporated a wider complement. All staff attached to the Periodicals Sections in the Main and Branch Libraries, except Library Attendants, received training initially on the Serials/Acquisitions module.

In addition, the Head of Periodicals (the Serials Librarian), among other staff drawn from the Systems Unit and the Cataloguing Section, received training in all ALEPH modules, as a trainer, to later impart the skills to the wider library staff in locally arranged training sessions. The Serials Librarian and Serials Cataloguer participated in the Tables Training, along with staff from the Systems Unit, while the Serials Librarian liaised with System to work out the mapping of records for transfer from the legacy system to ALEPH. Crucial to retaining the skills learnt from the series of vendor training, continuous training sessions were organized by our local trainers and held throughout the latter part of 2006.

In view of the impending centralization of the technical serials work, it might have been wise to include in the serials-acquisitions module training the Reference Librarian and support staff (including branch circulations staff) who were later transferred to what became Periodicals Circulations. Such training would have helped in orientating and equipping them with the requisite skills and knowledge to handle some of their serials inquiries—some of these staff had little prior knowledge of serials operations. Though not required to carry out technical serials functions, knowledge of how the system works can assist periodicals reference staff to forge better and more cooperative relationships and understanding with periodicals technical services. A broad knowledge of library operations can also help to build self-confidence and better public service skills in staff.

Staff selected to be trainers must as far as possible demonstrate a commitment to remain with the institution through the process of implementation. In addition, the person selected should be articulate and eager to impart the knowledge and skills learnt. Though paraprofessional staff may not be included in the tables-training and records-mapping processes, their knowledge of the workflow process, through their constant engagement in such processes, underscores the need for consultation with them during the implementation period. Paraprofessionals can provide practical insight and solutions to problems which arise during implementation. In order to boost staff morale and secure commitment to the process, paraprofessionals must also be made to feel that their contribution is valuable to the organization.

Of tremendous value to the implementation process is gaining preliminary knowledge by visiting other libraries which have experience in using the automated system. A post implementation visit by one member of the Mona staff to the Notre Dame University Library's Periodicals Department proved to be a worthwhile learning experience of a well-organized workflow using the ALEPH library automated system. Such visits are best organized prior to implementation at the local level, as they can assist in increased levels of preparedness in negotiating the contract and better organization of the implementation process.

Managing the Change Process while Centralizing Serials Work

Once the implementation process was on its way, transferring the technical functions of serials and finalizing the setup of the Periodicals Technical Services Unit began. With serials cataloguing centralized from as far back as May 2006, by the end of that year most of the other technical activities were transferred to the unit along with the Serials Librarian, as unit head, and two Periodicals support staff. By the end of 2006, however, the unit was faced with three resignations, and efforts to secure replacements were not achieved until early 2007. One replacement came from the Periodicals section in the science branch library, where the technical serials operations had already been downscaled, and another was drafted from the Acquisitions section.

More staff in the unit meant adjustments to ensure economic use of space, and displacement of others by negotiating for additional space occupied by other sections. The available location identified was a small office, which previously formed part of the space occupied by the Cataloguing Unit. The small office was enough to comfortably seat three staff and so further negotiations had to be done to acquire additional space from the Cataloguing Unit. The Cataloguing Unit was itself struggling to effectively and efficiently deliver on its own targets, due to inadequate floor space to accommodate its own operations. The chance of providing Technical Services with a new extension to the building was very slim since much of the budget was already being expended on migration to a new system. As the Cataloguing Unit was facing its own challenges, such negotiation required a strong, cooperative, and collaborative relationship between librarians, as well as support staff, for effective management of the transformation process.

Our experiences show that enlisting the support and commitment of all the staff involved in the process is the only way of ensuring a smooth transformation of the process. This can be done by providing reassurance to staff through stating explicitly the goals and objectives of the process and the future roles of the staff to be affected. This should be done at the earliest possible stage to remove any feeling of uncertainty by communicating planned changes to staff and preparing them for the impact such changes may bring.

Once the final batch load was delivered to ExLibris at the end of November, production ceased, and the following month was spent preparing for the arrival of the new catalogue by streamlining our operations. The first task was to rationalize and revise some procedures to ensure uniformity and consistency in our operations. Prior to centralization, each Periodicals Unit in the branch libraries followed their own manual of practices and procedures (though generic to that of Main Library), resulting in much inconsistency in our operations and procedures. The inconsistencies were evident, for example, in our catalogue public notes. Time was also spent organizing our vendor/invoice cards for our first project, as this data was not mapped from our legacy system to the subscription forms in the new system.

Once this was done, the next task was prioritizing the projects, which was no easy feat in itself. Once the migrated records were delivered by ExLibris in January 2007 and our new catalogue interface was about to be launched, a quick evaluation of the public display of serials records gave us a fuller picture of what task needed to be at the top of our prioritized list. The important steps in redesigning the workflow include understanding the current environment, identifying best practices, providing rationale for the benefits to be gained from the process, and planning and implementing the necessary changes in a methodical and systematic way (Fischer and Lugg 2005). While there is much to be said about multitasking, a serials workflow of completing one task after another in order of importance can be much more conducive to getting the work done efficiently and expeditiously. Dividing your attention between unrelated tasks can retard your work progress compared to finalizing one focused task after another.

Our first and most urgent project was to edit the holdings MARC by editing the 853 fields and adding 853X fields. Many of the patterns, which worked well in our legacy system when migrated to ALEPH, refused to display appropriately. Using the alphabetical invoice lists for 2007, which was divided amongst the staff, the patterns were adjusted, 853X fields added and subscription data entered to create check-in lists for arriving of over 2,000 current titles. The possibility of having to complete this task was raised earlier by one of our staff members during the initial training sessions, and so we were fully prepared for dealing with this setback. A dress rehearsal was done on how to construct the 853X field, locating or creating irregular patterns, filling out the subscription forms, and generating the check-in. The migration process also revealed that other areas, such as gift and exchange title records, required further rationalization as the manual records did not make suppliers and exchange partners' information readily available. Feedback from our clientele suggested that during the first month when many of our holdings did not display properly, it would have been a good idea to correct these problems before shutting down our legacy system and launching our "new look" public interface.

Another project was to continue retrospective bar coding of items, on the fly, while bar coding all new items from 2007 onward during the arrival in process. In our new dispensation, the workflow for retrospective bar coding was adjusted so that instead of entering the data at the circulations point, duplicate slips are completed by the client, and this is passed to Serials Technical Services for data entry. This solved the problems of some of the inconsistencies which resulted in part from some Circulations staff not being able to distinguish between books and some periodicals, as well as other data such as the enumeration and chronology information.

The success of any such venture requires the maintaining of a strong relationship between Technical Services and Public Services staff and a reliance on the support from the paraprofessionals who often guide the clients in filling out the duplicate issue slips and for ensuring accuracy of the data passed to Technical Services. The road forward was not an easy one for serials, but preparing ourselves for the job ahead of time made the difference. On most projects, we worked as teams. With staff at all levels involved in doing every task without the boundaries of job position, we completed our first project in record time.

In conclusion, I must say that it was rough going initially. Our work culture does not lend itself easily to having clericals doing "paraprofessional and librarian work" without first getting an extra increment, or librarians doing clerical and paraprofessional work without feeling demoted. It is at these times that our management and leadership skills are most essential to motivate our staff into getting the job done quickly and efficiently. Those who are leaders should not be afraid to try new things and to sell the idea that performing tasks above one's level is an opportunity for our support to learn new things and to grow. In fact, as managers we should be doing this always to build a greater work environment.

The new system can be difficult to get comfortable with; therefore, constant training has to be a priority to break in your staff to the new system, as well to ensure standardization of the procedures, even in a centralized setting. Include in the training staff members from the Client Services section to help them get a better understanding of the system's functionalities so that they can better appreciate the need for cooperation between the two groups of staff. Once you overcome the initial hurdles of the implementation process, ensure documentation of new procedures and workflow and constantly update your procedural manual.

A reminder is that serials technical work can be monotonous and painstaking, especially during the migration process, so a careful selection of your work team is essential to a smooth transformation process and to avoid high staff turnovers. Any such advertisement for new staff to join your technical services team should probably read as follows:

Help wanted! Essential qualities: Candidate must be a team player, willing to per-form tasks at any level, have a high tolerance for monotonous, repetitive tasks, and a genuine love for serials work would be an asset.

Finally, library automated systems are costly. Therefore, the need to maximize the benefits from the various modules is essential. The more of your data you input into the legacy system, the better you fare when mapping your records to a new system or updating to a new version of the legacy system. The road to managing change in serials workflow when migrating to a new automated system was not an easy one, but we persisted and have been reaping the rewards.

Note

1. *The Distance Student Handbook 2006–2007.* St. Michael, Barbados: University of the West Indies, Distance Education Centre, Cave Hill Campus, 2006.

Works Cited

Fischer, R., and Rick Lugg. (2005). *From Recommendation to Reality: Implementing Workflow Changes in Collections and Technical Services.* Paper presented at Charleston Pre-Conference, November 2.

Kerr-Campbell, M. *The Transitional Library and the Changing roles of Librarians: Case Study of the Library, University of the West Indies, Mona, Jamaica.* Unpublished paper.

Mclean, E. (2006). "Providing Library Instruction to Distance Learning Students in the 21st Century: Meeting the Current and Changing Needs of a Diverse Community." *Journal of Library Administration* 45, no. 3/4: 315–337.

COUNTER USAGE REPORTS: WHAT'S GOOD FOR THE GOOSE IS NUTS FOR THE GANDER

Laura Cox, Managing Director, Frontline Global Marketing Services Ltd., Towcester, United Kingdom

Sasha Gurke, Senior Vice President and Co-Founder, Knovel, New York, New York

How do you measure the value your organization receives from online collections you subscribe to?

There are a number of considerations which may vary slightly from institution to institution, but measuring the value of journals has become increasingly assisted by the widespread adoption of COUNTER-compliant usage statistics. In the e-book and reference work arena, the utility of COUNTER statistics is still under scrutiny.

COUNTER released the *COUNTER Code of Practice: Books and Reference Works* in March 2006. This Code of Practice covers a wide range of different publication and service types. E-books and reference works are not uniform in nature and are used for different purposes. Comparing the usage of such diverse content can be ambiguous, and factors affecting it are not addressed by the current format of COUNTER statistics.

Knovel is a service providing access to aggregated STM e-references which has recently implemented COUNTER-compliant usage statistics. In the course of the implementation process, Knovel has encountered some reports that do not make sense for its service or that provide problematic results. Consequently, we felt it would be useful to specifically address the problems and ambiguity caused when applying COUNTER usage reports to reference works.

COUNTER defines a reference work as: "An authoritative source of information about a subject used to find quick answers to questions."

This is a good definition, but COUNTER does not favor "quick answers to questions" because it favors comprehensiveness, desirable in a journal search, over relevancy, desirable in a reference search.

In order to find answers to specific questions quickly and easily, some technical reference services offer sophisticated searching facilities enabling users to specify the exact properties and conditions applicable to their circumstances, be it for research or as part of a production process. The search performed is usually across all the titles available in that particular service, and the results are ideally few but very specific. Further enhancements to reference work services include indexing tabular and graphical content, ensuring that all the objects within tables, graphs, and equations can be accessed in a search, further enabling users to find exactly the data they need with ease.

We analyzed the six COUNTER reports and applied them to the type of technical reference works mentioned to ascertain the value derived from each report. We will demonstrate that some of the reports provide skewed statistics and are not very useful for this type of resource; however, COUNTER compliance is frequently a requirement and certainly desired by institutions wishing to subscribe to the content.

The COUNTER Code of Practice for e-books and reference works measures the following statistics:

- Turnaways by month and service
- Turnaways by month and title
- Total searches and sessions by month and title
- Total searches and sessions by month and service
- Successful title requests by month and title
- Successful section requests by month and title

Turnaways

COUNTER only requires those services using a concurrent user model to provide turnaway reports. Whilst this is very useful for librarians to gauge the need to increase the number of simultaneous user licenses, it does not provide information for content provided under other business models. For example, there are many e-book and reference work vendors which provide content by subject collection or individual title under a site-wide license. This model enables libraries to subscribe to the subject collections and titles which they have determined would be of most use to patrons, and for all patrons to have access all of the time. COUNTER does not require the provision of turnaway reports under this model and therefore libraries may not be aware of users being turned away from subject areas and titles to which they do not subscribe.

Whilst turnaway reports for content provided under different business models may not actually be comparable, they would enable libraries to ensure that all content for which users have a need would be included in a subscription.

Sessions

NISO defines a session as "a successful request of an online service. It is one cycle of user activities that typically starts when a user connects to the service or database and ends by terminating activity that is either explicit (by leaving the service through exit or logout) or implicit (timeout due to user inactivity)."

COUNTER requires vendors to provide reports that are relevant to the business model being used. Vendors may provide usage statistics for sessions within a service or title. Whilst it makes sense for individually procured titles to provide sessions by title and collections of e-books to provide sessions by service, the actual reports are not comparable, and service-based reports provide very little information on the usefulness of the content.

Usage reporting by session within a service does indicate that users are aware of a service and using it. However, it does not determine that particular service's value. Reporting on sessions in a service makes sense only for successful sessions, i.e., those involving the viewing of the content. Lots of sessions may be useless and users leave the service without finding or viewing information. This report provides ambiguous results and interpreting the true value of a resource from it is difficult. As a result, some customers demand session reports by title even though they subscribe to a service or collection. This creates a problem for vendors that are required to log sessions both ways.

Searches

Most technical reference collections are searchable across the entire service, and this is usually the option that users take, searching for specific data within multiple resources, very few searches are performed within individual titles. COUNTER acknowledges this and requests that vendors provide the appropriate report for searches depending on the content provided and its use. If searches are performed across several titles simultaneously, usage data reports the searches by service. Conversely, if searches are performed within a title, the usage data should be recorded against that title.

Reference works are used in different ways. Technical references users normally require very specific data and therefore will search across many titles to obtain that specific information. However, it is common to search within an individual dictionary or encyclopedia. At Knovel, both searches are possible, and hence both reports are required. This, as in the case of session reports, complicates logging and reporting.

Another problem with search reports is their ambiguity. A high number of searches performed within either the service or title can be interpreted in two ways:

- The content is valuable and users find the data they are looking for with ease and return to the service to search again and again.

- The search is less useful and users have to refine searches to find what they are looking for—performing multiple searches to find one piece of information.

Successful Requests

COUNTER defines "successful request are those with specific return codes as defined by NCSA." In plain English, successful request is when a user requests to view, download, or print part of a title successfully and certain http return codes result.

Successful Requests by Section

What exactly is a section? COUNTER defines it as a chapter or entry, a subdivision of a book or reference work. An entry is defined as "a record of information in some categories of reference work."

A section is actually the next level down from the full title, for example, a chapter, entry, or record. So the usage data from these reports can vary wildly and depend entirely on how each particular vendor indexes its content. When comparing reference works and e-books, a database service like Knovel receives a huge advantage over full-text content providers, as each row in an interactive table is a separate record. A user may be viewing hundreds of them in one go when only looking for one particular item, whereas for full-text publishers and aggregators a section may be an entire chapter. The results for section requests can be dramatically skewed because of the differences in data architecture, making the reports impossible to compare. Furthermore, to ascertain the value of an individual service, the librarian would need to know how that particular vendor has indexed their content, what a record is in that particular service, and then decide what should be expected from the usage reports.

Successful Requests by Title

Of all the metrics COUNTER applies to reference works and e-books, only successful requests per title give any real indicator of value. As the data for successful requests by section can be seriously skewed, the successful requests by title report becomes the most relevant usage report. We cannot find out whether users actually used the material that they found, but at least we know that it was relevant enough to access. Or did they? As stated, technical reference users are usually looking for specific data. A quick answer to a question.

Let's compare an optimized search in a technical reference collection (Knovel) to full text search on Google (not an e-book provider but an example of wider keyword searches).

Suppose a user wants to find a solvent with a boiling point between 60 and 70 degrees Celsius. Using Knovel's advanced search and the query

keyword=solvent AND boiling point = 60–70°C,

the user retrieves two titles. The title with 100 percent relevancy has two records that contain data matching search criteria. The whole process including viewing the results takes less than one minute.

Using Google and the query

solvent boiling point 60 70 C,

the user gets 2,100,000 hits. Viewing the 10 documents on the first page only takes three minutes but there is no relevant answer.

When using high-usage statistics as a positive measure of value, the COUNTER reports favor Google even though the user did not find what he or she was looking for. Put simply, COUNTER-compliant reports favor comprehensiveness over relevancy.

One reason for this bias could be that COUNTER was developed originally for measuring the usage of journals. If we look at how journals are used in comparison with technical references, you will see how the difference in the intent of the user affects the usage pattern.

People using journal collections typically have one of four intents:

1. Find all the latest material written on the subject of their particular scientific interest or niche

2. Conduct a survey of all that has been written on a topic

3. Locate an article that has been recommended or referenced in another publication or that they want to revisit

4. Find specific answers, for example, a doctor looking for articles about the treatment of a specific condition, such as new drugs and therapies

What are the drivers of value for these use cases?

Use Case/Intent	Value Driver
1	Comprehensiveness Currency
2	Comprehensiveness
3	Relevancy
4	Comprehensiveness Reliability Relevancy

The table clearly shows that comprehensiveness is one of the key drivers in three out of four cases. A high number of successful requests for content in a journal strongly correlates with perceived value.

Typically journal articles do not contain extensive collections of technical data. Therefore, users do not search journals for specific technical data. For this they use reference collections and databases.

People using technical reference collections typically have one of four intents:

1. Find a solution to specific problem, often related to production

2. Locate a piece of data, for example, material property value, equation, procedure, or composition

3. Learn in general about a process, physical phenomenon, chemical reaction, or material

4. Find out the state of the art in a particular technical field (For example, in R&D, it is essential to check on existing patents and the research already undertaken so as not to spend time and money reinventing the wheel.)

The drivers for value in these use cases are:

Use Case/Intent	Value Driver
1	Reliability Relevancy
2	Relevancy Reliability
3	Relevancy
4	Comprehensiveness Currency Relevancy

The table clearly shows that relevancy is one of the key drivers in all cases.

With most people using reference works conducting searches for highly specific data, a small number of extremely relevant results (possibly only one result) are the ideal. So a lower number of successful requests for content in technical references can correlate with perceived value. Whilst this seems counterintuitive, what it really demonstrates is that different intents in usage will deliver different usage patterns which are not really comparable.

Quite clearly COUNTER reports favor comprehensiveness as an intent. Users searching for comprehensive content are likely to generate high usage data for successful requests. Technical reference users clearly require relevancy. With the use of a good search function, they will return very few results and view much less.

Comparing Usage Data for Different Resources

There are other factors affecting usage statistics that can skew data. In 2006, Phil Davis and Jason Price undertook a study of six of the major journal publishers, which found that publisher and vendor online interfaces can skew usage statistics as the "number of full-text downloads may be artificially inflated when publishers require users to view HTML versions before accessing PDF versions or when linking mechanisms, such as CrossRef, direct users to the full text rather than the abstract of each article."[1] Davis and Price found that when comparing one title's (*Embo Journal*) HTML and PDF downloads, that the platform on which it was being used dramatically affected the data. Use of the journal of the *Nature* interface resulted in twice the PDF to HTML ration of the Highwire platform, even when controls were set for content and the popularity of the platforms.

The implications of this on using usage data to compare resources or services is clear even in the relatively homogenous would of journal publishing. Davis and Price assert that "librarians need usage reports that can be deemed credible and comparable. How can this be done when usage statistics are heavily influenced by publisher interface?"[2]

Whether factors concerning vendor interfaces and linking mechanisms affect e-book and reference work usage statistics in a similar way is uncertain, but given the diverse nature of content provision in the e-book market, it would seem likely.

Conclusions

By assessing the statistics in the *COUNTER Code of Practice: Books and Reference Works,* we have been able to show that it is extremely difficult to compare the use of different types of reference works.

To summarize:

- Turnaway reports are dependent on the vendor using a concurrent user business model. Libraries may be missing out on important data for subject collections or single titles to which they do not subscribe under a sitewide license.

- Usage reporting of sessions makes sense only for successful sessions. Recording all sessions creates ambiguous data, and it is difficult to ascertain the value of a service.

- The type of searches performed dramatically affects the usage data. Recording the number of searches can yield ambiguous data. Not all searches are successful, and users refining searches can create the undesirable effect of increasing the usage statistics for services which are of less use or have inferior search functionality.

- The reporting of successful requests by section can be dramatically skewed by the manner in which a vendor indexes their content.

- The reporting of successful requests by title is a valid method of recording usage, but it still has flaws. The very essence of the usage statistic is to record the highest number of requests as being a positive measure of value, favoring usage which is intended to find a comprehensive selection of materials on a particular topic rather than usage which has the intention of finding very specific data—a quick answer to a question.

COUNTER is trying to compare apples with apples; in the reference work and e-book area, apples are not the only fruit. There are a large number of different types of e-books and reference works which are not really comparable. Current COUNTER-compliant reports do not take this into account. COUNTER has acknowledged this and stated at the recent Charleston Conference that comparisons of usage between e-books and reference works have to be made more cautiously than for journals.

However, the intent of the user when searching and requesting content on a service is not taken into account. COUNTER was originally set up with journals in mind, and the translation of usage statistics to e-books has not been fully thought through. COUNTER usage statistics may be good for the goose in comparing journals but are nuts for the gander in comparing the diverse e-book content available, as not all services are used to find comprehensive content.

So has the standardization of usage reports for e-books and reference works really assisted librarians? In some ways maybe, but librarians need to know more about the service and the vendor in order to interpret them and to assess which reports are relevant, which are not, and what would be an appropriate level at which to find good usage. Comparing usage data across different providers is extremely difficult and potentially misleading.

COUNTER statistics are much more valuable for tracking the usage of an individual service or reference over a period the time, particularly when taking into account the effect of publisher and vendor interfaces on data. This enables librarians to monitor fluctuations and trends in usage and to determine whether a service is declining in use or increasing, when that service is most used (due to undergraduate assignment deadlines or exams) and whether these patterns call for any action on the part of the librarian. It is here that successful requests come into their own. Users will go back to services they have found helpful and access more content; a service with an increasing number of successful requests over time can be interpreted as having value to the user.

We are not pretending to know how to solve all these problems, some of which are inherent to the nature of usage statistics themselves, but we have thought of a few ways in which to improve what is currently in existence.

1. Split the reports into three sections:

    a. e-books—titles typically used for comprehensive research

    b. data—databases and handbooks used to find specific answers to questions

    c. interactive book which contain both types of data

Each of these are more likely to be comparable to the other services in that section.

2. Create turnaway reports for different business models to ensure librarians are receiving the data they need to decide upon the addition of resources within a service.

3. Separately record usage data for sessions in which a successful request was made from sessions where no request was made. Include a report of the amount of time each session lasted. For technical reference and some other reference works, short sessions with a successful request is desirable. For e-books, longer sessions in which the user has requested several items may be more desirable.

4. Combine the searches and successful request reports to show how many searches ended in failure and how many created requests.

5. It would be desirable to include the amount of time taken in viewing the actual content and whether it was saved or printed out. Unfortunately this would disadvantage those vendors providing PDF delivery because once users have downloaded the content, we are unable to trace what they have actually done with it.

In the recent session at the Charleston Conference, Peter Shepherd, Director of COUNTER said that more work would be done on COUNTER reports for e-books and reference works and that a second release of the Code of Practice would occur in the near future after consultation with publishers and librarians. We hope that this paper will assist with that process.

Notes

1. Davis, Philip M., and Jason S. Price. (2006). "eJournal Interface Can Influence Usage Statistics: Implications for Libraries, Publishers, and Project COUNTER." *Journal for the American Society for Information Science and Technology* 57, no. 9: 1243–1248.

2. Ibid.

DEEP INDEXING OF EMBEDDED ARTICLE INFORMATION: A HISTORICAL ACADEMIC PERSPECTIVE AND RESULTS OF A SURVEY OF RESEARCHER BEHAVIOR

Helle Lauridsen, Illustrata, Product Manager, Proquest, Aarhus N, Denmark

Anne Langle, Coordinator of Public Services Assessment and Chemistry Librarian, Duke University, Durham, North Carolina

Abstract

A vast amount of important information is often unfindable for researchers because it is deeply embedded within research articles, sometimes in the form of tables or as part of the methods or discussion of the research itself. For many years, chemists have created their own versions of what we now call deep indexing. Chemical articles often contain data, such as chemical or property data, that have a life of their own beyond their birth in a research article; chemists create and use indexes and databases that offer specific deep indexed information. This joint article not only looks at using deep indexing from a historical academic perspective but will also present results and discussion from a recent in-depth survey of researcher behavior showing that making these objects visible by indexing each table and figure makes an extremely valuable research tool to focus literature searches and allows researchers to draw connections between disparate subjects, identifying avenues of new research rather than simply providing answers and as a side benefit.

Introduction

Scientists communicate their findings from laboratory or field research by writing a research article. Within articles, these findings, or facts, normally take the form of graphs, tables, figures, or images, which then are used as the base of the written article. However, once the article is published, the publisher often sees such illustrations as artwork and not as data and does not index them. This means that when searching for information, through full-text on the Internet or in professionally indexed databases, researchers can miss crucial data because their searches will not retrieve articles that contain the data that they are looking for.

This nonindexing of scientific data and facts is one of the reasons that many (often older) researchers still like to have the opportunity to browse through print versions of the most relevant journals for them—not only because most human brains "scan" image content a lot faster than written text but because images and data from tables and graphs can only be found by browsing articles from start to finish.

Pulling away from manually browsing journal articles is modern technology's "strong emphasis on tools for search, selection and distillation [which] seems to promote the identification of and extraction of smaller information units, fragments, pulled loose from their original surroundings." Levy argues that if the late eighteenth century witnessed the transition from intensive to extensive reading, the late twentieth century marked another transition to reading, that involves "hyper-extensive search for just the right, the most relevant, minimal units or fragments. If extensive reading has consisted of deep, sustained, continuous reading of books, hyper-extensive reading might be characterized as a frenzy of short bursts of shallow attendings [sic] to information fragments."[1]

Based on data gathered in various interactions with academic researchers, it is clear that journal article components are used by researchers throughout the cycle of identifying relevant documents, reading them and incorporating ideas from them into their own written work. Intellectual and material practices are interwoven in the continual play of disaggregating and reaggregating knowledge. The nature of component use is complex. A particular component may be used at any stage of this cycle. Author affiliations and bibliographic references, for example, may be used to either find relevant documents or to assess the relevance of documents retrieved. The same component may also be used in somewhat different ways within one stage. For example, a professor uses figures as a synopsis of a paper to assess its relevance, while an undergraduate used figures to gauge whether reading the paper would hold his interest—another type of pre-reading relevance assessment.[2]

An average scientific article contains seven to ten illustrations, most of them containing valuable data, which until very recently have not—or not in any extensive way—been indexed, thus rendering the data lost for searchers. An exception to this can be found in the field of chemistry. Chemists have along history of indexing their literature, and with the advent of digitization, have created multiple resources that apply deep indexing to the literature, which allows researchers to conduct very deep data mining of the chemical literature.

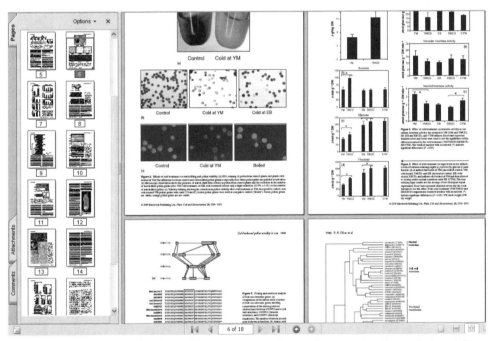

Figure 1. Academic article in *Natural Sciences:* note the number of normally not indexed figures.

Part I: Brief History of Deep Indexing in the Chemical Literature

Chemists have a long history of organizing the information they create. They realized quite early that chemists could save time and resources by making sure that they were not reinventing the wheel. There is a well-known aphorism about chemists and the literature that goes something like, "Why spend thirty minutes in the library when you can spend three months in the lab?" This section will briefly discuss two secondary information resources created by chemists that have a history of deep indexing and give a cursory look at the types of information indexed. This discussion is intended to show the intense usefulness of deep indexing of scientific literature to scientists and scholars. The two resources discussed here are Chemical Abstracts via SciFinder Scholar and Beilstein/Gmelin via CrossFire. There are many other chemical secondary resources that use or benefit from deep indexing. A few of these are the *CRC Handbook of Chemistry and Physics* (a compilation of facts, constants, data and more), KnowItAllU from BioRad Laboratories (indexes and allows searching of over 1.3 million spectral records of chemical compounds), and the Cambridge Structural Database (crystal structure information, chemical, and bibliographic data for about 400,000 organic and metal-organic compounds).

One of the earliest chemical indexing publications was the German Chemical Society's *Chemisches Zentralblatt* (1830), while the immediate precursor to Chemical Abstracts was the *Review of American Chemical Research* (1895), which became a supplement to the *Journal of the American Chemical Society* in 1897. This then became *Chemical Abstracts* in 1907. First edited by William Noyes, *Chemical Abstracts* has always been a part of the American Chemical Society. Considered to be the largest database in the world, *Chemical Abstracts* aims to abstract and index any and all information related to chemistry from all over the globe. Initially, indexes included only Author and Subject. In 1947, a *Molecular Index* was added, which cumulated the previous twenty-seven years. Also in 1947 a Patent index was added with ten years of cumulation. The Index of Ring Systems began in 1967 and was discontinued in 1995. The Index Guide (or the thesaurus for chemical terminology) started in 1967. The General Subject Index began in 1972 as well as the Chemical Substance Index. And in the 1960s the Chemical Abstracts Registry was created. This allowed for much better indexing and organizing of compounds, as every unique compound now had a unique identifier. This registry system helped pave the way for deep indexing as it allowed more automated indexing of chemical structures and data.[3,4]

In the 1980s automated indexing began in earnest, greatly enhancing the search experience for chemists the world over. As a member of STN International, CAS was able to offer chemical information everywhere. Since then, with improvements in computing technology, searching has improved exponentially. Because Chemical Abstracts was able to build on early indexing and took advantage of web technology, chemists are now able to search the chemical information via a variety of search options: citation information, structure, formula, registry, reaction, experimental data and more. At latest count Chemical Abstracts contains data on more than 27 million articles and patents, over 31 million organic and inorganic substances, over 13 million single and multi-step reactions, and as of the writing of this sentence, the Registry contains over 33 million organic and inorganic substance and more than 59 million sequences. In its 100th year (2007), Chemical Abstracts has shown the usefulness and vitality of deep indexing.[5] The Beilstein and Gmelin databases as offered via the CrossFire software interface are yet another example of the power of deep indexing. Begun in 1771 by Friedrich Konrad Beilstein, what now comprises the Beilstein and Gmelin databases initially were called the Beilstein Handbook of Organic Chemistry and the Gmelin Handbook of Inorganic and Organomettallic Chemistry. These have always had very deep indexing but were extremely difficult to use because of the language (German) and indexing.

In the mid-1990s the CrossFire software was created which opened up a wealth of information for chemists on millions of compounds. To create the data structure, the information in the handbooks was extensively indexed to included over 300 unique types of data. The searchable data included literature citation information as well as chemical and property data, structures, reactions and synthesis; pharmacological and environmental data. This allows chemists to quickly find the data they need in the millions of articles and patents that have been published since the late 1700s. This type of deep indexing offers phenomenal support to researchers in chemistry and related fields.[6,7]

Part II: Results of a Survey of Researcher Behavior Using Deep Indexed Information

In 2005 CSA, now ProQuest, started exploring a different way of extracting data from scientific articles and especially from the primary research data found in figures and illustrations. This was a giant leap in database indexing in an era when even the most affluent college and special libraries have to cope with searching in expensive information retrieval systems that completely omit, or remains silent, in their full text records about informative graphic material.[8] Before undertaking this new venture, CSA/Proquest asked Carol Tenopir, Margaret M. Casado and Robert Sandusky to conduct a thorough market research project.

Market Research[9]

In the spring of 2006 the in-depth market research was launched. CSA identified librarians at universities and research institutes in Europe and North America who would assist with the recruitment of scientists to test the system. In all, sixty scientists in nine organizations participated (seven universities and two research institutes; three in Europe and six in the United States):

	Universities	Research Institutes	Totals
United States	5	1	6
Europe	2	1	3
Totals	7	2	9

Table 1. Participants in usability test.

Methods

One member of the research team visited each of the participating organizations, to provide introductory sessions, gather data, distribute passwords, and provide instructions on additional data collection. Multiple methods of data collection allowed data validation and triangulation for both quantitative and qualitative data. The various methods allowed the team to study both predictive questions, such as how indexing of tables and figures might be used by scientists; and functional questions, such as what type of search and interface features are particularly useful for a tables and figures system.

Data collection methods included: pre- and post-search questionnaires to describe potential usefulness, expectations and current practices; observation sessions to discover, through initial and real-time interactions with the system, potential usability and functionality issues;

and structured diaries of searches performed by the participants, on topics of their own choosing in the weeks following the introductory sessions to gather more detail on potential uses of the Tables and Figures index prototype, encourage additional participant experiences with the system, and identify both useful functions and concerns with the prototype.

Findings

The ability to search for figures in support of research (45 responses considered) was cited as "absolutely essential" by 18 of 45 respondents (40 percent), and 17 respondents (38 percent) ranked figures at 6; combined, this represents 35, or 78 percent, of the participants who responded to this item.

Forty-five responses were provided when respondents were asked about the importance of searching for tables in support of research. Twenty of those 45 (44 percent) rated the ability to search for photographs as "absolutely essential." Another 12 (27 percent) indicated this was a very important capability by ranking searching for tables at 6. Combined, the 32 responses of 6 or 7 represent 71 percent of all responses to this question. The ability to search for graphs in support of research shows a similar pattern compared to the responses regarding figures.

Impacts on Practice

Participants were asked on the summative questionnaire if the ability to search for specific objects, as provided by the Tables and Figures index prototype, made a difference in their search and discovery process. Forty-three (93 percent) of the 46 respondents said yes, their search and discovery processes were changed, while 3 (6 percent) said they were not.

A follow-up, open-ended questionnaire prompted the respondents to elaborate on how this capability made a difference in their search and discovery process. Overwhelmingly, participants alluded to the fact that this capability saved time and provided quicker access to information. "I can find the tables and figures that I need quickly, [and] it can save me a lot of time. I can work more efficiently" (Post Doc, Biology). One participant mentioned the increased efficiency of the search process, stating, "It makes the search much quicker when it is focused" (Post Doc, Biology), and another noted that "the tables and figures are really helpful for scanning large sets of data first" (Post Doc, Oceanography). Some participants specifically noted that this quicker access and search time was a convenient aid to presentation preparation: "It takes less time to find the information I want, and especially I would find this useful when making a presentation" (Student, Biology). Another wrote: "I could find relevant information more quickly and images that were useful for presentations and research" (Professor, Engineering).

However, the scientists pointed out that it was of crucial importance that the images were closely linked to the full text, as this was the only way to evaluate the value of them. Also rights management was an important issue.

Survey Conclusion

The results were positive enough to start developing in earnest with the changes suggested by the scientists and in January 2007 CSA Illustrata: Natural Sciences were launched with over 600,000 indexed objects.

Image Indexing

The indexing of the Images in Illustrata is not a trivial matter, as shown in Figure 2.

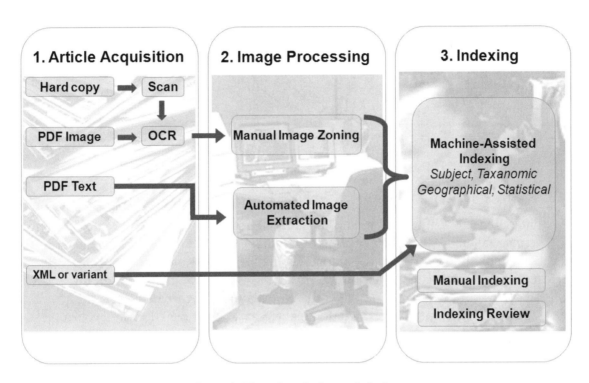

Figure 2. Flow chart for image indexing.

Qualified indexers identify the key variables (or data) that best describe the data illustrated in the images. For example, they know that the terms along the axes of a graph are important or the terms that are column/row headers in a table. If the caption has some important terms, they are supposed to capture those as well (e.g., names of organisms, geographic terms, or other subject terms that are important but may not always be displayed in the actual figure or table).

To assist the indexers, the entire caption, table, and other relevant text is sent through some automated indexing routines, which match terms in the caption, for example, with terms in our controlled vocabularies. Any of the matches may be useful for the index, although these terms may be removed at the discretion of the indexers thus providing a natural language index to the images.

Figure	Graph	3D Surface Plot	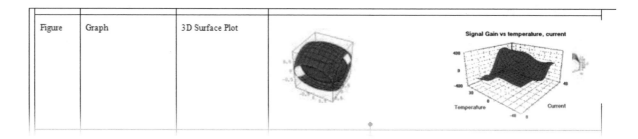

Figure 3. Example from object indexing guide, surface plot.

The indexers of CSA Illustrata have two "pick lists" of terms to choose from, which they use to classify the Object Categories and Statistical Terms.

Figure	Illustration	Flow Chart	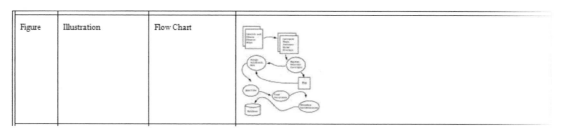

Figure 4. Example from object indexing guide, flow chart.

Around 30 percent of objects in the database fall under the category of table. The remaining 70 percent fall under the broad heading of "figure." The five main Object Categories for figures are Graph, Illustration, Map, Photograph, and Transmission/Emission Image. Each of these categories are then subdivided further (except for Transmission/Emission Image), allowing the search to be very specific or quite broad in the type of figure being searched for. Each level of the hierarchy is indexed so an individual record could have all three levels represented in the category field.

Figure	Map	Geological Map	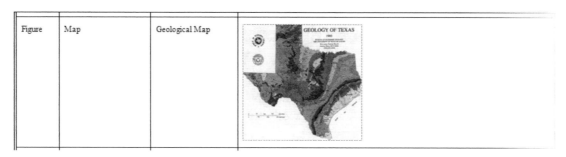

Figure 5. Example from object indexing guide, geological map.

There are over 140 different Statistical Terms, 26,000 geographic rules, and 200,000 taxonomic names in use within CSA Illustrata.

Figure	Photograph	Vertical Section Photograph	Sediment/soil/geological/ice etc. 

Figure 6. Example from object indexing guide, Vertical Section Photograph.

Content of CSA Illustrata: Natural Sciences

CSA Illustrata: Natural Sciences is interdisciplinary, covering a wide variety of journals from all major areas such as:

- Biology
- Earth Sciences
- Environmental Studies
- Medical Sciences
- Agriculture
- Fish and Fisheries
- Education
- Geography
- Veterinary Science
- Food and Food Industries
- Pharmacy and Pharmacology
- Meteorology
- Public Health and Safety
- Water Resources
- Conservation
- Forests and Forestry

Almost 5,000 journal titles have been indexed so far, bringing the total number of indexed images the first year up to a whopping 3-million-plus records. Most journals are indexed from 2000 on, but as the indexing teams labor not just to add new titles but also to expand coverage backwards, several titles have reached the target coverage starting in 1997.

Searching

It is possible to make a simple "Quick Search" for indexing terms in images and text, but "Advanced Search" gives much better opportunities for exploiting the full power of Illustrata.

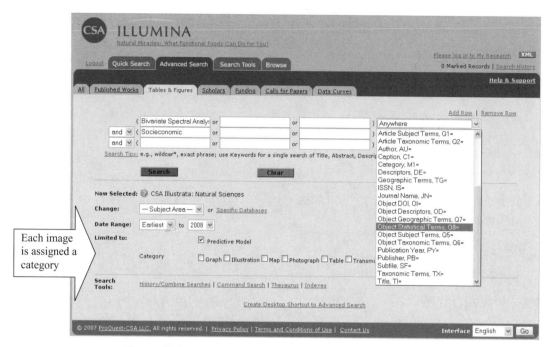

Figure 7. Screenshot of Advanced Search, descriptors and categories.

In advanced search, it is possible not only to pinpoint the categories of the image but also to utilize the object index terms fully.

The results are presented in a clear and easily navigable presentation. If you search for *Carbon Budget and ecosystem** in the entire natural sciences subject area, you will find that seventeen images contain these index terms. This is clearly indicated in the so-called pinky-nails, which show not only small thumbnails of all the images, but also where the object-bearing records are brightly rimmed in red. There is, of course, a direct link to the full text from this page, as approximately 50 percent of the users find the information here perfectly adequate and go directly to the full text.

However, if more information is needed, the user can go to the so-called object-bearing record, which displays clear, large thumbnails of all images in the article, where a quick mouse-over can give a full caption of the individual image.

In this view, the difference between indexing the article text and the article images really shows itself, the number of object descriptors is vastly higher than the number of descriptors assigned to the article, and the difference in the level of detail is obvious. It is possible to continue a search using one or more of the descriptors.

The rights to use the individual images are governed by each individual country's copyright law, and to make this easier for users and librarians ProQuest has added a direct link to rights management.

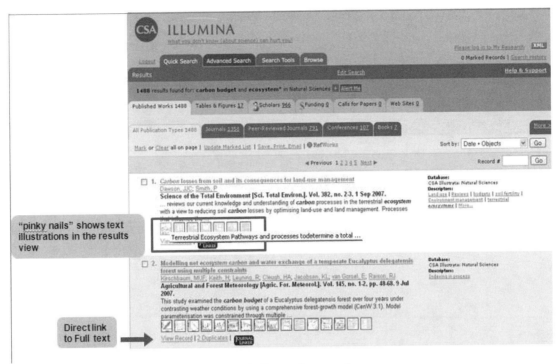

"pinky nails" shows text illustrations in the results view

Direct link to Full text

Figure 8. Screenshot, results.

Conclusion

With technological advances making the indexing of deeply imbedded data and facts more feasible, database creators and researchers alike stand to gain. Looking at a historical example in the field of chemistry of the gains to researchers who use databases with deep indexing, and the advantages found and reported by researchers at all levels in its initial study of deep indexing, Proquest is beginning an exciting new era of deep data indexing in many other academic fields. Based on the results of this survey, it is obvious that researchers use and think about literature searching in new and very productive ways when deep indexing is a part of their searching capabilities.

References

1. Bishop, A. P. (1999). "Document structure and digital libraries: How researchers mobilize information in journal articles." *Information Processing and management* 35: 255.

2. *Chemical abstracts web.* Retrieved January 20, 2008, from http://www.cas.org.

3. CrossFire Beilstein brochure. Retrieved January 20, 2008, from http://www.beilstein.com.

4. *Crossfire gmelin brochure.* Retrieved January 20, 2008, from http://www.mdli.com/products/pdfs/cfg_brochure.pdf

5. Jacso, P. (2007). CSA Illustrata by Jacso. *Online* 32, no. 3.

6. Levy, D. M. (1997). I read the news today, oh boy: Reading and attention in digital libraries. *ACM DL '97: Proceedings of the Second ACM International Conference on Digital Libraries,* 202–208.

7. Massie, R. J. (2007). At the CUSP of a new century. *Chemical & Engineering News, 85(24),* 56–57.

8. Powell, E. C. (2000). A history of chemical abstracts service, 1907–1998. *Science and Technology Libraries* 18, no. 4: 93–110.

9. Tenopir, C., Sandusky, R. J., & Casado, M. M. (2006). The value of CSA deep indexing for researchers. White paper.

10. Vawter, E. (2007). CSA Illustrata: Is a picture really worth a thousand words? *The Searcher: The Magazine for Database Professionals* 15, no. 5: 39–41

WEEDING A PERIODICAL COLLECTION

Tinker Massey, Serials Librarian, Embry-Riddle Aeronautical University, Daytona Beach, Florida

Why?

There are some very good reasons for weeding serial collections in an academic environment: keeping the collection current and appropriate to the primary needs of the teaching and research in the institution, preservation or conservation purposes, or to make room on the shelves for more titles or volumes. Most academic libraries are not blest with unending space, so room on the shelves becomes a mandate of sizeable proportions. Since this is the greatest cause of weeding projects, we will base the presentation on those needs.

Possibilities?

First is an assessment of the condition of the Collection. If you can do some minor reorganization of the Collection to use boxes, binders, or other means to compact the materials already housed, that is good. We found that creating half-sized boxes that were only two inches wide, instead of four inches, saved us a great amount of space as we moved through the Collection. Many times you are housing only a few issues that could not be bound among others that are bound, so wasting those extra two inches is unnecessary. Perhaps there are completed volumes that have not been bound yet, and binding them will save some space, as well as look better. Will you continue to keep ceased titles on the open shelves, or move them to storage areas? If they ceased over ten years ago, they are probably seeing very little use and can reside in a less used/visited area of the library or even an off-campus storage site. We did not have that option available to us.

Once the assessment has been done, note the areas which can be changed to save space and proceed with those changes. Will you be reassessing subject matter? Will you consider replacing some print items with a microform or electronic substitute? Make sure you consider as many alternatives as possible so that your options are numerous.

Procedure?

Assess the collection—Reorganize the materials—Review titles—Review Holdings of Titles—Change Formats where possible—Physical removal.

Congratulations, you now have a new concise Collection. At Embry-Riddle Aeronautical University, our Reference Librarians evaluate titles we submit to them and decide on what we will keep or change. I create an Excel sheet with the journal titles, holdings, status (current/ceased), price, shelving requirements (number of shelves of occupancy), full-text availability, microform availability, and price per reel. The Reference Librarians, sometimes with the help of their liaison connections, split the list among themselves and determine the necessity of the journal to classroom and research needs, whether it is better to keep older volumes on another format, and how many years to keep on the shelves; they then give this advice to me, so that action can be taken for the good of the Collection. We try to do evaluation in a subject arrangement, so that all the engineering or computer journals, for example, are done at the same time. We do acknowledge that there are a core of journals that we will continue to receive and house no matter what, so those need not be reevaluated. As we get extra monies assigned to binding, we are replacing the boxes with permanent bindings to reduce encumbered space on the shelves. We also try to limit the evaluation time to just several weeks per list, so that we can continue to "lean" the Collection and make room for newer and sometimes more valuable materials. We are learning more about the process with each list we tackle, and we are revising our strategies as we go further.

More information involving the usage of microfilm was presented this year. We are in the process of reproducing acetate film onto the new polyester film, which will last for approximately 300 years. Deterioration can be detected by a faint aroma of vinegar around the film. We have identified our film needing the reduplication process and are in the process of sending them to NAPA for the fix at a nominal fee. The other suggestion would be to add a new reader/printer system that allows the patron to send the pages to any offsite computer or print onsite if he or she wishes. The patrons find this to be very helpful, and it negates the need to print costly copies. More and more titles are available each year on film, and both the backup and primary source possibilities are fantastic. We have already used microfilm heavily following weather crises such as tornados and flooding of servers. You never know when you will need it, and we are always happy to have the microfilm in our collection. It does relieve space on shelves and works well over the years with a minimum amount of conservation needs. I place small packets in the shelving area that provide absorption of moisture and check them periodically. There is no binding, there are no repairs, and it offers longevity that can't be matched by other formats—a real winner.

Bibliography

Bourne, Toss, ed. (1980). *Serials Librarianship* (Handbooks on Library Practice). London: Library Association, 1980.

Brooks, Colette. (2002). "So Many Books, So Little Space." *New York Times*, October 26, p. B9.

Gorman, G., E., and B. R. Howes. (1990). *Collection Development for Libraries* (Topics in Library and Information Studies). London: Bowker-Saur.

Hall, Blaine H. (1985). *Collection Assessment for College and University Libraries*. Phoenix : Oryx Press.

Lee, Sul H., ed. (1981). *Serials Collection Development: Choices and Strategies* (Library Management Series). Ann Arbor, MI: The Pierian Press.

Morgan, Steve. (2001). "Weeding Library Collections: Library Weeding Methods/Developing Information Leaders: Harnessing the Talents of Generation X," *Journal of Documentation* 57, no. 4: 561–564.

Osborn, A. D. (1980). *Serial Publications; Their Place and Treatment in Libraries*. Chicago: American Library Association.

Slote, Stanley J. (1989). *Weeding Library Collections: Library Weeding Methods*, 3rd ed. Englewood, CO: Libraries Unlimited.

Tuttle, Marcia. (1983). *Introduction to Serials Management* (Foundations in Library and Information Science). Greenwich, CT: JAI Press.

Tuttle, Marcia. (1996). *Managing Serials* (Foundations in Library and Information Science). Greenwich, CT: JAI Press.

Wortman, W. A. (1989). *Collection Management; Background and Principles*. Chicago: American Library Association.

OPEN ACCESS: GOOD FOR SOCIETY, BAD FOR LIBRARIES?

Rick Anderson, Associate Director for Scholarly Resources and Collections, University of Utah, Salt Lake City, Utah

T. Scott Plutchak, Director, Lister Hill Library of the Health Sciences, University of Alabama at Birmingham, Birmingham, Alabama

Introduction

In order to explore in some depth the likely impacts of an open access (OA) world on libraries, we presented a "debate" using the following proposition:

"As open access becomes more widespread, and more scholarly material becomes available either in open access journals or institutional repositories, libraries will become more marginalized in higher education institutions as funds formerly devoted to collections are diverted to other institutional priorities."

Rather than taking a pro or con position on the statement, however, we each approached it from the standpoint of the risks inherent for libraries from the technical services side of things (Anderson) and from the public services side (Plutchak). What follows are the prepared remarks with which we each laid the initial groundwork for our positions.

Anderson:

Our topic assumes that open access (OA) will eventually become widespread enough that the library's role as purchaser of expensive information on behalf of those who can't afford it themselves will, for all intents and purposes, be obviated. While I fully acknowledge the possibility of that happening, I also continue to be skeptical. OA is certainly here to stay. But whether it will become the default arrangement for scholarly publishing in general, even within the physical sciences, remains a very open question. There are some major OA initiatives operating right now that look very successful from the outside but that may look substantially less so in the future when the third-party funding that is currently keeping them afloat runs out.

All of that said, though, let me continue from the assumption that OA does, in fact, take hold and becomes the primary model for the dissemination of scholarly content.

Currently, patrons need libraries for three basic reasons:

- To buy them access to information they can't afford
- To organize and ease access to that information
- To help them use the information better

The problem is that on two of those points, patrons might beg to differ with our assessment of their need. Our users are becoming less and less convinced that they need the information to be organized—now that large-scale searching of documents is both possible and easy (and a normal part of every Google user's everyday life), many would just as soon search all available information at once, rather than be guided to what we tell them are relevant sectors of a preselected subset. And while some of our patrons would like help in making good and responsible use of our resources, most of them would—for better or for worse—just as soon be left alone to use the information as they see fit.

That leaves one fundamental function for us: that of broker on behalf of those who can't afford to buy for themselves all the access they need.

And therein lies the problem for libraries in an OA environment. If everything is free, then there are no subscriptions, and nothing needs to be bought. This obviously poses a threat to the job security of our acquisitions and serials staff, but more fundamentally, it poses a threat to the library itself. A university library that is spending $2 million per year on journals that have gradually stopped costing anything will not get to keep the $2 million to use for other purposes. Unless the university's provost is incompetent, the $2 million will get redirected to one of the university's other urgent needs. And if that $2 million dollar serials budget constituted half or more (as it often does) of the library's total allocation for collections, then the library has the makings of an existential crisis on its hands.

So here's the hard question: in an environment where one of the library's core functions has been obviated, is the library itself now marginal? The answer to that hard question is that it depends. And it depends on two things:

1. How important the library's remaining functions are to the institution that it serves

2. Whether the library has found new ways to be needed

As for the first variable, I'd like to suggest that our traditional nonbroker functions are a slender reed on which to hang if we want to remain an essential part of the institutions we serve. The importance of those traditional functions has been eroding for years, but that fact has been camouflaged because the library has retained an essential role as the purchasing agent for research content on campus. How can I say that the library's traditional services are losing their place? Because our time is short, I'm going to be brief, and that means the things I am about to say will sound harsher than I mean them to, but:

First, traditional reference service does not work. It seems like it works, because it works well for the very few patrons to whom we can provide it. But when you look at the populations we're trying to serve and the tiny fraction of them who benefit from personal reference service, it is simply not justifiable. Nor is the answer to expand the reach of traditional reference service, because no library has (or could possibly afford to have) all the staff that would be required to provide that level of service to all the patrons it serves. *Traditional reference service functions now only because so few patrons take advantage of it.* Add to this the increasing ease with which most patrons can answer most reference questions on their own, and you end up with a service whose days are numbered. (For more on this, you can look at my column on reference service and the "starfish problem" in the November 2007 issue of *Against the Grain*.)

Second, traditional cataloging has been a questionable enterprise for about five years now, and recent developments have marginalized it almost completely. If our goal is to describe collections well, then traditional MARC-based cataloging is as good a tool as any. But describing collections should not be our goal. It is a means to an end, and the end is connecting users with the information they need. If what we are really trying to do is connect users with information, then it may well be that a combination of full-text searching and folksonomical tagging will work just as well as, if not better than, traditional cataloging, and at a fraction of the cost.

Third, to the degree that OA takes hold, the concept of interlibrary loan (ILL) will lose all meaning. This is obvious. If scholarly information is all freely available online, then the very idea of exchanging copies between libraries becomes nonsensical.

Acquisitions, serials, collection development, reference, cataloging, ILL—what library functions remain?

Well, there is still one. In theory, at least, an OA environment will mean that there's an even greater need for discrimination, a need for people who can make it easier for users to find the good information and the relevant information (these are not the same thing) from among a bewildering array of no-cost choices. Librarians would no longer decide what to acquire but rather would decide what should be identified as worthy and/or relevant. The big question here is how necessary that service will be—or, to put it more starkly, how necessary our users will feel that service to be.

This obviously brings up the issue of searching. As we all know, the kinds of searching that happen in libraries can be divided into two general categories: searching for a known item (we could call this "targeted searching") and searching to find out what's out there (call it "speculative searching"). Library services tend to be organized as if both were variations on the same theme, but they're actually fundamentally different tasks, and I think an OA world will make the differences between them much more clear. In a world where there are functionally no price barriers between the user and the content, targeted searching may be much easier (because you can be certain that the desired item is available, and search tools like Google are ideally constructed to lead you to known items), and speculative searching may be harder (because formulating those kinds of searches requires real skill, and it can be difficult to cull relevant items from potentially massive results).

Librarians have always been more directly involved with speculative searching than with targeted searching, and there will probably continue to be a role for us in that regard into the foreseeable future.

However, that is not a role that will employ many librarians, and speaking as a librarian who's going to need a job for another twenty-five years or so, it doesn't give me a lot of confidence. So I think we need to look very hard for some new ways to be important to our sponsoring institutions. In the time that remains to me, I'd like to touch briefly on three specific possibilities.

One of the possibilities I think we need to explore—quickly, and with a sense of urgency —is **expanding our role from that of information receptacle to that of information creator.** One of the things an OA environment encourages is the creation, population, and maintenance of institutional repositories (IRs). I think the opportunities for libraries are tremendous in this regard. Now more than ever, we need to be getting out from behind our desks and working directly with faculty, and the creation of an IR gives you the perfect opportunity to do so in a natural, unforced way—asking faculty members to provide copies of their CVs (so that IR staff can use them to identify publications and add them to the database) and to submit future articles. Many of us are working in this direction already.

A second possibility is **the creation of a specialized on-campus repository for large data sets**—a massive memory facility in which raw data can be housed, and from which the data can be served to the campus and, as appropriate, beyond. A number of university libraries are working in this direction as well, and having quite a bit of success with it. It's a real boon to quantitative researchers and to those working with large image files, most of whom do not have the resources in their academic departments to house and serve out the huge sets of data that they create in the course of their research.

A third is **the creation and distribution of virtual journals.** This one, I think, can be especially fun. A virtual journal isn't really a journal at all, but rather a carefully edited compilation of links to recently published journal articles on a particular topic. In an OA environment, a virtual journal would look and feel just like a real online journal, although the look and feel would vary somewhat from article to article, depending on the layout and writing style in each original publication. The possibilities for tailoring such a journal to institutional (or even departmental, even faculty-specific) needs are potentially unlimited. For those of us who have long felt that the future of serials cataloging lies in targeting articles rather than journal titles, this is a clear step forward. And it would allow librarians to do what they do best in a flexible, user-centered, creative way.

Plutchak:

I've always found there to be an odd disconnect in the way that librarians have enthusiastically supported open access, in light of the general sense of angst and anxiety with which we look at our futures. Coming from a medical library background, I'm very sensitive to the wailing and gnashing of teeth of some of my hospital librarian colleagues, who often seem to be extremely vulnerable to the pressures of cost-cutting and mergers and acquisitions that have characterized healthcare in the United States over the past couple of decades. Often, they see the Internet, the rise of ubiquitous computing and the Googleization of everything as a tremendous threat. Arguing for the importance of the library becomes increasingly difficult in a world in which so much information is so freely and widely available.

The phrase that they hate the most, the phrase that characterizes for them the unassailable ignorance of hospital administrators is, "But it's all free and on the Internet!" And much of the work that librarians have done over the past several years has gone into exploring and explaining all of the reasons that this statement is very, very far from being the truth. We have to believe that it is far from being the truth, else how do we argue with those administrators for the value of keeping our libraries open and funded?

And at the same time that we are fighting those battles, we have become enthusiastic supporters of open access, carrying on the moral crusade to create a world in which it is all free and on the Internet.

One can't help wondering if we aren't becoming our own worst enemies, advocating for an environment in which we will put ourselves out of business because we have made ourselves irrelevant and unnecessary.

I would submit, however, that this bleak vision is only the case if one's view of the essential activity of libraries is the buying and organizing of stuff—the buying, in particular. For many people, this *is* the essential role of libraries, and I suspect that is the case for many of the people in this room. But as I have argued in other contexts, this is far too narrow a view of the role of librarians, and inaccurate both in its representation of our past and, more importantly, of our possible futures.

Lately, I've been reading a book by Frances Groen, former director of the health sciences library at McGill, called *Access to Medical Knowledge* (Groen 2007). She starts her discussion by talking about values, the fundamental values of librarianship, and I think it is worth our while in these interesting times to pay attention to the bedrock on which our profession has been built.

Groen identifies the three core values as:

1. Access to information for all

2. The promotion of literacy

3. The preservation of the accumulated wisdom of the past

She argues that, to some degree, these values are shared by all librarians in all contexts, although how they may be interpreted in any given context is determined by the type of library and environment.

Obviously, support for open access is in line with the first value, although true "access" requires much more than that.

The activities implied in the third value are clearly as necessary in an open access environment as in the world that we've lived in previously. Indeed, the challenge of preservation is far more difficult now than it was in the past, and open access will do nothing to diminish the importance of those critical activities.

I'd like to take the remainder of my time to focus on the second value—the promotion of literacy, which, if we take a very broad view, encompasses all of the activities that we typically associate with the public services side of the house, and which, I will argue, are even more essential in the world that we are creating.

When we use the word "literacy" in its common context, we tend to think of it as functional literacy—simply the ability to do the basic reading and writing tasks that are essential to function effectively in the modern world. And yet, the literacy that librarians should be concerned with goes beyond that. UNESCO (the United Nations Educational, Scientific and Cultural Organization) defines literacy this way:

> Literacy is the ability to identify, understand, interpret, create, communicate and compute, using printed and written materials associated with varying contexts. Literacy involves a continuum of learning to enable an individual to achieve his or her goals, to develop his or her knowledge and potential, and to participate fully in the wider society. (UNESCO 2004)

Most of our service programs are directed toward helping the users of our libraries achieve these goals. "Bibliographic instruction," back in the days of print, was intended to help our users become "library literate," and virtually all academic libraries now have a wide range of educational programs directed toward this end. Whether it be through reference consultations, the development of systematic reviews, support for bioinformatics, curriculum development, or the myriad other activities that we engage in, promoting literacy in its broadest aspect is a fundamental part of the mission of academic librarians.

In the digital world, the situation has become far more complex than it was in print. To the extent that open access initiatives increase the amount of material that is freely available to the students, faculty, and researchers in our institutions, OA does its part to increase the need that they have for the kinds of literacy support that we can provide.

Where we were once concerned with helping people find the right book or journal article (or, very occasionally, the right videotape or slide set), we now are plunged in a vast swirling universe of complex and conflicting information resources—electronic journals and electronic books are merely the tip of what can now be found in databanks and institutional repositories and point-of-care services. The gray literature that has bedeviled librarians for so long is increasingly more findable and usable. The full data sets on which researchers base their articles are more frequently becoming available as well. The task of helping people attain the skills that they need to effectively and efficiently navigate this sea of information is vastly larger than it was in print. The services of librarians who can provide this kind of instruction and assistance are more essential than ever.

Peter Morville recently published a book titled *Ambient Findability* (Morville 2005). He uses that title to refer to a world in which virtually any piece of information can be accessed from anywhere at anytime—if only we can figure out how to sort our way through to actually find it. In a presentation that he gave earlier this fall, he quoted that profound management consultant Dogbert, who has taken the old trope "finding information on the Internet is like drinking from a firehose" that was popular a decade ago, and rephrased it for the twenty-first century: "Information is gushing toward your brain like a firehose aimed at a teacup" (Adams 1996). Librarians can help.

It was nicely coincidental that I heard Morville speak as the 2007 Matheson Lecturer during the annual meeting of the Association of American Medical Colleges. The Matheson Lecture was named in honor of Nina Matheson, one of the most visionary leaders ever to come out of medical librarianship. More than a decade ago, in a lecture she gave at the annual Medical Library Association conference, Matheson spoke about "The Idea of the Library in the 21st Century." She said, "In the coming era of knowledge capitalism, those individuals and organizations will flourish who are able to apply knowledge to create knowledge and to organize it to produce knowledge" (Matheson 1995).

The OA debates are only a small part of the dramatic changes that we are encountering in the way that information is developed and shared. It seems fairly clear that OA business models will become more prevalent, although I suspect that the subscription-based models will continue to thrive for a very long time. In any case, the requirements and opportunities created for librarians in this very complex world are great. It may be that we are coming to the end of the age of libraries, but we certainly need librarians more than ever.

Summary and Conclusions

Following our prepared remarks, we made some extemporaneous comments on each other's presentations and then took questions from the audience. While we both tried to present an optimistic view of the opportunities available to librarians, we are well aware of the difficulties, risks, and dangers. We believe that it need not be the case that libraries will become marginalized, as our debatable proposition suggests; but to avoid it librarians will need to be creative, aggressive, and innovative, continually assessing their skills and the contributions that they can make to their institutions.

References

Adams, S. *Dilbert* [comic strip]. August 18, 1996.

Groen, F. K. *Access to Medical Knowledge: Libraries, Digitization and the Public Good*. Lanham, MD: Scarecrow Press, 2007.

Matheson, N. W. (1995). The Idea of the Library in the Twenty-First Century. *Bulletin of the Medical Library Association* 83(1):1–7. Retrieved January 18, 2008, from http://www.pubmedcentral.nih.gov/picrender.fcgi?artid=225988&blobtype=pdf.

Morville, P. (2005). *Ambient Findability: What We Find Changes Who We Become*. Sebastopol, CA: O'Reilly Media.

United Nations Educational, Scientific and Cultural Organization. (2004). UNESCO Education Sector. The plurality of literacy and its implications for policies and programmes. UNESCO Education Sector position paper. Retrieved January 18, 2008, from http://unesdoc.unesco.org/images/0013/001362/136246e.pdf.

REPORT ON THE PANEL: THE EXPANDING JOURNAL LITERATURE

Mary Summerfield, Director, Business Development, University of Chicago Press, Chicago, Illinois

The journal literature continues to expand with both more pages in existing journals and launches of new journals. This panel explored the issues related to this expansion for disciplines, publishers, and libraries.

Mary Summerfield[1] developed the concept for the panel after receiving many inquiries about the interest of the University of Chicago Press in publishing new journals. Those inquiring fell into three categories: (a) groups starting a new society and seeking to sponsor a related journal; (b) individuals or groups with a concept for a new journal but no society base; and (c) groups with a fledgling journal, that is, one that has been out for no more than five years and has modest exposure and subscription levels. These individuals and groups realized that they needed to work with a publisher in order to launch a journal or to take a fledgling journal to maturity.

Panelists were:

- David Colander, professor of economics at Middlebury College and a member of the task force of the American Economics Association that recommended launching four specialist journals;

- Robert Michaelson, head librarian, Science and Engineering, Northwestern University

- Zac Rolnik, currently publisher, NOW Publishers; has been an editor or publisher for twenty-one years

The journal literature is growing in many ways.

- Existing journals expand by adding issues or making existing issues larger. This happens so commonly that it is unfair to point fingers by giving examples. Commercially owned journals are more likely to take this approach as their publishers will understand the value of expanding share of publication in a field.

- Publishers launch journals when they see an opportunity because existing journal(s) in a subdiscipline is/are not moving aggressively to serve the field, or the field is sufficiently large that it can absorb another journal, or a new subdiscipline has matured.

- Societies can seek to establish additional or different journals when they believe that the scholars in their disciplines have insufficient outlets or their current publishing partners are not compatible. The American Economic Association falls in this category for its launch of four journals, each titled *American Economic Journal* and having subtitles *Macroeconomics*, *Microeconomics*, *Economic Policy*, and *Applied Economics*.

- As new subdisciplines evolve, new societies come into existence to serve them. These new societies often want to establish a journal which can be at the center of its focus. New societies see a journal as a focal point for members' work and also as a potential source of funds to underwrite their activities. In 2007, Chicago talked to several groups that were in the process of starting societies—for example, for neuroeconomics, psychology of science, and history of intellectual property—and wanted to learn about how to begin a journal.

- University centers or departments can see a gap in the journal literature and look to a journal as an underpinning for their work and an opportunity for students to become involved with the publishing process. Chicago's newly launched *Journal of Human Capital* falls in this category. Founder and editor-in-chief Isaac Ehrlich has a Signature Center of Excellence on Human Capital, Technology Transfer, and Economic Growth and Development at SUNY Buffalo.

- Groups of individuals who are concerned about an issue, especially a public-policy-related interdisciplinary issue, can seek to start a journal to provide a forum for the discussion of this issue. Such a group sought to launch a journal of food security.

Robert Michaelson cited Michael Mabe's July 2003 article in *Serials,* which examined data from the summer 2001 *Ulrich's Periodicals Directory* in attempting to estimate the growth of the journal literature. (The author of this report unsuccessfully searched for more recent comprehensive data on this topic.) This study found that there were 14,694 active, refereed academic/scholarly serials in summer 2001 (p. 192). The realism of this value was confirmed with ISI data on titles and citations and other data about the number of active researchers and their rate of publishing articles. By reviewing Ulrich's data since 1965, Mabe found that "the growth rate of active peer reviewed scholarly and scientific journals has been almost constant at 3.46% per annum. This means that the number of active journals has been doubling every 20 years." He found that the annual rate of growth was 3.23 precent from 1900 to 1940; 4.35 percent from 1945 to 1976; and 3.26 percent from 1977 to 2001 (p. 193). Mabe found a strong correlation between the growth in the number of journal titles and the growth in the number of researchers. "An increase of about 100-refereed papers per year globally results in the launch of a new journal" (p. 196). Mabe did not investigate whether journals were increasing in size.

Michaelson noted that the number of research and development workers affects the number of papers and pages in journals. This output could be managed in part by the evolution of online-only science, technology, and medicine (STM) journals. He observed that researchers in many fields related to physics use arXiv to disseminate their findings. This e-print archive provides open access to 459,742 e-prints in physics, mathematics, computer science, quantitative biology, and statistics (arxiv.org, January 21, 2008).

Michaelson wondered why the journal literature continues to grow. He acknowledged that some new journals add value to the STM community by serving emerging disciplines of value or providing important articles at lower cost than existing journals. He sees value in virtual journals that have been created by AIP and the Royal Society of Chemists.

The American Society for Engineering Education (ASEE) has established a list of best practices in provision of scholarly resources, for example, in the terms for providing articles via interlibrary loan. ASEE hopes that libraries will shun publications that ignore these rules.

Michaelson challenged the launch of new journals with high prices in fields that are already well served, giving Nature Publishing Group as an example of a publisher using this tactic. Libraries should refuse to acquire these journals. The increase in prices for STM journals has exceeded the increase in health care costs.

David Colander reported that the American Economic Association (AEA) is expanding its journal portfolio from three titles to seven in 2009 "because it can." With the general expansion of economics in academia and the need for young scholars to publish articles in order to obtain tenure, there is a need to expand the journals in economics. The AEA's flagship journal, *The American Economic Review,* has been expanding, but it is still rejecting strong articles. The AEA could have continued to expand the AER but decided to create four quarterly subject journals instead. Doing so will enable the AEA to serve its members as authors and readers more fully and increase the diversity of editors of AEA journals.

The launch of the new journals will have no impact on the high prices of commercial publishers like Elsevier, as they will contain a small fraction of the articles in economics and will not enable libraries to change their subscribing patterns.

The AEA bundles its journals; libraries pay $375 for the three journals in print form and the same amount again for a site license for the online version of all three journals in combination with the print copy. An online-only subscription to the three journals costs $625. The base price with the four new journals is planned as $630. The result will be higher subscription prices to libraries overall for the AEA bundle, but a lower average cost per AEA journal. The journals have 4,000 institutional subscribers. This large volume of subscriptions leads to lower unit costs for the AEA.

The AEA is a high-cost publisher as it pays editors and coeditors for their work; this makes it easy to recruit editors, who also appreciate the power that role conveys. The average cost to publish an article is $10,000 to $15,000. The AEA has $2 million in reserves so it can afford the cost of launching these journals. It is easy for the AEA to maintain its publishing program in house; it feels no need to work with a publisher.

Online access is important for journals, but print editions will be offered for the new AEA journals as well. Print editions indicate quality and are important to those who are seeking tenure. AEA members will receive free access to the online editions of the new journals as part of their membership.

The AEA will provide electronic tables of contents and article packaging for subject specialties. The new journals are expected to be among the most cited in economics five to six years after launch.

The journal literature is directly tied to tenure in economics. Universities subsidize scholars' research and then must pay for access to the results through journal subscriptions. The lack of a hard budget constraint in libraries means that publishers can demand relatively large price increases.

Working papers are the means by which economists disseminate their thinking to the discipline. Journals are the tombstone of the literature and the means of preserving and effectively disseminating it to those who were not involved with it at the working paper stage.

Universities need to deal with the economics of scholarly communication. Universities and university presses are the source of knowledge and need to disseminate this knowledge.

Zac Rolnik began his talk by agreeing with Bob Michaelson that there are too many journals. He asserted that 50 percent of journals could be eliminated without affecting science, but this would affect the tenure process as young scholars need to be published to obtain tenure. The STM publishing industry could be killed with a change in the tenure system that eliminated the dependency on journals to judge the quality of scholarship. At this time, however, journals provide the metric for advancement in the sciences. Working papers are the key tools for sharing knowledge, but journals contain and preserve the "minutes of science."

Journals typically start at a quarterly frequency. As content increases beyond the page budget, publishers either reduce the acceptance rate, which can open the door for competitive journals, or increase frequency. In order to maintain quality, it is important not to increase the acceptance rate as submissions increase. Some publishers look to increase page budget and frequency to increase prices; it is easier to capture more content than new subscribers.

Launching new journals occurs when there are:

- New areas of study: for example, the advent of AIDS brought *AIDS* in 1987, *Journal of Acquired Immunity Deficiency Syndrome* in 1988, and *International Journal of STD and AIDS* in 1990;

- Paradigm shifts or new areas of interest: *Journal of Economic Growth* in 1996 and *Machine Learning* in 1986 after first conference in 1980; and

- Omnibus journals unable to focus on new topics or bring discriminating reviews to bear on articles: *Quarterly Journal of Political Science* in 2006 with an analytical approach focusing on positive political theories.

Vibrant and active fields yield new journals:

- The top ten journals in Cell Biology were all created after 1973, and nine of the ten were launched after 1985.

- Seven of the top ten journals in computer science, theory and methods were launched after 1984.

- Four of the top ten journals in economics were launched after 1985.

- One of the top ten journals in history was launched after 1985.

The "Big Deal" lowers barriers to entry for large publishers to start new journals as they are able to add these journals to their packages without obtaining consent from libraries. The journals face increased pressure to expand content and add more pages as the publishers want to expand the content in their databases. The result is that new journals are being launched that would not have existed in the print-only world in which libraries bought each journal by itself, and significant costs were incurred in expanding content.

Note

1. Ms. Summerfield was director, business development, University of Chicago Press Journals Division; she is now a consultant in the scholarly communications industry. She can be reached at marysummerfield@ameritech.net.

INVESTIGATING WOMEN'S STUDIES CORE JOURNALS: LIBRARIANS' TOOLS, CITATIONS, AND SPECULATIONS

Wm. Joseph Thomas, Electronic Resources Librarian, Cornell University Library, Ithaca, New York (Formally at East Carolina University)

Leigh Younce, Library Fellow, East Carolina University, Greenville, North Carolina

Abstract

Having a list of "core" journals in a subject area can help librarians justify new subscriptions or protect highly regarded titles in tight budget times. Women's Studies is a broad interdisciplinary field that may effectively be resistant to the development of a core list, despite having customary librarians' tools for creating such core lists. Thomas and Younce have compared title lists from various standard sources, including the 2006 ISI Journal Citation Reports, the 2002 Association of College and Research Libraries (ACRL) Women's Studies Section core list, and titles indexed in a variety of Women's Studies indexes and databases, and collated those lists to arrive at a potential core journal list for Women's Studies. The purpose of this study is two-fold: to propose a current core list of journals for Women's Studies, and to examine the challenges of creating core lists.

Introduction

Core journals lists can have many uses, from providing support for a newly developed program or evaluating subscription requests to identifying journals to protect against cancellation. Lists of core titles help libraries determine start-up subscriptions to support new programs, or decide which journals must stay within reach rather than going to remote storage.[1] Janice Lewis and John D. McDonald also suggest that core journals lists can help when librarians are "evaluating the content of full-text aggregated databases," preparing accreditation reports, or creating materials for "instruction sessions and other educational programs."[2] Librarians may seek core journals lists in their efforts to prove that they have "a reliable, defensible, demonstrably fair empirical basis for their decisions."[3] Not everyone will agree on the same list of journals, but it is important that librarians have made the effort to proceed in a methodical manner and can explain how they arrived at the list they generated. Librarians often try to create core lists that are unbiased. Whether this is even possible is debatable. Katherine Corby writes that core lists can still be useful for offering a standard against which to judge a local collection, for beginning librarians to become more familiar with a discipline, or for helping set other priorities—the example she quotes is converting print to electronic subscriptions.[4] In addition to concerns about methodologies for arriving at any list of core journals, there is the very real issue of the applicability of a generalized core list to the campus specifics of curriculum, research practices, library budgets, and other local factors. Whether a campus offers graduate degrees or undergraduate, minor only, or only specific courses in the subject area all affect the ability of the library to support that field. The research interests of the professors teaching in the subject area will certainly vary, and this variation may directly affect the types of research their students do.

There is a variety of prior scholarship available on the creation of core lists. Several of these directly informed the current project by delving into methods for generating core journal lists, including Corby's "Constructing Core Journal Lists: Mixing Science and Alchemy" and Thomas E. Nisonger's "Journals in the Core Collection: Definition, Identification, and Applications." There are others, of course, but Corby and Nisonger provided insights into several methods for arriving at core journals, in addition to their cautions to librarians in how they should proceed. There were also several especially directly relevant studies of women's studies resources, including articles by Thura Mack and Linda A. Krikos, and a special issue of the *Serials Librarian* devoted to women's studies serials. Mack published "A Model Methodology for Selecting Women's Studies Core Journals" in 1991. She rejects a review of abstracting and indexing sources, preferring instead to design a citation analysis of *Signs*, a women's studies journal that most would agree is central to the field.[5] At that time, Mack asserted that "there was not an adequate number of journals published to develop a selected list reflecting only women's studies titles."[6] Krikos published a comparison of women's studies periodicals indexes in the *Serials Review* in 1994; it provides insight not only into some of the indexing resources but also into the development of the subject area and some of the journals serving it. "Women's Studies Serials: A Quarter-Century of Development" was published in 1998 as a special issue of *Serials Librarian;* it contained thirteen articles on topics ranging from faculty use of women's studies periodicals to citations within dissertations. It is important to note the age of the articles dealing specifically with women's studies journals—this really caught our attention because we believe this field has changed significantly since the majority of these articles have been written.

There are several other notable resources as well. Krikos and Cindy Ingold's book *Women's Studies: A Recommended Bibliography* (2004), which builds on *Women's Studies: A Recommended Core Bibliography, 1980–1985* by Catherine Loeb, Susan E. Searing, and Esther F. Stineman (1987), and on Esther Lanigan and Catherine Loeb's *Women's Studies: A Recommended Core Bibliography* (1979). These bibliographies provide some recommended periodical titles. The journal *WLW* (Women Library Workers), published by McFarland in North Carolina, had a short-lived column that reviewed women's studies periodicals. It lasted only from volume 14, no. 4 (Summer 1991) through volume 16, no. 4 (Winter 1993/94). During that time, columnist Audrey Eaglen reviewed around 80 journals, several of them appearing on our list of cross-indexed journals. The Women's Studies Section (WSS) of the Association of College and Research Libraries (ACRL) maintains a Core List of Journals for Women's Studies, last updated May 13, 2002. The WSS also provides access to "Defining Women's Studies Scholarship: A Statement of the National Women's Studies Association Task Force on Faculty Roles and Rewards" (1999), which contains an appendix listing scholarly journals in women's studies.

Definitions

A central issue in creating a core list of library materials is the ability to define the field these materials serve. And that's a tough job for Women's Studies. Interdisciplinarity is a critical issue—the field is not yet fully discrete nor bounded, which means that in addition to self-defined women's studies journals, its scholarship will also cite and be produced within a variety of potentially-related subject areas: sociology, history, english, education, and many others. In her essay, "Some Thoughts about the Future of Women's Studies," Bonnie Zimmerman understands that like all disciplines, women's studies is faced with defining its subject. She defines the subject matter as, "a cluster of concepts centering around woman as a category of analysis, gender as a system of power relations, interlocking systems of power, feminism and social change."[7] The National Women's Studies Association itself does not define Women's Studies as much as it suggests a pedagogical method. Rather than saying that students should, for instance, study the lives of both men and women in history or compare communication styles between men and women, the National Women's Studies Association puts forth what might be a much more radical approach—to reorient teaching and learning at all levels to recognize "gender, race, class, sexuality, region, ethnicity, and ability as important research variables…and constraints on objectivity."[8] "Above all," the Task Force concludes, "women's studies promotes access to institutions and to paradigms of knowledge for persons historically underrepresented in Western traditions of scholarship and knowledge production."[9] This emphasis on giving voice to people traditionally silenced is also neatly summarized within the Mission Statement of the Department Women's Studies at the University of Maryland: We work to "achieve intellectual freedom, social justice, and equality for all people."[10]

What is women's studies locally? The Women's Studies Program at East Carolina University (ECU) describes its intent to "[draw] on a variety of academic perspectives to research and study women's experiences in the United States and around the world."[11] The Women's Studies Program has a director and executive committee whose members are all faculty members within other departments of the University—as with other interdisciplinary programs of study at ECU. The program explicitly encourages its students to "re-vision societal patterns—especially those leading to prejudice—and to explore new frameworks from which to analyze contemporary conditions in women's lives." The university offers an undergraduate major and minor, and a graduate minor. Women's studies classes at ECU include an introduction to women's studies, a class on feminist theory, directed readings, and selected topics. Students must also have credit applied to the major from approved classes in related subject areas. These subject areas include the following: Anthropology, Child Development & Family Relations, Classical Studies, Communications, English, Ethnic Studies, Foreign Languages, Geography, Health, History, Nursing, Philosophy, Political Science, Psychology, Social Work, and Sociology. While there are only about a dozen professors listed on the Women's Studies Executive Committee, there is a pool of around eighty who have requested to teach courses for Women's Studies credit and/or to participate in an e-mail discussion list.[12] The diversity of departments and professors involved in women's studies fosters students' ability to "examine how women are affected by such factors as gender, race/ethnicity, sexual orientation, class, political and economic structures, and social systems" from a variety of perspectives.[13]

There have been many attempts over the years to define core lists, core journals, and other concepts of core library holdings. Nisonger suggests that the concept of "core" materials "refers to the fundamental collection development/collection management concept that certain materials are of such vital importance that they not only should definitely be included in the collection, but also constitute the collection's center."[14] Core lists of journals can also be defined in a more pragmatic way as journals that should be protected from cancellation or journals that best meet the needs of undergraduate or graduate students. Corby suggests that librarians have a "clear definition of purpose" for creating a core list, and that simplicity for nationally recognized lists is attractive.[15] We believe her, and believe that the concept of core applies most reliably to specified fields of study, rather than vaguely to some other subset of a library's holdings. Our primary purposes for creating a core list of women's studies journals are to demonstrate the advances in publication of women's studies periodical literature, and to raise awareness of some of the complexities in creating core lists for interdisciplinary fields. For the current study, we define a core list of journals as *a group of periodicals necessary to support teaching and research for specified field or discipline*.

Methodology

There are multiple methodologies for generating core lists, including citation analysis, overlapping library holdings, faculty publication data, and indexing coverage.[16] We also believe that core journals must be indexed in a generally available index for the subject matter, and that indexing is more important than reported circulations. In her article on women's studies indexes, Linda Krikos suggests that the periodicals addressed not focus exclusively on academic titles but also include mainstream magazines and small/radical/alternative press publications. Content of women's studies journals, she says, extends beyond activism or narrow academic boundaries to include titles that pertain to women of various ethnicities and cultural backgrounds, multiple sexualities, and international issues.[17] Other important characteristics of core journals include that they be currently published and appropriate for academic libraries.[18] Related characteristics that may interest librarians include WorldCat holdings and ISI impact factors, among others. Building on previous work of Nisonger, Mack, Krikos, and other librarians, we set about constructing a methodology.

Our method began with selecting women's studies resources and obtaining title lists from them. There were nine sources. Among these were the subject indexes Contemporary Women's Issues (which provided a title list of 384 journals), GenderWatch (120), LGBT Life with Full Text (88), Studies on Women and Gender Abstracts (1,053), and Women Studies Abstracts (25). Contemporary Women's Issues and Studies on Women and Gender Abstracts include books, which we manually eliminated before running the comparisons. Chesire Calhoun has identified coverage of lesbian issues as being subsumed under an umbrella of women's studies, so we were curious about the overlap between this database and other women's studies databases.[19] We were constrained to use the print issues of Women Studies Abstracts (WSA) because it is only available electronically as part of Women's Studies International (WSI), and this database did not provide an exportable title list. We chose the full volumes of WSA from 2004 to 2006, but because WSI incorporates such a respected index and claims to have citations from around 15,000 periodicals, we wanted to use it in some fashion. We decided to weight journals in our shared list in part based on the number of citations to that publication in WSI. We also used the undergrad-oriented Women's Interest Module from ProQuest Research Library (62 titles), in part due to the encouragement of the Research Agenda for Women's Studies Librarianship, suggesting that women's studies librarians examine coverage of women's studies journals in general databases.[20] We also chose several librarians' tools: the core list from ACRL Women's Studies Section (with 40 journals), ISI's Journal Citation Reports list for Women's Studies (26), and a specific report from Ulrichsweb that we ran, which yielded 102 titles, mostly peer-reviewed academic journals. We constructed this report by searching for actively published periodicals which were assigned women's studies as an Ulrichs subject heading, and reviewed by Magazines for Libraries.

We proceeded next to compare all title lists looking for shared and unique titles, and then focused our attention on all titles represented in more than one source. There were 143 shared titles, many of them solidly focused on women's studies, with two-thirds of them classed with women's studies rather than any other subject field. For this list of shared titles, we would compile related information, including whether it had appeared on any previous authoritative list, the year the publication began, peer-review status, format type (scholarly journal, magazine, newspaper, etc.), WorldCat holdings, number of subscriptions reported in Ulrichsweb, and number of citations in Women's Studies International. The authoritative lists we used were Thura Mack's core list, titles found in Krikos's and Ingold's *Women's Studies: A Recommended Bibliography,* and Krikos and Ingold's two predecessors by Stineman and Loeb. We also examined the 15th edition of *Magazines for Libraries* for reviews no matter in which subject area the journal was reviewed, and to see which journals on our list were considered basic for the gender studies subject area (the most immediately relevant to women's studies).

Several of these pieces of related information must be used in a cautious manner: for instance, WorldCat holdings do not show whether the institution currently receives the periodical, and online access may not be reported to OCLC. Peer-review status and format type do not carry the same kind of weight for women's studies journals as they do for other subject areas. Women's studies' commitment to activism (illustrated by *off our backs* or *Bitch Magazine*) and use of both the mainstream magazines (like *Ms.*) and of radical/alternative presses (for instance, *Hecate*) force a more inclusive approach to status and format when considering what kinds of journals should be considered core.

Results

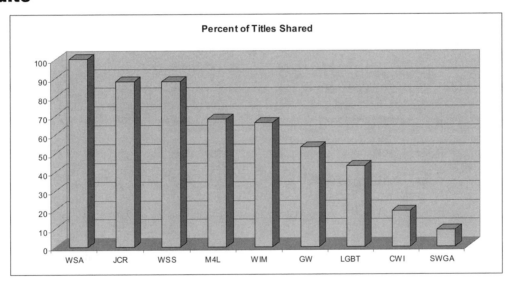

Figure 1. Percent of titles shared.

As we began examining the data, we wanted to relate the shared titles back to the sources we used. Women Studies Abstracts has the highest percentage of shared titles: all 25. Titles from the Journal Citation Reports (JCR) and the Women's Studies Section core list had the next highest degree of overlap with 88 percent each (23 shared of 26, and 35 of 40, respectively). The Ulrichs/Magazines for Libraries list had 69 of 102 shared, or 68 percent, and the Women's Interest Module of ProQuest Research Library had a similar 66 percent, with 41 of 62 shared. GenderWatch is the last resource with more than half its titles shared: 63 of 120. LGBT shared 38 of 88 titles for 43 percent shared, and Contemporary Women's Issues had only 19 percent of its titles shared, or 74 of 384. The resource with the smallest percentage of overlap was Studies on Women and Gender Abstracts (SWGA): 95 of 1053 shared, for 9 percent. See Figure 1.

Does this focus on shared titles suggest any action for librarians looking at women's studies indexing resources? Not necessarily. We were looking for overlap as an indicator of the journal's importance, not as a means of making a collection development decision to subscribe to or cancel women's studies databases. Further comments on these databases regarding their shared and unique titles follows in the discussion of our core list.

There were 143 journals that were found in more than one of the nine women's studies sources (see Figure 2). When we started examining that data and began to construct our core list, we included the 45 journals shared by four or more indexes, not only because they were shared by four but because of other factors like which indexes shared the titles, whether they were recommended by an authority, the number of citations in Women's Studies International, the age of the publication, the relation to Women's Studies (this includes activist, alternative/radical/small press, etc.), the format type, and peer-review status. We also selected some titles that were shared by only 2 or 3 indexes because of these factors. We finally arrived at a list of 60 core journals for Women's Studies. This list is appended below.

---

143 journals were found in more than 1 of the 9 indexes

- 69 journals only shared by 2 indexes
- 29 journals shared by 3 indexes
- 14 journals shared by 4 indexes
- 15 journals shared by 5 indexes
- 6 journals shared by 6 indexes
- 9 journals shared by 7 indexes
- 1 journal shared by 8 indexes

The characteristics of our core list suggest a maturing field with a coalescing set of supporting journals. Some relevant characteristics include subject area, start date, format, and publisher. Two-thirds of these titles are pretty solidly women's studies: thirty-six are classed with women's studies call numbers between HQ1101-2030, and four others have related HQ call numbers for sex roles and customs, lesbianism, and child rearing. Other subject areas represented include Social Work and Criminal Justice (five titles), Psychiatry (three titles), Education (two titles), Literature (two titles), and OB/GYN (two titles). One title appears from each of the following fields: Judaism (BM), Geography (GF), Business (HD), Visual Arts (N), Linguistic Theory (P), and Librarianship (Z). They average 1,422 citations in Women's Studies International, and the average holdings reported to WorldCat was 604. The average number of subscriptions reported to Ulrichs (of the forty-eight which did so) was more than 4,500.

The average start date is 1983; there are only two newer than 1995. The earliest start date is 1970, and about a third of the titles began that decade. Of the sixty titles, fifty-three were academic/scholarly journals, five magazines, one newsletter, and one "consumer journal." The five magazines were *Herizons, Lilith, Ms., off our backs*, and *Women and Environments*

International Magazine. The consumer magazine was *Feminist Collections*, the review of women's studies resources published by the Women's Studies Librarian office of the University of Wisconsin system, and the newsletter was *Al-Raida*, published by the Institute for Women's Studies in the Arab World at Beirut University College. American university presses publish sixteen of our titles, and commercial academic presses publish another thirty-two. Among these commercial publishers, Haworth has the most titles, with nine. Routledge publishes seven, and Sage publishes six of the titles on our list. Mostly published in the United States and United Kingdom, there were also several Canadian publications and journals published in Sudan, Lebanon, and India

A comparison of our titles to other authoritative lists provides some ideas about development and relative stability of the field. All sixty have appeared in some edition of *Magazines for Libraries*, with 57 reviewed in the 15th edition of *Magazines for Libraries*. Of these fifty-seven, thirty-four were reviewed in the Gender Studies category, half of them considered basic periodicals for this category. Categories containing reviews for the other twenty-three titles included Psychology (four titles), Lesbian Gay Bisexual and Transgender Studies (three titles), Cultural Studies (two), Health and Fitness (two), and twelve other categories with only one title each. Two-thirds of our titles have appeared on at least one of our other authoritative lists. Mack's 1991 list had twenty titles, with only nine in women's studies. (Many of the others were staples in their subject areas, like *American Anthropologist*, *American Economic Review*, *American Journal of Sociology*, etc.) Of the nine women's studies journals in Mack's list, one has ceased publication; the other eight are also in our list. Twenty-nine of our titles have appeared in at least one of the three editions of Krikos's women's studies bibliography.

One of the other questions that arose concerned the titles not part of that group of 143 with which we started. That is, what journals were unique among the title lists for various women's studies resources we used? Among other observations related to the unique content of various sources, we saw that LGBT Life retained the most activist publications and the greatest variety of format types, including many newsletters. ProQuest Research Library's Women's Interest Module contained unique titles which included many general interest commercial magazines like *Cosmo*, *Essence*, and *Vogue*. GenderWatch retained some relevant titles, like *Hurricane Alice*, the *Beltane Papers*, and *Women's Research Network News*. GenderWatch also contained some of the subject-oriented periodicals, like *International Journal of Childbirth Education* and literary review *FemSpec*. Contemporary Women's Issues (CWI) had some reasonable titles, like *Perspectives on Sexual and Reproductive Health, Lila: Asia Pacific Women's Studies Journal,* or *Peace and Freedom*. There were also some publications that might inform women's studies, but by and large, CWI's unique titles were not related to women's studies—these were periodicals with names like *Billboard,* the *Northern Miner,* and a lot of Crain's business publications. CWI also included major newspapers, which may or may not have value when searching for women's studies issues.

Studies on Women and Gender Abstracts had the same problem CWI had: there were some very reasonable women's studies titles (like *Women's Studies Journal* or the *Canadian Journal of Women and the Law*) that got buried in the list of more than 950 titles by non-relevant journals. And like CWI, there were publications that would provide greater depth to research in women's studies topics, for instance *AIDS Care, Journal of Gay and Lesbian Issues,* or the *Journal of Sexual Aggression*. When we reviewed the lists from Journal Citation Reports, Ulrichs/Magazines for Libraries, and the Women's Studies Section, we saw quite a few of their unique titles that would make excellent candidates for a women's studies core list, such as the *Journal of Women's Health*, *Calyx*, the *Harvard Journal of Law and Gender*, and *Kalliope*. Why weren't they included?

After we ran our shared lists and started comparing, we quickly realized that there were significant journals that did not make our list and wondered why. Indexing played a major part, particularly two events: the way we chose to run our Ulrichs search and the fact that Women's Studies International has no exportable title list. Within Ulrichs we chose to use the subject heading Women's Studies rather than its relative Women's Interest. That choice excluded some of significant titles, like *Calyx*, *Feminist Economics*, *Sinister Wisdom*, and *Feminist Teacher*, as well as a whole bunch of titles we didn't want, like *Cosmogirl, Playgirl*, and *Family Circle*. Some of these titles appeared on our list anyway (like *Feminist Economics* and *Feminist Teacher*), primarily because they were indexed in multiple places. Maybe in the future we could find a way to shift our design slightly to bring in these titles that have appeared on other authoritative lists, and certainly if Women's Studies International would provide an exportable title list, that would aid similar research efforts.

Robin Lent expresses concerns with the generation of core lists, especially in the potential for creating a self-sustaining cycle whereby core journals get indexed; indexed journals get higher subscriptions, higher subscriptions and indexing equate to core, etc.[21] But this current project does have value, to demonstrate advances in the subject coverage of women's studies, and for libraries looking for a starter or comparison list for providing access to the subject area. Certainly additional cautions must be offered. One of these is the need for maintaining journals that are classed within other subject areas but also provide support for women's studies—for example, the literary reviews *Calyx* or *FemSpec*. Another caution is the assessment of indexing support for women's studies: this project is a case where overlap is more important than uniqueness of titles indexed. GenderWatch, Studies on Women and Gender Abstracts, Contemporary Women's Issues, and Women's Studies International do provide broad indexing across women's studies and a variety of related disciplines, and comments above are not intended for libraries to use in subscription decisions for these indexing resources. Last is the most difficult or most subjective (or both) limitation: how does this list of core journals apply to the individual library's local needs? That is a question each library must answer for itself.

What does this core list mean for women's studies? Writers who address women's studies as a discipline indicate growth in international issues and express a concern not to leave behind the activist roots of women's studies. Our own title list indicates that women's health is an area of women's studies that is growing but hasn't yet stabilized. Our list also suggests that women's studies is making a move away from its activist roots and is becoming more populated with scholarly journals produced by mostly university and commercial academic publishers. Does the development of core journals within "women's studies" suggest that the subject is becoming more discipline-based or developing its own theory? And if the field is developing its own theory, how does it compare to previous and concurrent theories?

There are surely other changes in the field itself, and librarians must monitor and respond to them within the context of changes in the librarian's work to provide access to information. Further research opportunities exist, including the comparison of core lists generated by various methods in order to arrive at what might be the most effective methodology for women's studies, and continuing the work urged within the Research Agenda for Women's Studies Librarianship to investigate the coverage of women's studies journals within general databases. According to Kennedy and Beins, "Women's Studies offers the best opportunities for productive interdisciplinary theorizing about women, gender, knowledge and society."[22] We hope the present core list contributes to libraries' ability to offer access to these opportunities.

References

Eaglen, Audrey. (Summer 1991–Winter 1993/1994). "Spreading the Word on Women." *WLW Journal* 14–16.

Gerhard, Kristin H., editor. (1998). "Women's Studies Serials: A Quarter-Century of Development" (special issue). *The Serials Librarian* 35 (nos. 1–2).

Krikos, Linda A. (1994). "Women's Studies Periodical Indexes: An In-Depth Comparison" *Serials Review* 20 (no. 2): 65–78+.

Krikos, Linda A., and Cindy Ingold. (2004). *Women's Studies: A Recommended Bibliography* (3rd ed.). Westport, CT: Libraries Unlimited.

LaGuardia, Cheryl, editor. (2006). *Magazines for Libraries* (15th ed.). New Providence, NJ: CSA.

Lanigan, E., and Loeb, C. (1979). *Women's Studies: A Recommended Core Bibliography.* Littleton, CO: Libraries Unlimited.

Loeb, Catherine, Susan E. Searing, and Esther F. Stineman. (1987). *Women's Studies: A Recommended Core Bibliography, 1980–1985.* Littleton, CO: Libraries Unlimited.

Olson, Hope A., editor. (2002). *Information Sources in Women's Studies and Feminism. Guides to Information Sources.* München: K.G. Saur.

Searing, Susan E. (1985). *Introduction to Library Research in Women's Studies.* Westview Guides to Library Research. Boulder, CO: Westview Press.

Notes

1. Janice Steed Lewis and John D. McDonald, "Defining an Undergraduate Core Collection," *Serials Librarian* 43, no. 1 (2002): 45–46.

2. Ibid.

3. Katherine Corby, "Constructing Core Journal Lists: Mixing Science and Alchemy," *portal: Libraries and the Academy* 3, no. 2 (2003): 207.

4. Ibid., 213.

5. Thura Mack, "A Model Methodology for Selecting Women's Studies Core Journals" *Library and Information Science Research* 13 (1991): 131–145.

6. Ibid., 133.

7. Bonnie Zimmerman, "Beyond Dualisms: Some Thoughts on the Future of Women's Studies," in *Women's Studies for the Future: Foundations, Interrogations, Politics,* eds. Elizabeth L. Kennedy and Agatha Beins (Piscataway, NJ: Rutgers, 2005), 36.

8. Marjorie Pryse, "Defining Women's Studies Scholarship: A Statement of the National Women's Studies Association Task Force on Faculty Roles and Rewards." (NWSA Task Force, 1999). Introduction and Statement of Purpose.

9. Ibid.

10. "Mission Statement." Department of Women's Studies. University of Maryland. Retrieved October 29, 2007, from http://www.womensstudies.umd.edu/about/missionstatement.shtml.

11. "Home." Women's Studies. Thomas Harriott College of Arts and Sciences, East Carolina University. Retrieved October 28, 2007, from http://www.ecu.edu/wost/.

12. Cheryl Dudasik-Wiggs. Personal correspondence. October 11, 2007.

13. "Home." Women's Studies. Thomas Harriott College of Arts and Sciences. East Carolina University. Retrieved October 28, 2007, from http://www.ecu.edu/wost/.

14. Thomas E. Nisonger, "Journals in the Core Collection: Definition, Identification, and Applications," *Serials Librarian* 51, nos. 3–4 (2007): 51–73.

15. Corby 213–214.

16. Thomas E. Nisonger, "Journals in the Core Collection: Definition, Identification, and Applications," *Serials Librarian* 51, nos. 3–4 (2007): 51–73.

17. Linda A. Krikos, "Women's Studies Periodical Indexes: An In-Depth Comparison" *Serials Review* 20, no. 2 (1994): 66.

18. "Core List of Journals for Women's Studies." ACRL Women's Studies Section. Retrieved July 16, 2007, from http://libr.org/wss/projects/serial.html.

19. Among other publications, see Cheshire Calhoun, "Separating Lesbian Theory from Feminist Theory," *Ethics* 104, no. 3 (1994): 558–581.

20. "Research Agenda for Women's Studies Librarianship." Research Committee of the Women's Studies Section. The Section. Last updated March 21, 2006. Retrieved July 16, 2007, from http://www.libr.org/wss/committees/research/researchagenda.html.

21. Robin Lent, "Women's Studies Journals: Getting the Collection Right!" *Serials Librarian* 35, nos. 1/2 (1998): 52.

22. Kennedy and Beins, Introduction, 34

Appendix: Thomas and Younce's Core List for Women's Studies Journals:

1. *Affilia* (0886-1099)

2. *Ahfad Journal* (0255-4070)

3. *Al-Raida* (0259-9953)

4. *Atlantis* (0702-7818)

5. *Australian Feminist Studies* (0816-4649)

6. *Camera Obscura* (0270-5346)

7. *Canadian Woman Studies* (0713-3235)

8. *Differences* (1040-7391)

9. *European Journal of Women's Studies* (1350-5068)

10. *Feminism and Psychology* (0959-3535)

11. *Feminist Collections* (0742-7441)

12. *Feminist Economics* (1354-5701)

13. *Feminist Review* (0141-7789)

14. *Feminist Studies* (0046-3663)

15. *Feminist Teacher* (0882-4843)

16. *Feminist Theory* (1464-7001)

17. *Frontiers* (0160-9009)

18. *Gender and Education* (0954-0253)

19. *Gender and History* (0953-5233)

20. *Gender and Society* (0891-2432)

21. *Gender Issues* (1098-092X)

22. *Gender Place and Culture* (0966-369X)

23. *Gender, Work, and Organization* (0968-6673)

24. *Hecate* (0311-4198)

25. *Herizons* (0711-7485)

26. *Hypatia* (0887-5367)

27. *Journal of Feminist Family Therapy* (0895-2833)

28. *Journal of Gay and Lesbian Psychotherapy* (0891-7140)

29. *Journal of Gay and Lesbian Social Services* (1053-8720)

30. *Journal of Gender Studies* (0958-9236)

31. *Journal of Lesbian Studies* (1089-4160)

32. *Journal of the History of Sexuality* (1043-4070)

33. *Journal of Women and Aging* (0895-2841)

34. *Journal of Women, Politics and Policy* (1554-477X)

35. *Journal of Women's History* (1042-7961)

36. *Lilith* (0146-2334)

37. *Manushi* (0257-7305)

38. *MS* (0047-8318)

39. *NWSA Journal* (1040-0656)

40. *off our backs* (0030-0071)

41. *Psychology of Women Quarterly* (0361-6843)

42. *Resources for Feminist Research* (0707-8412)

43. *Sex Roles* (0360-0025)

44. *Signs* (0097-9740)

45. *Social Politics* (1072-4745)

46. *Tulsa Studies in Women's Literature* (0732-7730)

47. *Violence against Women* (1077-8012)

48. *Woman's Art Journal* (0270-7993)

49. *Women & Environments International* (1499-1993)

50. *Women and Criminal Justice* (0897-4454)

51. *Women and Health* (0363-0242)

52. *Women and Language* (8755-4550)

53. *Women and Therapy* (0270-3149)

54. *Women: A Cultural Review* (0957-4042)

55. *Women's Health Issues* (1049-3867)

56. *Women's History Review* (0961-2025)

57. *Women's Review of Books* (0085-8269)

58. *Women's Studies International Forum* (0277-5395)

59. *Women's Studies Quarterly* (0732-1562)

60. *Women's Studies: An Interdisciplinary Journal* (0049-7878)

A COLLABORATIVE, CURRICULUM-BASED PERIODICALS COLLECTION DEVELOPMENT PROJECT

Sue Wiegand, Periodicals Librarian, Saint Mary's College, Notre Dame, Indiana

Some Collection Development evaluation projects are necessitated by lack of space, but the recent curriculum-based Periodicals Evaluation Project at Saint Mary's College was inspired more by a desire to correlate our periodicals collection more closely with departmental needs. I also wanted to increase collaborative discussions both with other, non-serials librarians and with disciplinary teaching faculty, and cut subscriptions that weren't needed as a cost-saving measure. The project actually started as a cancellation project, mainly to eliminate duplication of formats. Usage studies will come later as we refine the ongoing evaluation process.

To get started, I did the spreadsheets for each department with information on each title (see Appendix A for a sample spreadsheet.) Then I e-mailed the spreadsheet to each department head and asked for a meeting with the department to discuss their periodicals in the library. Some departments have yet to respond. We started in 2003, and I plan to continue to rotate through the departments on a regular basis.

Who Was Included

As the project developed, some decisions had to be made on who was to be included in the discussions. The final composition of the decision-making team included:

- The Periodicals Librarian

- Disciplinary Faculty by Department (In some departments, all faculty participated; in others, selected faculty joined the discussion. I left it up to the departments and their respective Chairs.)

- Other Librarians—any who were interested could come to the meetings (Those who did included those from Reference, Cataloging, Acquisitions [monograph], Instruction, Interlibrary Loan, and the Library Director.)

As the project continued, I found that faculty collaboration was key. The conversations began to include all library resources and nonprint formats also, leading to many fruitful discussions as awareness of library resources increased. The Evaluation Project eventually became a more positive communication tool for both building the periodicals collection and weeding, for the non-Periodicals Librarians as well as the faculty who became involved. Weeding the bound Periodicals on the Lower Level was added later (see Appendix B for a sample weeding checklist). This detailed process was only possible because we have fewer than 600 current print periodicals.

Advantages of Spreadsheet Presentation

I found several advantages to using spreadsheets for the evaluation, including:

- Concise presentation

- Ease of sharing information through e-mail and printed lists

- Lists of titles for each department (not an allocation)
- Criteria for evaluation—spreadsheets and checklists—can be annotated, updated, and compiled

The criteria to be included for the spreadsheets and checklist sheets was taken from the current Collection Development policy and included such items as Title, SMC Holdings, Other Holdings, and a Rating, first from the librarians and then with the other faculty involved.

We also considered if a title was:

- Indexed, abstracted, or full-text in any of our databases or Abstracting/Indexing sources

- Recommended by Katz/LaGuardia's *Magazines for Libraries* or by a particular faculty member

- Had any other pertinent criteria, such as publication dates, run, relevance to curriculum, demonstrated need, scholarly reputation, price, availability of other formats or replacement, condition, significance of authors, illustrations, etc.

The Discussions

Two major advantages of the ensuing discussion were improved communication and outreach to the teaching faculty, which I hope will herald a new era in the library. The faculty discussions were great—we moved from the discussion of print resources to online needs and wants, and I was able to introduce topics such as scholarly communication issues, including archival preservation and emphasizing the importance of the scholarly record—a topic of great interest to faculty. I could highlight what the library had available in print and online, and how to find it (aggregators vs. "real" online subscriptions; Table of Contents alerts and RSS feeds for current awareness and how to find them). I also talked about library instructional services that were available to help their students find, use, understand, and evaluate online resources in the changing scholarly/academic environment.

Then, when the librarians met afterward to discuss what had been learned, we were able to include actual disciplinary observations and concerns, to the benefit of both Collection Development for periodicals and also later weeding discussions. The spreadsheets provided a good, concise summary of the discussions and literally kept everyone on the same page, especially since we could share spreadsheets through e-mail.

Disadvantages

There were some disadvantages to this intensive evaluation project. The spreadsheets were a lot of work and very time-consuming, plus were almost instantly outdated, given price fluctuations and aggregator licensing changes. Eventually, the librarians started meeting in a room with computer access to check current information as questions came up, using CUFTS (http://cufts.lib.sfu.ca/tools.shtml) for finding where full-text was available; WorldCat for publication history and other holdings; and SFX as well as our individual databases and online catalog for title lists and years held. We also found some problems using this procedure, such as inaccurate holdings, that could then be corrected.

Another disadvantage was that the columns and abbreviations had to be explained repeatedly. As for the included information itself, even with student help (problematic in itself), this level of detail was probably only possible with our small number of print periodicals, though I think it could be extended to an amendable core list for each department in the preferred format, with continuing meetings on a rotating basis.

Faculty typically had a cancel one title, then add two mind-set and often wanted more expensive online titles, which we weren't always able to provide (although it did increase awareness of prices and the library budget. This may have helped put the library in the forefront of the College President's Strategic Plan).

Other disadvantages—other librarians sometimes disagreed on what information was needed and/or provided, and, not understanding the changing nature of serials, they wanted it perfect, with all the latest pricing and indexing information. In a way, this was not really a disadvantage, except for the time factor—because it led to great discussions!

Towards a New Collection Development Policy

For future direction of this project, I'd like to find time to build all the information into an evaluation database to help in making future decisions. In spite of the head-banging from non–Technical Services Librarians, I'd like to continue the consensus-building, educational, and informative discussions with the other librarians as well as disciplinary faculty, as the discussions were of great educational and consensus-building value in learning to understand periodicals in this transitional environment.

I'd also like to include a section in the Collection Development Manual that includes format as a criterion—when is it appropriate, when is aggregator inclusion enough, what are our guidelines for archival concerns for storage of print and also for weeding our lower level? How will JSTOR titles be handled? What areas will we concentrate on for collecting deeply? Right now, none of these concerns is addressed in our 1999 policy, and it should be updated. My goal is that this collaborative, curriculum-based collection development communication tool will become an ongoing discussion.

Note: this presentation utilized questions from the participants as inspired by an article on "The Cephalonian Method," citation in the Resources that follow.

Resources

Brier, David J., and Vickery Kaye Lebbin. (1999, November). "Evaluating Title Coverage of Full-text Periodical Databases." *Journal of Academic Librarianship* 25, no. 6.

Duranceau, Ellen Finnie. (n.d.). "Beyond Print: Revisioning Serials Acquisitions for the Digital Age." Retrieved September 8, 1999, from http://web.mit.edu/waynej/www/duranceau.htm.

Hall, Blaine H. *Collection Assessment Manual for College and University Libraries.* Phoenix, AZ: Oryx Press, 1985.

Hardesty, Larry, and Collette Mak. (1994). "Searching for the Holy Grail: A Core Collection for Undergraduate Libraries." *Journal of Academic Librarianship* 19, no. 6.

Lafferty, Cindy. (2006). "Serials Usage Statistics in a Small Academic Library." *The Serials Librarian* 49, no. 4.

Lee, Sul H. (1981). *Serials Collection Development: Choices and Strategies.* Ann Arbor, MI: Pierian Press, 1981.

Metz, Paul, and John Cosgriff. (2000, July). "Building a Comprehensive Serials Decision Database at Virginia Tech." *College and Research Libraries* (July 2000).

Metz, Paul. (1992, May). "Thirteen Steps to Avoiding Bad Luck in a Serials Cancellation Project." *Journal of Academic Librarianship* 18, no. 2.

Morgan, Nigel, and Linda Davies. (2004, Summer/Autumn). "Innovative Library Induction—Introducing the 'Cephalonian Method.' " SCONUL Focus 32. Library, Information Science & Technology Abstracts. Retrieved August 19, 2008, from http://www.sconul.ac.uk/publications/newsletter/32/2.rtf.

Nisonger, Thomas. (1998). *Management of Serials in Libraries.* Englewood, CO: Libraries Unlimited.

Sapp, Gregg, and Peter G. Watson. (1989). "Librarian-Faculty Relations during a Period of Journals Cancellations." *Journal of Academic Librarianship* 15, no. 5.

Slote, Stanley J. (1997). *Weeding Library Collections.* Englewood, CO: Libraries Unlimited.

Appendix A: Sample Spreadsheet—Business

Current Periodical Titles in Business

	Periodical Title	SMC	Price	Rating	ND	IUSB	ASE	Katz/LaGuardia	Notes
1	Accounting Today newspaper	12 mo.	$105.04	+	nf	nf	nf	surveys of particular interest	BSP 03-
	includes Marketplace, Accounting Technology							some content free at	current online free
	includes Practical Accountant Alert							WebCPA.com	
	includes CPA Wealth Provider								
	includes Year in Review								
2	Advertising Age	12 mo.	$149.00	+	6 mo.	60-	96-,H	highly rec college libraries	BSP
	Advertising Age (mf)	75-	$210.00	+	60-02	nf			
3	American Economic Review	11-	$265.25	2	11-	11-	nf	very highly rec	JSTOR-catalogued
	includes American Economic Assn mbshp								BSP 11-3 yr mw
	includes Directory of members—online								
4	includes Journal of Economic Literature	69-		2	69-	69-	nf	core; highly rec colleges, etc.	JSTOR-cat.,BSP 69-
5	includes Journal of Economic Perspectives	87-		2	87-	87-	nf	core; bargain,highly rec	JSTOR-cat.,3 yr mw
	includes Papers & Proc. of the Annual Mtg.							lg public & acad libraries	
6	American Enterprise	97-	$29.71	1	93-	90-	nf	conservative,1 topic in	BSP 93-
	includes Am Enterprise Inst for Public Pol							depth; valuable surveys	
	Research membership								
7	Barrons newspaper	2 yr.	$155.00	+	mf 94-	94-	nf	recommended	not in Newspaper Src
8	Brandweek	92-	$158.09	3	92-01	94-	94-,H	important	BSP 94-
9	Business Horizons	96-	$326.79	2	58-	58-	65-01,P,H	of interest to all libraries	BSP 65-01
	includes ScienceDirect Web edition online								
	includes12 mos. Backfile; link in catalog								
10	Business Week (was 2 copies, now 1)	49-	$60.00	1	29-	43-	96-,H;BSP 96-	this 1 if only 1	on CR's list to keep
11	Challenge: the magazine of economic affairs	96-	$233.42	2	54-03	73-	nf		BSP 64-6 mos mw
12	Consumer Reports	43-,inc.	$27.59	1	42-03	69-	90-3 mos.	core; this 1 if only 1	BSP 90-3 mos.
	includes Buying Guide (annual)								BSP 98-
13	Consumers' Research Magazine	73-89 mf	$31.83		73-87	76-04	90-04,P,H	good for acad & public	ceased; BSP 90-04
14	CPA Journal	75-	$50.93	1	73-01	nf	nf	1 of most imp., online 89-	CR—keep

Appendix B: Sample Weeding Checklist

Title & SMC holdings	Other Holdings	Indexed/Abstracts	Full-Text	Recommended?	Notes	Initial if OK to withdraw
Gebrauchsgraphik v.30-41, inc. 1959-71 cont. by Novum Gebrauchsgraphik SMC 1972-88	ND 1954-68	nf	nf	nf	pub. history 1924-31 wd	
Geographical Magazine v.8-47, inc. 1941-75	nf	nf	nf	nf	pub. history 1935-88 wd	
Georgia Review v.35-41, inc. 1982-87	ND 1947-	ASE 93-	nf	4401 **core (bold)**	pub. history 1947- wd	
German Quarterly v.9-40, inc. 1936-67 cont. by Membership Directory, not at SMC	ND 1928- IUSB 1937-	nf	nf	2806 should be in libraries supporting German Studies	pub. history 1928- wd	

Golden Book Magazine

v.1-9	ND 1925-35	nf	nf	pub. history 1925-35
1925-34, inc.	Readers' Guide			"pop.magazine for brainy people"
cont. by Fiction Parade, not at	has own index also			"odd"
SMC				kept

Good Housekeeping

v.192-239	IUSB 1935-38	nf	ASE 01-	6726
1982-2004			core	wd

Good Work

v.23-32	ND 1937-70, inc.	nf	nf	pub. history 1959-70
1959-69				previous titles: Christian Social Art,
conts. Catholic Art Quarterly				SMC 1937-41
SMC 1941-59				Catholic Social Art Q, not at SMC
				kept

ARE THEY BEING INDEXED? TRACKING THE INDEXING AND ABSTRACTING OF OPEN ACCESS JOURNALS

Elaine Yontz, Professor of Library and Information Science, Valdosta State University, Valdosta, Georgia, eyontz@valdosta.edu

Jack R. Fisher II, Acquisitions Librarian, Valdosta State University, Valdosta, Georgia, jrfisher@valdosta.edu

Abstract

If open access journals are to fulfill their promise, their inclusion in the indexing and abstracting services used by scholars and researchers is essential. The purposes of this project are to design a model for tracking the inclusion of open access journals in recognized indexing and abstracting services and to test the model.

As a pilot study, the 78 Library and Information Science (LIS) journals in the Directory of Open Access Journals (DOAJ) were checked for inclusion in Library Literature & Information Science (LibLit), Library & Information Science Abstracts (LISA), Library, Information Science & Technology Abstracts (LISTA), Information Science & Technology Abstracts (ISTA), Trade & Industry Index (T&I), and Social Science Citation Index (SocSCI). Ulrich's, the home pages of the journals, and the lists of the indexing/abstracting services were consulted to verify inclusion or exclusion.

The study revealed that 52.63 percent of the LIS journals were not included in any of the indexing/abstracting services and that only four journals were indexed by half of the services. Feedback from conference attendees will be used to revise the model and to extend it to other scholarly and research disciplines.

Research Design/Pilot Study

The Directory of Open Access Journals (DOAJ) was chosen as the source for journals to be considered due to the site's reputation as a stable collocation point for open-access journals and because the titles in DOAJ are organized into subject groups. The discipline of Library and Information Science was chosen because the number of LIS journals was considered to be workable for a pilot study and because the researchers have the requisite knowledge of LIS to identify the "recognized indexing and abstracting services" for that field. The six indexing and abstracting services are the ones included in Péter Jacso's October 2006 comparative review of LIS indexing services (http://gale.cengage.com/reference/peter/lista.htm).

The seventy-eight Library and Information Science journals in the DOAJ were checked for inclusion in Library Literature & Information Science (LibLit), Library & Information Science Abstracts (LISA), Library, Information Science & Technology Abstracts (LISTA), Information Science & Technology Abstracts (ISTA), Trade & Industry Index (T&I), and Social Science Citation Index (SocSCI). Ulrich's, the home pages of the journals, and the lists of the indexing/abstracting services were consulted to verify inclusion or exclusion.

An Access database was created to store the data that was collected. The database also allowed for the sorting of data and the movement of data into Excel for calculations. See Figures 1–3.

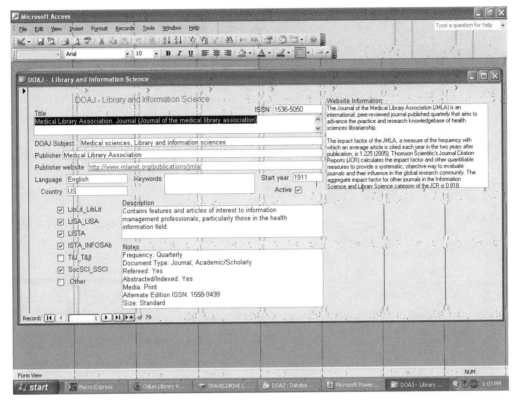

Figure 1. Data entry form.

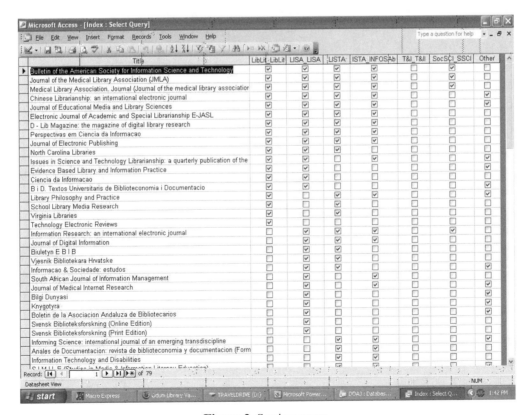

Figure 2. Sorting query.

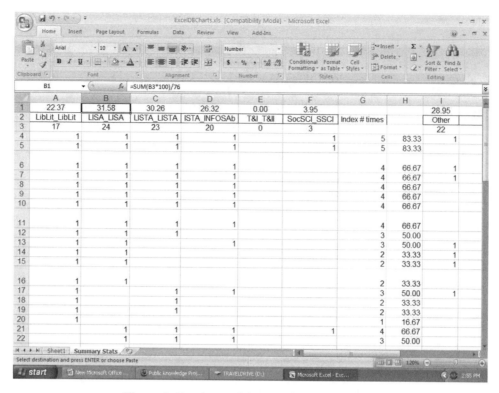

Figure 3. Excel spreadsheet used for calculation.

At the beginning of the project, the print version of Ulrich's was used for gathering data. This proved to be tedious, so the online version was used to complete the data collection. The Web sites of the indexing services were consulted to confirm that the journal was listed. Again, this proved somewhat tedious, as there are variations of title that sometimes made searching confusing. Finding and searching the homepages of the journals was also a tedious task and frequently provided little or no additional information that was not included in Ulrich's. Many of the journal Web sites were simply access points to the content of the various issues. The basic question of the proposal, whether the open access journals were being indexed by the six indexing services, could be answered most efficiently by consulting Ulrich's and verifying on the indexing services' Web sites. Information tangential to the basic question, including language, country of publication, start year, frequency, and peer-review status, was collected for possible use if the project parameters are extended. Additional indexing services, including some that focus on non-English language publications, were noted.

The Conference Session

The purpose of the session was to present the results of the research for the seventy-eight Library and Information Science journals in the DOAJ and to seek input from the audience. The project was briefly explained and results were presented. See Tables 1–3.

Table 1. Percentage of the DOAJ Library and Information Science Journals Indexed.

LibLit_LibLit	LISA_LISA	LISTA_LISTA	ISTA_INFOSAb	T&I_T&II	SocSCI_SSCI
22.37%	31.58%	30.26%	26.32%	0.00%	3.95%

Table 2. Number of the DOAJ Library and Information Science Journals Indexed.

LibLit_LibLit	LISA_LISA	LISTA_LISTA	ISTA_INFOSAb	T&I_T&II	SocSCI_SSCI
17	24	23	20	0	3

Table 3. Other statistics.

Number of journals indexed at least 1 time	36	47.37%
Number of journals indexed at least 3 times	13	17.11%
Number of journals not indexed	40	52.63%

2 titles are included in 5 of the 6 indexes

7 titles are included in 4 of the 6 indexes

4 titles are included in 3 of the 6 indexes

14 titles are included in 2 of the indexes

9 titles are included in 1 of the indexes

Approximately half of the session was spent in discussion with the audience. Those present made many useful suggestions for refining the model and developing the project.

- The contribution of scholars and researchers from the discipline being studied is vital for identifying "recognized indexing and abstracting services" that are pertinent to the discipline.

- The difficulty of searching by title, where some journals are listed by acronym and not their official title, could be alleviated by using the ISSN.

- Abstracting and indexing services may not have a mechanism (staff or time) to seek out additional journals to service.

- Many open access journals are relatively new and may not yet have the content, longevity, or reputation to warrant an abstracting and indexing service's attention. Most journals are not indexed until at least three or more issues are published or they have existed for at least one year.

- Some open access journals are not published in the traditional volume and issue format, which may make them incompatible with indexing services' processes.

- Open-access journals that resemble newsletters or are not peer-reviewed may not justify inclusion by the traditional abstracting and indexing services.

- Citation rates might be compared to indexing rates to see if a relationship is suggested and to test the usefulness of finding sources other than traditional indexing services.

- Creators of open-access journals in the DOAJ may not know how to navigate the indexing services' requirements and processes, resulting in relatively low numbers.

- A Public Knowledge Project article "Getting found, staying found, increasing impact: Enhancing readership and preserving content for OJS journals" by Kevin Stranack (2006; http://pkp.sfu.ca/files/GettingFoundStayingFound.pdf) was suggested as a useful article to read.

- Efforts to educate creators of open-access journals about the indexing process might be targeted to subject-area journals and to librarians who work with faculty. Stranack's article is an example of such outreach and contains much useful information for such efforts.

- Information about non-English language indexing services and journals should be promulgated.

Conclusion

From the results of the pilot study and input from conference attendees, the researchers concluded that the project is valuable and will be continued. The use of an Access database for data management has been successful and will continue. One adjustment to the model will be that only Ulrich's and the indexing services' Web sites will be used for data collection. Consultation with subject specialists to identify pertinent indexing services will be incorporated. Indexing services' requirements regarding longevity and peer-review status will be studied and the model adjusted to eliminate consideration of non-eligible journals. Interested readers are invited to contact the authors with additional comments and input.

This year the Charleston Conference had several programs dealing with technical services and cataloging issues. Key topics discussed were Library of Congress subject changes, changes in technical services workflows, using Jtacq (a freeware product) in technical services, and enhancing our catalogs.

Technical Services and Cataloging

THE VANISHING GYPSIES

Alice Crosetto, Coordinator of Collection Development/Acquisitions, The University of Toledo, Toledo, Ohio

The summer of 2001 saw a change in language of the Library of Congress classification, DX. The Cataloging Service Bulletin (#93) informed us that what for years had been the subject area for Gypsies was now renamed, Romanies—the politically correct term for this ethnic group. Was this a response to society's attempt to embrace diversity or, as the documentation supports, a politically motivated change brought about by lobbying individuals in Washington who were in a position to effect change—especially those who could pressure the Library of Congress?

Available documentation reveals what events occurred that appear to have influenced this change in the Library of Congress classification. Which leads one to ponder—should the Library of Congress be above any political influence?

Running an almost parallel question is the value of subject headings and their place and importance in accessing information.

Let's look at the pieces of this puzzle—

LC, the ethnic group, the change, and subject headings.

The Library of Congress was established in 1800 as a resource center for the nation's congressional members, a legislative Library. From the mid-1860s to the late 1890s, under the leadership of Ainsworth Rand Spofford (1864–1897 term as Librarian of Congress) bipartisan congressional support secured its national role. Under the leadership of Herbert Putnam whose term began in 1899 (1899-1939—term as Librarian of Congress), LC began an active role in the American library movement—moving toward assuming a service role for other libraries. By World War II, LC had been recognized as a national, even international, resource of unparallel dimension.

Over the years, the Library of Congress has evolved into so much more—by the 1950s, it was on its way to becoming the unofficial national library; by this time, it was widely recognized as one of the world's leading cultural institutions. It is our national library—albeit de facto; it sets the standards for libraries even beyond the U.S. borders, and in doing so provides leadership for us all.

And because of this—what we want, what we expect, what we need from LC is an entity above reproach—above any political ties or partisan obligation.

The Librarian of Congress is not only the chief operating officer of the national library but, as John Berry (1987) states, "many see the Librarian of Congress as an American Minister of Culture, even the Ambassador of the Intellect." Even as a political appointee who, in taking the administrative lead in the day-to-day operations of LC, sets policy and upholds the Library mission, this Librarian needs to be working toward the benefit of society as a whole and the benefit of the library profession, not catering to any special interest group nor submitting to the pressure of politicians.

Now let's turn toward the Romanies/Gypsy puzzle piece.

So, who are the gypsies, and who are the Romanies? Has there ever been an ethnic group that possesses such dual reputation, dual imagery? Say the word "gypsy" and what comes to mind? A Romantic rogue, mysterious, full of music, or a deceitful man; now for the female—the female is seen as a femme fatale, a seductress. How many of us start humming the tune to Cher's popular song from the early 1970s, Gypsies, Tramps and Thieves. Or does a caravan of transient individuals come to mind?—or the image of a fortuneteller? And if you're a fan of classic horror movies, one of the most famous and enduring images of a gypsy is the old woman in the Werewolf movies.

This secretive, mysterious ethnicity has obscure origins. The term gypsy comes from the words Egypt and Egyptian—a mistaken heritage. The term is first identified in the *Oxford English Dictionary* as having appeared in the beginning of the sixteenth century. Those individuals identified as gypsies at this time probably came from the Indus Valley. This is the ethnic group that is referred to as Roma/Romanies today. Attention needs to be taken when using the term Roma—this is sometimes confused with the Eternal City in Italy—Roma is Rome in the Italian language. Be careful not to confuse Romanies with the modern-day country Romania.

However, this is not the only group to consider when discussing gypsy ethnic groups. The challenge arises because not all groups historically named gypsy are the Rom/Romanies from the Indus Valley. "Gypsies (Romanies) and Travelers" are introduced under the umbrella term Gypsies even though there is continuing, even heated, controversy over what to call them without appearing to be disrespectful or ignorant.

In order to educate our community about these different groups, a colleague and I created a display for the Library about the DX group. The brochure that we created for distribution contains a good preliminary introduction to the term gypsy. All the groups that are addressed are listed here:

Rom and Roma: Gypsies of Eastern Europe

Ludar: Gypsies from the Banat area/Rumanian Gypsies

Romnichels: English Gypsies

English Travelers: took shape in England; associated with Romnichels

Irish Travelers: ethnically Irish but does not identify itself as "Gypsy"; sometimes called "Irish Gypsies"

Scottish Travelers: Ethnically Scottish; originally known as Tinkers and Tinklers

Hungarian-Slovak Gypsies: mainly sedentary Gypsy

Cale: Spanish Gypsies, or Gitanos

Roaders or Roadies: Native-born Americans who have led a traveling life similar to that of the Gypsies and Travelers but who were not originally descended from those groups

Sinti: German Gypsies; both non-Gypsy and Romnichel populations

Yenisch: ethnic Germans, misidentified as Gypsies

If the majority of individuals in the variety of ethnic groups that have traditionally been called gypsy demand anonymity, why, then, has there been this action to draw attention to them? And when an ethnic group that resides on society's fringe, as the gypsy groups have for centuries, is suddenly thrust into the mainstream, the question *cui bono* should be asked. One might wonder what other benefits exist—that is, in addition to embracing multiculturalism within a diverse society? And do the individuals in these various gypsy communities want to be in society's mainstream? *Cui bono*?

As with many ethnic terms, the past fifty years has witnessed many changes. Some gradual, some obvious, some long time in changing, some long over due.

The next piece of the puzzle . . .

The next piece of the puzzle reveals the political strategies used by some prominent individuals identified by Sheila Salo (2002) of the Gypsy Lore Society to pressure the LC to change the language of the DX. My research colleague states that these individuals employed the same model used by those during the Civil Rights Movement of the 1960s. Salo states that over a period of thirteen years, numerous letters and e-mails were sent to LC. Salo also notes that there may be more correspondence that was not retained, or at least not provided for public viewing. I agree with her.

Beginning in 1988, a librarian for Romani Materials, New York Public Library, sent a letter to LC. At the same time, copies of his letter were sent to Sanford Berman and Ian Hancock. Before proceeding, who are these individuals? Berman is known to most librarians as a crusader for politically correct language in the LC subject headings. Author of *Prejudices and Antipathies: A Tract on the LC Subject Heads Concerning People* (1971). Ian Hancock, based in Texas, is a national activist on behalf of Roma. Salo states that Hancock appears to be the common thread, even at this time.

More letters are sent to LC in 1991. In 1995, Berman launches his protest over the continued use of the term "gypsies." It should be noted that in 1987, Hancock wrote a six-page article titled, "Gypsies in Our Libraries" for Berman's column, "Alternatives," in the journal *Collection Building*. One question does arise: Did Hancock contact Berman, knowing that he could or would know the means to effect change at LC?

In his 1993 edition of *Prejudices and Antipathies,* Berman states in the preface that "Gypsies, it's true, are no longer tarred as "rogues and vagabonds," but neither are they called by their own, self-preferred name: ROMANIES (or ROMA) and no heading yet denotes their experience during the Third Reich, which directly parallels what happened to Jews. Berman expands this discussion in the chapter titled "Races, Nationalities, Faiths, and Ethnic Groups," (# 29. Item: GIPSIES).

Correspondence is lacking after 1995. Then in May 2000, CPSO (Cataloging Policy and Support Office) notifies Berman that it had no plans at that time to change the "Gypsies" subject heading. June and August 2000 finds more correspondence to LC. Citizens, one senator, and members of Congress write directly to Dr. James H. Billington, the current Librarian of Congress, appointed in 1987. Among this correspondence to LC is Hancock, who in mid-June 2000 writes directly to Dr. Billington urging LC to change the term gypsy. Hancock calls LC stubborn by continuing to maintain the status quo of prejudice against his people.

In June 2000, a notice is sent within the CPSO that due to the use of gypsy by both the *New York Times* and *Washington Post,* LC will continue to follow the usage in current general reference sources in the United States. "I think we could offer to monitor the situation and change our headings in the future if there is a shift in usage in the general reference sources." Two days later, Paul G. Weiss of CPSO writes to the *New York Times* stating that LC is currently under pressure from various individuals and organizations, to change the LC subject heading Gypsies to the term Roma. One of the reasons there has been resistance is that the national news media use the word gypsies much more commonly than the word Roma—therefore, gypsies is the more familiar term to most American library users. Weiss should be commended in reaching out to a national media organization in order to seek input into this challenging dilemma.

Within two weeks, the Director of Cataloging at LC writes to Hancock stating that there is a strong case to retain the current subject heading in an attempt to reflect common usage among the educated American population. Citing standard general reference sources and most of the national news media, the letter continues to state that the word gypsy is not a disparaging term. Then in July 2000, one Gypsy scholar writes to Tom Yee of LC regarding an upcoming meeting of the Gypsy Lore Society. In her correspondence, she has agreed to discuss acceptable terms that are being proposed. Interesting to note is her concern for several groups that comprise the whole gypsy concept: "My remaining concern—whether or not the major groups, such as the Sinti, would find this term acceptable." She continues, "I know that here is also opposition to a change among scholars, because the groups are so disparate, their languages vary greatly in some cases, and they call themselves by different names."

And we know how this story ends. The language is changed. One unconfirmed piece of this puzzle needs to be mentioned. This piece due to lack of primary evidence is the role that the late Paul Simon, long-serving Congressional leader from Illinois, may have played in this change. In September 2002, Simon's Public Policy Institute on the campus of Southern Illinois University hosted a two-day symposium titled, "Addressing the Plight of the Romani People." Several names in the working group for the symposium were familiar, including Hancock. We know the time involved in setting up a conference or symposium—this was years in the planning—around the same time that LC show an increase in the pressure to change DX.

How concerned should we be when subject headings are changed?

For years when a user relied solely on the card catalog, the importance of subject headings ruled searching strategies. If one could master this concept, then research was not a challenge. The controlled vocabulary, or, as Marydee Ojala (2007) calls them, "magic words," were the information professional's ace in the hole. Using these words enabled us to find information that our patrons couldn't. The advent and the perfecting of online database searching created an easier strategy—the keyword search. And even today, keyword seems to be preferred. It is easier, faster—how easy is it to use Google? Jeffery Beall (2007) states that keyword searching is becoming extremely popular. However, the flaws and weaknesses, according to Beall, are most grievous: overlooking synonyms, being unable to match homonyms, functioning poorly for common terms or names, being unable to search vague terms and concepts, and failing to pull up documents in languages other than that of the original search. Even with all its flaws and weaknesses, keyword searching will dominate. He continues to say that it does have its uses and can be an effective tool for information discovery, especially in casual information seeking. However, keyword searching is not for serious information seeking. Ojala states that identifying the most appropriate terms to use in a search strategy depends upon whether you're in a database that uses controlled vocabulary or whether you're in a free-form environment such as the Web.

Suzanne Bell (2007) feels that using a controlled vocabulary allows the user to get all the database has to offer on a topic without having to think of all the possible synonyms. It should also ensure that your results are more precise and not littered with false drops. Bell states that it provides a safe and helpful entry point into an unfamiliar subject area. Even if you know nothing about the subject, you have the assurance that the terms in the subject list are correct and appropriate. She adds this thought—and isn't this true for most of us: "as one who has to delve into unfamiliar subject areas on a regular basis, I am always grateful for databases that offer a subject list of some kind."

Ojala also knows that terminology is always changing—at least, in some disciplines. She states that terminology in the business literature changes in an almost faddish fashion. Therefore, a thesaurus becomes a moving target. She notes YouTube: given the unique product name, you don't need controlled vocabulary to search for YouTube; you can simply search the name.

Current research has shown that the subject heading cannot not be so easily dismissed. In a study at Northwestern by Jeffrey Garrett (2007), it was proven that keyword searching was successful because the keyword actually tagged words in an item's subject heading. Garrett cited a study which examined searches and discovered that individual cases exist in which 80, 90, and even 100 percent of the retrieved records would not be retrieved in the absence of subject headings.

How ready are we to dismiss the subject heading and the value its language has in accessing information?

In older item records, if the term gypsy is anywhere in the records, the user will find and retrieve the item by employing keyword searching. Often, even with many of the more recent resources, even after the political correctness push, the term is still used. In losing the term as a subject heading, we lose the connection to all the different ethnic groups historically termed gypsy. As Beall states, "subject headings create multidimensional networks between works, complexities of relationship going far beyond the classificatory power of linear arrangement of books on shelves."

So, why target LC subject headings?

As mentioned earlier, the power and impact of the Library of Congress is far more reaching than its de facto existence as our national library. When LC accepts and embraces societal trends and changes in new terminology, these changes are in fact made legitimate by the LC. Remember the role of LC and remember its power. LC approves and sets the standard in librarianship in this nation and beyond. With LC controlling the terminology used throughout information hubs—libraries at every level—then this truly is the hallowed halls of power. Romani activists knew this—this was an important bastion to conquer or, should it be said, won over. As Hancock wrote in 1987, "I entitled this essay 'Gypsies in our Libraries' because this is where the seeds of the Gypsy stereotype are planted." What a general indictment of our libraries. Hancock examined primary school holdings and discovered the use of the word and the depiction of the gypsy group less than accurate or flattering. Therefore, action taken by Romani activists was deliberate—by pressuring influential individuals in Washington, lobbying key political leaders, they would be successful.

And what remains is a note in the LC authority record that alludes to a variety of sources addressing the correct language for this ethnic group.

In the continued wave of political correctness, more changes are inevitable. I am not suggesting that society employ long-standing ethnic terms deem offensive by the very ethnic group itself. Who among us would question that the term Negro still be used as a Subject Heading?

However, as Berman stated, changing gypsy was what the group preferred—is this statement accurate? In recalling the description of this ethnic group, by its very nature and overwhelming anonymity, how can anyone speak of its behalf? This ethnicity is so spread out—how can one person, one group, speak on behalf of an amorphous ethnicity?

Some would give credit to Berman who had the support if not the impetus supplied by the Roma activist Hancock; some would give credit to society. There may be truth in both, but was this pressure necessary? I do believe that the professionals at LC are competent and do their best to maintain the status required of a national library. When language needs to be addressed and possibility changed, then I propose to leave this decision in the hands of LC. LC appears to be most accommodating in accepting input regarding subject headings; the LC Web site contains a Subject Authority Proposal Form for submitting a subject heading proposal through the Subject Authority Cooperative (SACO). Some would suggest that this change was instigated for the advancement of the ethnicity. Some might say that this change was inevitable within a world of political correctness forcing the dominant culture to embrace multiculturalism. And there are those who say that the individuals who drove this change did so for personal profit and gain, both financial and political.

What I do know is that the gypsies have indeed vanished.

Works Cited

Beall, Jeffrey. (2007). Search Fatigue. *American Libraries* 38, no. 3: 46–50.

Bell, Suzanne. (2007). Tools Every Searcher Should Know and Use. *Online* 31, no. 5: 22–27.

Berry, John. (1987). Profession, Politics, and LC. *Library Journal* 112, no. 2, 4.

Encyclopedia of the Library of Congress: for Congress, the Nation & the World. (2004). John Y. Cole and Jane Aikens, eds. Washington, DC: Library of Congress; Lanham, MD: Bernan Press.

Garrett, Jeffrey. (2007). Subject Headings in Full-Text Environments: The ECCO Experiment. *College Research Libraries* 68, no. 1: 69–81

Hancock, Ian. (1987). Gypsies in Our Libraries. *Collection Building* 8, no. 4: 31–36.

Ojala, Marydee. (2007). Finding and Using the Magic Words: Keywords, Thesauri, and Free Text Search. *Online* 31, no. 4, 40–42.

Salo, Sheila (2002). "Gypsies" Vanish from Library of Congress. *Gypsy Lore Society Newsletter*, 25:1, 6-7.

A FREEWARE SOLUTION TO TECHNICAL SERVICES TEDIUM: SAVING TIME AND MONEY WITH JTACQ

Don Butterworth, Technical Services Librarian, Asbury Theological Seminary, Orlando, Florida

Is there another word that can send a shudder through the technical service department like the word "outsourcing"? Practically every book vendor, even Amazon.com, now offers the outsourcing of technical services functions. Conscientious, budget-strapped administrators must consider this option even when it results in major restructuring or personnel layoffs. Outsourcing services are not cheap, and a significant level of local control is lost, but when a technical services department is not highly efficient, outsourcing becomes both attractive and viable in the eyes of an administrator.

One reason for the growth of outsourcing is that integrated library system (ILS) vendors have failed to recognize the need to automate collection development processes and fully integrate them with acquisitions and cataloging. This results in less than optimal workflows and has allowed book vendors, with vested financial interests, to take up the slack. The freeware product called JTacq (pronounced Jây-tăk) addresses this oversight. **JTacq is a comprehensive solution to the automation of collection development.** It is intended to supplement the acquisitions and cataloging modules of your ILS. It is *not* intended to replace them. It provides most of the functions that are currently only available for an annual fee from vendors plus much, much more. JTacq now makes it possible to take the control of collection development away from vendors and return it to the librarian's desktop.

Technical services operations are highly complex and unique for each library. Because of this, JTacq was developed to be as flexible as possible. It contains dozens of time-saving features but does not require you to use them all or even to use them in a specific order. Simply pick out and use those features that you find most helpful. An example is JTacq's ability to electronically check large lists of titles against your local holdings in a matter of minutes. This feature alone can save enormous amounts of time and effort for someone in technical services.

Even though technical services workflows vary greatly, there are some general processes that tend to follow a specific progression. These are: 1) Compile, 2) Distribute, 3) Select, 4) Purchase, 5) Get MARC, and 6) Export. The purpose of the demonstration given at the Charleston Conference and of this paper is twofold: first, to describe many of JTacq's features and second, to outline a benchmark workflow that can be compared against other library workflows. For the purposes of demonstration, the specific steps outlined will take the "longest path." Please note that because the processes being described are detailed and technical, at points they may be difficult to visualize. However, in a live environment, JTacq becomes very intuitive. An online demonstration of JTacq will greatly enhance the understanding of its features and workflow options and is freely available on request from the software developer.

Getting Started

Because JTacq's goal is to offer a comprehensive solution with maximum flexibility to your collection development needs, a substantial number of parameters need to be set before it can be used to its best advantage. Probably the most important of these is the establishment of a connection between JTacq and your local catalog so that an automated holdings check can be performed. It is a rather technical, one-time procedure that the JTacq software developer will assist you with. This feature is currently operational on Horizon, Innovative, Endeavor, Dynix, Sirsi, and Sagebrush sites. The developer will work with you to establish this feature if your library uses another system.

If your library has standing orders for monographic series or publishers, entries for these should be placed in the **Filters area** so that as requests enter into JTacq, potential duplicate titles can be either deleted or sent to a junk bin. Settings in the filters area can also be set to screen materials by audience, age level, binding, media type, and availability.

Other parameters that should be set include: **Requestor profiles** that allow default budget, department and location data to be quickly applied to a title record; **Location, Collection, and Item code profiles,** which are used to generate item records; **Vendor/Publisher profiles** that will be used to compute and display discounts.

Finally you will want to create personalized files (referred to in JTacq as **Bins**), to supplement the default JTacq bins. These bins are used to organize titles any way your operation requires. Besides creating bins for your primary vendors, you may want to create bins for subject areas, requestors and selectors, or titles with a certain status such as "not yet published." The creation of bins and sets of bins is totally flexible and completely at your discretion.

The JTacq system has numerous screens that are used to establish parameters and perform the various collection development and purchasing functions. Interaction with these screens will depend on what features you choose to incorporate into your workflow. Most operations will require becoming familiar with six screens: Titles, Offers, Item Entry, Shopping Cart, MARC Processing, and MARC Retrieval. Of these, approximately 90% of the time will be spent using the Titles and Offers screens (see Figures 1 and 2).

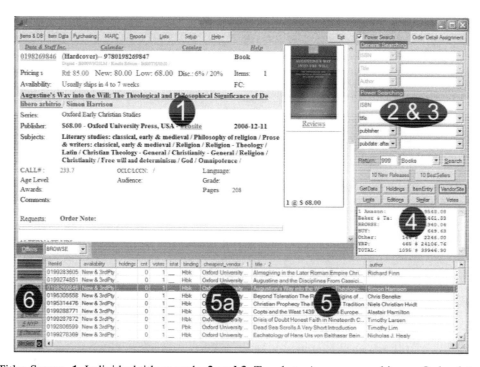

Figure 1. Titles Screen. **1.** Individual title records. **2 and 3.** Toggle to Amazon searching or Order data. **4.** Action buttons. **5.** Title list. **5a.** "Cheapest Vendor" column. **6.** Bins and Offers buttons.

The **Titles Screen** is used to display compiled title information and to perform various functions, including the retrieval of prices from multiple vendors, the local holdings check, the application of order and item data, the initiation of purchases and the launching of MARC record retrieval. Special note should be taken of **5a in Figure 1, the "Cheapest Vendor" column of the Title List.** Sorting on this column makes it possible to arrange groups of titles by vendors offering the lowest discount. Each group can be highlighted and moved into a designated storage bin with one mouse click. Order and Item Data can also be applied to groups of highlighted titles with a single click.

The **Offers Screen** displays listings of purchase offers from multiple vendors for selection and purchase. From this screen it is also possible to apply order data to specific volumes or items.

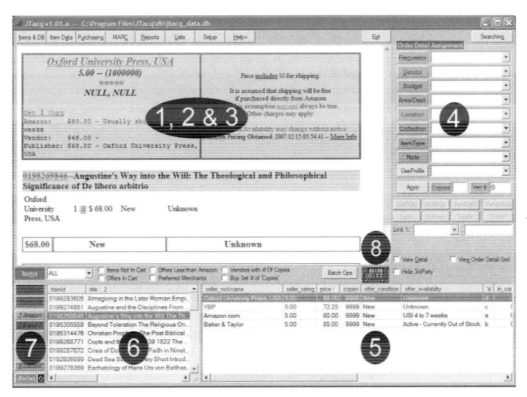

Figure 2. Offers Screen. **1–3.** Toggle to Individual title records, Vendor offer records, and Order details grid. **4.** Order data. **5.** Offers list. **6.** Title list. **7.** Bins and Title screen buttons. **8.** Shopping cart.

Compile

Titles and title data arrive in the collection development department in every imaginable form—everything from an electronic file provided by a book dealer to notes on napkins. JTacq provides multiple ways of bringing these requests and candidate titles into its lists.

When a request is received in hard copy or from an e-mail, a staff member must search for the request using traditional search methods against the Amazon.com database using the JTacq **Searching** options or **Drag-n-Drop** (see Figure 3).

Figure 3. Searching.

General searching is perfectly adequate for most titles, preferably using an ISBN search to minimize typing and provide the most specific results. But in cases when title information is not available from Amazon and can only be found in WorldCat, activate Drag-n-Drop and use the free WorldCat site (www.worldcat.org) to find the title, then highlight the URL in your browser and drag it into the Drag-n-Drop window. JTacq will capture the basic title information plus the OCLC number. Drag-n-Drop will also work with Choice Reviews Online, and with a number of online retail booksellers. In addition it is possible to highlight any ISBN online and drag it to the window; this ISBN will then be automatically searched using the Amazon.com database.

Yet another way of capturing data from WorldCat is to use **Zotero.** Files of titles captured in Zotero can be exported in the EndNote format and then imported into JTacq; unfortunately Zotero does not automatically capture the OCLC number. As a last resort, it is also possible to key-in title and pricing information by using JTacq's **Manual Item Entry** feature or to enter data on a spreadsheet and import into JTacq.

There is no escaping the necessity of doing individual searches for some titles, but it is more efficient and preferable to work with lists and batches when possible. **Power Searching** is one method to accomplish this. For example, let's say your university is starting a new degree program. By searching key subject terms, qualified by a range of dates, large lists can be quickly compiled from the Amazon database. A Local Holdings search will quickly identify the titles your library already holds. By sorting on the "Holdings" column, these "already held" titles can be deleted as a batch, leaving a filtered list of titles for your designated selectors to choose from.

The most efficient method of compiling titles, however, is to use an outside agency. This is accomplished in two ways. First, JTacq provides a **free online Patron Request** feature (see Figure 4). From your library's Patron Request page a patron can search the Amazon.com database by any combination of keyword, title, and author. When a title is found and requested, a request screen appears, populated with basic title information. The patron then can add comments into the Additional Info field; based on your library's policy, you can require the requester to include a name, ID number, and e-mail address.

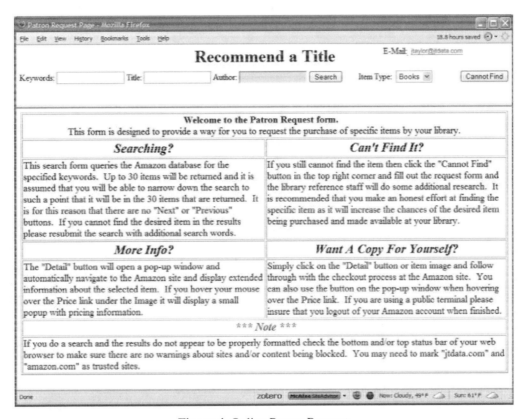

Figure 4. Online Patron Request.

When the request is submitted, an alert is sent to the appropriate JTacq console so it can be imported.

Second, JTacq allows for the **importing of Electronic Approval Records** that are provided by most major jobbers as delimited text files. It is also possible to import files from the Windows clipboard, direct SQL queries against databases, e-mail accounts, MARC records and files in JTacq's own native JTF format.

When a batch of candidate titles has been compiled into JTacq, it is a good idea to perform a local **Holdings Check** to determine and report what titles you have, do not have, or might have. JTacq identifies matches based on ISBN and other control numbers together with a character by character title search. Results of the check are displayed in the holdings column of the title list. When an exact match or possible match is detected, volume and item data is displayed in a grid on the main title screen to provide you with enough information to decide whether additional copies are needed or which titles should be deleted from further consideration. From this display, you can determine when the item record was created, how often it has been checked out, the most recent checkout date, and its current status (missing, lost, etc.).

After unwanted titles have been placed in the Discard bin, it is time to **acquire availability and cost information from multiple suppliers** by clicking the GetData button. Based on your settings, JTacq will search Amazon.com, various used book dealers, and vendors that offer VIP (Vendor Information Protocol) connectivity. Vendors that currently offer VIP include Baker & Taylor, Ingram, Book Wholesalers Inc., United Library Services, and Midwest Tapes. Search times will vary depending on your Internet speed and how many titles and vendors are being searched. Once the retrieval process is finished, each title screen will contain the information necessary for selectors to decide which titles to purchase. Information provided includes title availability, price offers, cover art, key subject terms, basic bibliographic description, content descriptions and Amazon reviews.

Distribute and Select

In many libraries, the selector(s) are not part of the technical services department and will not want to learn to use JTacq. When this is the case, JTacq offers a **free online selection feature.** With this feature, bins are created for the various subject or budgetary areas of each designated selector. The fully filtered and completed title records are then placed into these bins. When a sufficient number of titles have been compiled, an **Online Selection List** (see Figure 5) is created for one or more selectors. The selectors make their choices by clicking the Add buttons. After all selections have been made, the Finished button is clicked, the choices are stored, and an alert is sent to the appropriate JTacq console. The operator then imports the selection list into JTacq, where the choices are displayed as Votes. Once all selections have been imported, the titles are sorted using the Votes column. Unwanted titles are sent as a batch to the Discard bin. The remaining titles are now ready for purchasing.

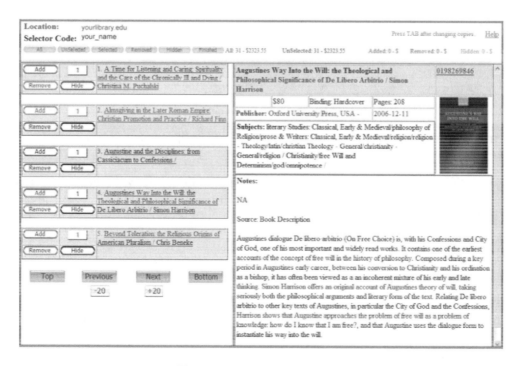

Figure 5. Online Selection List.

Purchase

At the purchasing stage, library policies and workflows vary widely. Some libraries regularly purchase used books, while other do not. Many libraries will want to use brief order records and only get the permanent MARC record when an item arrives, while others will want to obtain the permanent MARC record first so it can be used to generate an order. Some libraries will want to import records that contain order data and item data so that orders and items can be automatically generated in their local ILS. JTacq has features that can accommodate any of these variations, but for the purpose of this demonstration, the workflow described uses all of the purchasing and ordering processes available within the JTacq environment.

It is a good idea to do a second local Holdings check at the beginning of the purchasing process to ensure that duplicate titles were not added to your local database while the review and selection processes were occurring. The next step should be to sort your title list using the "Cheapest Vendor" column so that whenever possible batches of titles can be highlighted and transferred into vendor bins as groups.

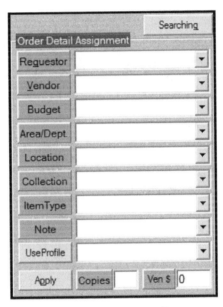

Figure 6. Order Details.

Order and item data should be attached to title records at this point using the **Order Detail Assignment** panel (see Figure 6), if you want to be able to automatically generate purchase order and item record information in your ILS. The key category is "Requestor." Creating a Requestor profile allows you to populate some or all of the order detail categories simply by selecting the appropriate requestor. This data can be applied both to individual records and groups of records. Once this information is applied, it displays on the main title record and will generate any 9XX tags required by your ILS. Then, using the appropriate "Buy all ..." command in the Purchasing dropdown menu sets the pricing information. It cannot be overemphasized how much time and effort this feature can save by providing the means to automatically populate purchase orders and generate item records.

At this point, the workflow will vary based on which vendor or publisher you will be ordering from. **If you are purchasing from Amazon or from used book vendors,** the green shopping cart icon found on the Offers screen will be used to display the JTacq Cart screen.

Once there, double clicking on the title menu listings will place the associated titles into the chosen Vendor's online shopping cart, ready for checkout. **If you are purchasing from other Vendors or Publishers,** after clicking the appropriate "Buy all …" command, you can proceed directly to the MARC screens.

Get MARC, Edit MARC, and Export

The next step is the retrieval and/or creation of the MARC records that will be imported into your local ILS. **JTacq can pull MARC records from any available Z39.50 source, including OCLC.** When an existing record cannot be found **JTacq can automatically create MARC records** from any data that was captured during the compiling processes.

From the **Get MARC** screen, either a specific batch of orders or a specific bin is highlighted for searching OCLC by the OCLC number and/or ISBN. The results are then displayed on the **MARC Processing** screen (see Figure 7). One file of titles is created for exact matches and a second file for any titles that cannot be found.

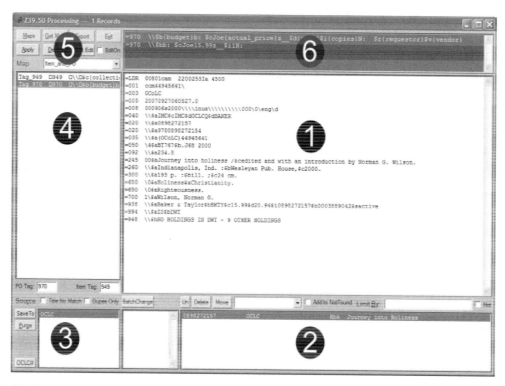

Figure 7. MARC Processing. **1.** Bibliographic record display. **2.** Title list. **3.** Menu of title files. **4.** MARC tag list of the active Map profile. **5.** Action buttons. **6.** Tag Data display.

Because ISBN searches in OCLC often result in multiple matches JTacq can limit the retrieved title list to display only duplicated records. One is then able to scroll through the list and delete the unwanted records. JTacq also offers the ability to do one final automated check against holdings to guard against duplicates by typing the word "held" in the "Limit by" field. Any record that has the term "Held by [your library symbol]" in the 948 tag will be displayed.

Retrieved MARC records are fully editable from the MARC Processing screen. In addition **JTacq provides the ability to add one or more fields, in a single operation, to all of**

the records in the list based on profiles that you create. This capability is used to apply the 9XX tags needed to generate Item and Order records in your ILS, but it can also be used to supply any kind of constant data that your local policies may require.

You create maps containing the tags and subfields you will want to add to records. To add tags to an entire batch of records with one click, choose the appropriate Map profile, press the Apply button, and then select "Apply entire map to all." **This same procedure is also used to generate full MARC records** when none were found during the Z39.50 search, or when library policies preclude obtaining a full MARC record at this stage in the workflow.

After all MARC records have been edited, it is time to **export the file.** Click Export to store the file on your local or network directory until it is ready for import into your local database. At this point, if you are using OCLC records, you are asked if you would like to save the file a second time. This is done so that another file can be created or added to, and sent to OCLC to have your library's holdings symbol attached. **Finally JTacq enables you to notify requestors by e-mail that their selections have been ordered.**

Conclusion

JTacq is a comprehensive solution to the automation of collection development. It was designed to minimize staff labor by reducing keystrokes in the compiling process by providing a comprehensive set of data import methods. It maximizes efficiency by providing multiple limiting and sorting features, an automated local holdings check, 1-click application of ordering and item data, and automated MARC record creation. Demands on technical services staff are further reduced by providing an online selection tool, an online patron request feature, and computer-generated notices.

In addition to saving money by reducing staff labor, JTacq can help a library save by minimizing duplicate purchases and by the compilation of purchase offers from multiple library vendors, publishers, and used book dealers so that materials can be purchased at the lowest available price.

The only cost for all of this functionality is the time it takes to set up the system and learn to use its many rich features. **Every library that incorporates JTacq into its workflow will save money and reduce labor.** For a live demonstration or download, contact Jim Taylor at jtaylor@jtdata.com.

TRACKING LIBRARY CHANGES: 2005 TO 2007

Shin Freedman, Head of Acquisitions & Serials, Framingham State College Library, Framingham, Massachusetts

In this paper, I will be discussing a number of changes that have been implemented at Framingham State College (FSC) while I served as Head of Acquisitions and Serials from 2004 to the present. FSC is located 20 miles west of Boston on a beautiful, 73-acre traditional New England campus in Framingham, the largest town in Massachusetts, and was the first state-supported school dedicated to training teachers in America in 1839. The FSC library mainly supports the liberal arts curriculum.

The majority of the library changes have been closely related to the impact of information technology and an attempt to improve library services. For example, we implemented proxy-server technology in 2006 to allow easier off-campus access to our library's electronic resources and Web-enabled resource, *Electronic Resources by Subject,* was introduced and developed. The library Web page had begun a makeover project in 2005, and I started building our library's electronic journal resources and supporting technology, as well as implementing a process for change. In addition, we also implemented OpenURL Link Resolver to facilitate seamless access to full text articles in 2006.

Let me explain how the library changes all started. In 2004, I came across a homegrown library survey of FSC faculty and students conducted by the library staff. When I asked about the results of the survey in terms of initiating library changes, no one seemed to know. My continuing observation of our library patrons' lack of involvement and alienation from the library services and resources struck me deeply.

Amos Lakos and Shelley Phipps who wrote "Creating a Culture of Assessment: A Catalyst for Organizational Change" observed that dealing with organizational culture is a challenge in terms of what the organization wants to achieve. The relative strength of an organization's culture depends on how well the group deals with external adaptation and internal integration in order for change to occur.[1] In this regard, the FSC library staff were truly novices in the area of library change. Change was not a word the library staff uttered in our library at all. As our library strived to become more relevant to our college community, we slowly began by adding a new faculty liaison program and began developing electronic resource subject guides in addition to providing traditional library instructional service, library material acquisitions, and cataloging services.

According to John Kotter's business model for change, eight critical steps are involved in changing culture and performance.[2] I will describe the library changes at FSC using Kotter's Change Model. This is a work in progress. To date, I feel that we have accomplished steps 1 through 4 well; the remaining steps 5 to 8 which include *Empower Broad-Based Action, Generate Short-term Wins, Consolidate Gains, Produce More Change,* and *Anchor New Approaches in the Organizational Culture* are yet to come.

Step 1. Establish a Sense of Urgency

First, I organized the Faculty Outreach Program (FOP) as a library service and proposed it to the Library Director. The idea immediately came about upon my being hired as Head of Acquisitions and Serials, through my observation of the Library's lack of involvement with the FSC college community. The FOP was presented as a major opportunity to link the Library and the academic departments. Essentially, what the Library needed was an advisory board or a group who could help us in our collection development efforts, library instruction services, faculty research needs analysis, as well as student needs integration. Often in the library material selection process, we were left in the dark without any information about what was being taught and how the curriculum was changing. When the program was understood as an urgent, community-building, library-supporting activity, it was up to me to move it forward. Without such an outreach program, any library decision making suffered from a lack of confidence in our patron support system. Therefore, a program of systematic meetings with the academic department chairs and the faculty library liaisons was begun in the summer of 2005. Kotter emphasized that change will not occur where there is complacency.

Step 2. Create a Guiding Coalition

In creating a group with the power to guide the FOP, essential group representatives were identified: the Library Directory, myself, Academic Department Chairs, and the Faculty Library Liaisons. Starting with a high sense of urgency, I began simply by verifying the FSC academic department chairs and faculty liaison persons' contact information including e-mail address, department alias, and telephone number. The information on the list represented the key stakeholders in our target group.

We had had a similar list to distribute library monographs selection information in the past. Along the way, we learned how much the list was not up-to-date. In the absence of direct feedback, there was a gap as to whether our sent information was received or not. Working together as a team to build the list had a great benefit as no one person had the institutional knowledge, expertise, or skills to pull the FOP together.

In addition, to support the IT infrastructure that would be needed, the IT director, the IT Network Director, the Library Director, and the Academic Technology Support and Distance Education were pulled together as a team.

Step 3. Develop a Vision and Strategy

We carefully developed and reviewed our meeting objectives. It took nearly three months on average just to set up a meeting with one academic department. The typical scenario I heard was that they didn't have the time to see me. One department chair questioned the necessity of a meeting initiated by the Library because the Library had never called a meeting with academic departments for the past twenty-five years. I politely replied that I was a new librarian and there was a good reason we should meet and discuss the departmental needs. I emphasized especially that there were a lot of exciting new resources just added and more to be added for the next five years, and we would like to show them off.

At first, many department heads who had agreed to meet with us did not show up at scheduled meetings (only two out of twenty-one departments agree). I called the chairs on the phone asking for an explanation. Being persistent, eventually they all obliged my request and showed up. In 2005, we met with nine departments; seven in 2006; five in 2007. This was a big first step of creatively establishing a link between the Library and the College.

At each meeting, my Director talked about the overview and the book budget allocated for each department, and we answered whatever concerns and issues the participants raised. Overall, the meetings were well received because a flow of information sharing began to occur: what specific library resources were available and what services were under development.

Every time I requested a meeting with a department, a packet of information was specifically prepared for the needs of that department: a meeting agenda including a set of goals, a meeting reminder, the resources available for the department along with faculty resources for teaching needs. It seemed to motivate the people when we shared the information. By having a focused goal, we were able to achieve a shared vision for the faculty outreach program.

Step 4. Communicate the Change Vision

We used every venue possible to get the message out, including formal and informal interactions—big or small meetings, memos, and e-mails. We also made an effort to communicate the change vision of having the FOP with the FSC Library be seen as a constructive resource and one deeply involved with the FSC faculty and student community.

Kotter's Steps 5 through 8 include *Getting Rid of Barriers to Change, Empower Broad-Based Action, Generate Short-term Wins, Consolidate Gains and Produce More Change*, and *Anchor New Approaches in the Organizational Corporate Culture*. These are yet to be accomplished, and there is much more to come in next few years.

Outcome of the Faculty Outreach Project

Starting in the second year of the FOP, the Library began getting more requests for library instructional services, and the Reference staff were getting overwhelmed with increased requests for student activities. In the third year of the FOP, we were invited back to department meetings to speak about library programs and services. We were often asked to talk at faculty-driven workshops on campus, that is, Critical Thinking Workshops, Faculty Development Workshops, and our Teaching Excellence Symposium. In other words, faculty-initiated demand was being expressed. Active input from faculty was sought and received in the library database selection process. An increasing number of faculty member inquiries for their own research or for students' needs were handled. More department chairs requested the creation of an *E-Resources Subject Guide* for their respective departments.

We have been told that the students and faculty appreciate the improved resources and services. Because of the technology upgrades, access to the electronic resources has become easier and more efficient both on and off campus. Off-campus access to major databases (i.e., Lexis-Nexis, American History and Life, and Project Muse) was made possible for the first time in 2006. As Laura Cohen has articulated in her "A Librarian's 2.0 Manifesto," we now mindfully recognize that the universe of information culture is changing fast and that our library needs to respond positively to these changes to provide the resources and services those users need and want.[3]

Finally, faculty began to feel comfortable with the librarians. They viewed the librarians as people who not only help students but also provide for faculty research needs and guidance. As described in recent literature, Denis Troll noted that the library is not the only information provider, thus many academic libraries are changing in response to changes in the learning and research environment and changes in the behavior of library users.[4]

Conclusion

The most positive transformation we achieved from 2005 to 2007 resulted from the faculty outreach program success. For each teaching faculty influenced, we figured at least 100 students are involved and influenced. In the FSC Library's history, for the first time, we made a relevant and meaningful connection with the teaching faculty. This change effort proved to be the most crucial support and a link to the Library. Our patrons appreciated our efforts and were engaged with us.

Notes

1. Lakos, A., and S. Phipps. (2004). Creating a Culture of Assessment: A Catalyst for Organizational Change. *Portal: Libraries and the Academy* 4, no. 3: 345–361. Retrieved from http://search.ebscohost.com/login.aspx?direct=true&db=aph&AN=13927185&site=ehost-live.

2. Kotter, John P. (2007, January). Leading Change. *Harvard Business Review* 85, no. 1. Retrieved from http://search.ebscohost.com/login.aspx?direct=true&db=buh&AN=23363656&site=ehost-live.

3. Cohen, L. B. (2007). A Manifesto for Our Times. *American Libraries* 38, no. 7, 47–49. Retrieved from http://search.ebscohost.com/login.aspx?direct=true&db=aph&AN=26279814&site=ehost-live

4. Troll, D. A. (2002). How and why libraries are changing: What we know and what we need to know. *Portal: Libraries and the Academy* 2, no. 1: 99–123. Retrieved from http://muse.jhu.edu/journals/portal_libraries_and_the_academy/v002/2.1troll.html.

FROM CHAOS TO EFFECTIVENESS: RESULTS OF A WORKFLOW ANALYSIS AT OLD DOMINION UNIVERSITY LIBRARIES

Tonia Graves, Electronic Resources & Serials Services Librarian, Old Dominion University, Norfolk, Virginia

My presentation focused on the results of a serials unit workflow analysis conducted at Old Dominion University in 2004. At that time, the University Librarian at Old Dominion University Libraries requested all units in the Bibliographic Services Department to conduct a workflow analysis. At the completion of the analysis, the Serials and Acquisitions Services Librarian submitted a report to the University Librarian containing several recommendations. For more information on the workflow analysis process and its recommendations, see "Developing a Crystal Clear Future for the Serials Unit in an Electronic Environment: Results of a Workflow Analysis."[1]

The number one recommendation from the 2004 workflow analysis called for the creation of a new unit within the Bibliographic Services Unit. The Electronic Resources & Serials Services Unit (ERSSU) was formed in fall 2006, and I moved from the Electronic Resources Cataloger position in the Cataloging Services Unit to assume the newly created Electronic Resources and Serials Services Librarian position and manage the new unit.

We not only created a new unit as recommended, but we also updated staff position descriptions to accurately reflect changes in workflows. We created new electronic resource responsibilities for the Serials Coordinator and transferred print journal collection related responsibilities from the Serials Coordinator to the Periodicals Assistant as recommended. The new responsibilities for the Serials Coordinator include:

- Downloading title and URL lists, determine local fields to be added, assign macros for local fields

- Downloading bib records from OCLC for electronic only journals

- Maintaining links in the OPAC

- Assisting with managing E-journal management system

- Assisting with populating and maintaining ERMS

Print journal management responsibilities that were transferred from the Serials Coordinator to the Periodicals Assistant include:

- Claiming

- Managing unsolicited and gift print journals

- Adding fields to bib records for print journals to reflect electronic access

The new and transferred responsibilities continue to be refined and reviewed. While staff could have been apprehensive about these changes, instead they have demonstrated flexibility and a willingness to embrace change.

In addition to nearly completely overhauling both ERSSU staff position descriptions in 2006–2007, we carried on with daily operations. Daily operations include:

- Access Issues
    - Lapsed access to a noteworthy collection of society journals due to switching subscriptions from the society to our periodicals vendor
    - A breach in access to back volumes of a noteworthy journal collection
    - Outdated HTML code causing inconsistent search results in our e-journal management system
    - Refining our link resolver results page
- Public Service
    - The ERSSU staff provided 231.5 hours at public service desks in FY 06–07
    - Technology upgrades
    - New staff computers
    - Expected but significant vendor database/interface upgrade
    - Unexpected and significant ERMS vendor database/interface upgrade
- New standing orders vendor

In addition to overhauling ERSSU staff position descriptions and managing daily operations, we assumed the new responsibilities and expectations of our new unit. Included in the new responsibilities are:

- Setting up resource trials and documenting evaluations
- Collecting usage statistics for print journals and electronic resources
- Managing a MARC records service

Some of the training and development necessary to proceed included:

- Excel training
- Creating lists in our ILS
- ERMS webinars

I am happy to report that since the 2007 Charleston Conference a staff position has been transferred to the ERSSU. The position's title is Electronic Resources Assistant, and the new hire started January 10, 2008. Responsibilities associated with the position include:

- Assisting with trial management
- Improving population of ERMS
- Assisting with usage statistics
- Access issue resolution

Although it might have seemed a tedious process when it started in fall 2004, the workflow analysis team produced a report whose recommendations have been supported by library administration. Our library collection assessments show that the appropriate format for many of our research collections is electronic. Therefore, library organizations and operations should be appropriately staffed to manage electronic collections. The Old Dominion University Libraries have effectively reduced some of the chaos related to electronic resources and their management by reallocating library staff and providing them with tools and skills necessary to provide successful service and access to our valuable electronic collections.

Note

1. Graves, T., and M. A. Arthur. (2006). Developing a Crystal Clear Future for the Serials Unit in an Electronic Environment: Results of a Workflow Analysis. *Serials Review* 32: 238–246.

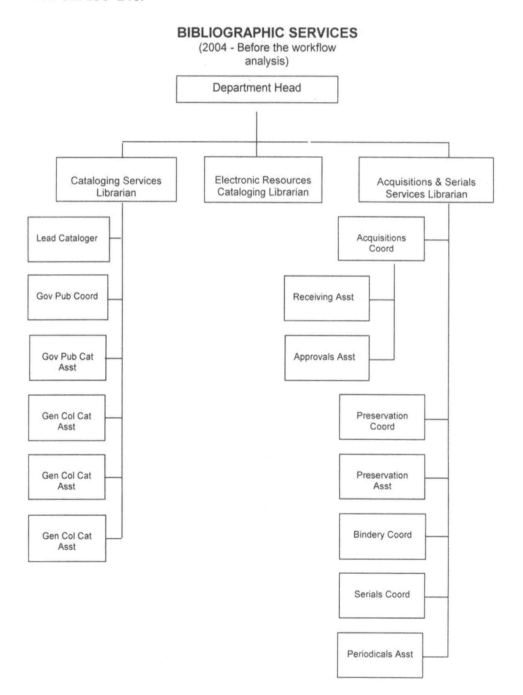

BIBLIOGRAPHIC SERVICES

(2008 - After the workflow analysis)

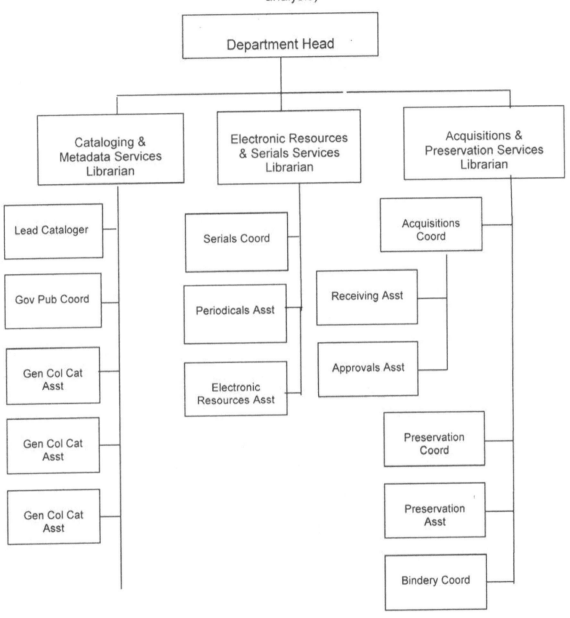

CATALOG COLLECTIVISM: XC AND THE FUTURE OF LIBRARY SEARCH

Eric Lease Morgan, Head, Digital Access and Information Architecture, University Libraries of Notre Dame, Notre Dame, Indiana

Collections without services are useless, and services without collections are empty. The future of library search lies between these two statements. It is about making search smarter and putting search within the context of the user.

Collections and Services

From my point of view, libraries spend most of their time around four processes: collection, organization, preservation, and dissemination. Collection managers and bibliographers identify the needs of the library's patrons and amass content to fit those needs. Catalogers use controlled vocabularies and standardized methods to describe and bring together this content to form a coherent whole. The content, in whatever form, is saved for the long term and future generations by the preservationists and conservators. Reference librarians provide access to the collection by interpreting the needs of patrons and suggesting solutions to fit their "information needs."

None of these processes are independent of the others. None is above the others. Each is required in order to fulfill the goals of a library. This is not a chicken-and-egg problem. A library that has great collections but provides no services against them cannot call itself a library. Such collections are literally useless. Similarly, an institution or organization cannot provide information services without collections and call itself a library. Such an institution is not a library but more like an intermediary—an index, as it were. We can all name the world's largest indexer. It has no content, per say, but it provides many services. It is a library? Collections without services are useless, and services without collections are empty.

Search plays a critical role between collections and services. Right alongside browse, search facilitates the discovery of content in collections. Search and browse are probably the two most fundamental services applied against collections. Again, without access via search or browse (or both), the collections are useless.

Databases and Indexes

When people think of search, they often—and incorrectly—think of databases. Databases, specifically relational databases, are wonderful tools for organizing and maintaining data. Through the processes of normalization, databases enable people to quickly and accurately record and update data in discrete locations, avoiding the need for duplication and massive find/replace operations. Ironically, databases are notoriously difficult to search because users need to know the structure of the database in order to query it; you need to know what fields you want to search before you can do a search.

Instead, when you think of search, think of indexes. Computer-generated indexes are not very much different from back-of-the-book indexes. In both cases, they are lists of words or phrases associated with a pointer to where the words or phrases can be found in context. In the case of back-of-the-book indexes, the pointers are page numbers. In the case of traditional library catalogs, the pointers are call numbers. In the case of journal indexes, the pointers are citations. In the case of Internet indexes, the pointers are URLs.

Indexes make search easy. Enter a word or phrase. Get back a list of pointers. In such an environment, it is not necessary to give your query very much structure. That is done for you by the software. Adding "syntactical sugar" for phrases, field searches, truncation, and so on makes search results more accurate, but increasingly the underlying software does that sort of thing for you.

Moreover, through the combined use of linguistics, pattern matching, statistical analysis, and the wisdom of crowds, it is not unrealistic to support result-set sorting by author, title, and date but also by relevance. This relevancy ranking is literally calculated based on the number of times a word or phrase is found in a particular document, the length of the document, their location in the document, and the number of times the word or phrase is found in the entire corpus of the index. Thus, the word "human" never accounts for very much in PubMed because just about every record is contains the word "human."

Future of Search

The future of search lies in 1) the enhancement of the discovery process and 2) providing services against collection beyond simple identify. Putting the user's needs and characteristics at the center of the query process will greatly enhance the discovery process. By knowing more about the searcher—placing the query in context with the searcher—it will be possible to improve find significantly. For example, if you know the searcher is a freshman, then it is safe to assume his or her experience or knowledge is less than a senior's, and therefore a different set of resources may be appropriate for the user's needs. Search can take experience into account and present results accordingly. Suppose the searcher is an expert in anthropology but is searching for information on microeconomics. Given this, it is unlikely the searcher will want advanced microeconomic data, at least not right away. Present the results accordingly. Assume the searcher has a history of doing many microeconomic searches. Either the searcher is not finding the desired information or he or she is looking for more specific information. Return search results accordingly. Put another way, ask yourself questions about the searcher, and modify the results. Who is the searcher? What is his or her level of skill or education? Is the searcher new to the subject or an expert? Who are the searcher's peers, and what are they using? Use these resources as a guide. Does the searcher want help? To what degree does he or she desire privacy? By knowing the answers to these sorts of questions, search results can be tailored to meet individual needs; search can be put into the user's context.

Once the discovery process is improved, it will be easier to move to the next step, providing enhanced services against the found items. People do not want to know simply that a library owns an item. They want to do something with the item. Get it. Read it. Buy it. Have it delivered to them. Compare it to other items. Annotate it and take notes against it. Review it. Add it to their personal collection. Use the ideas and facts it contains to find and trace other ideas and facts. Delete it from their collection. Share it with their friends. Cite it. Summarize it. Rank it. Index it along with the other items in their collection. In an academic setting, these services can be characterized as activities supporting learning, teaching, and research. In the future, it is these services that will distinguish libraries from commercial search engines. Libraries, by definition, serve a specific use population. They never exist unto themselves. They are there to support their particular constituents. By knowing and understanding their constituents in ways commercial services can not, libraries will continue to have a role when it seems as if everybody and their brother is getting into the library act.

XC

The University Libraries is proud to be a part of the XC project. Our responsibilities are clear: 1) dump/extract our bibliographic, holdings, and authority data from the ILS; 2) make this data accessible via OAI; 3) enable a patron authentication service; and 4) enable real-time item status reports. The folks of XC will then: 1) harvest/ingest our data, 2) normalize it into a central store (a database), 3) make it searchable (an index), and 4) give Notre Dame the resulting software. It will then be Notre Dame's responsibility to implement the software in a test environment and provide XC with our feedback.

The model XC is proposing is not very much different from the model proposed by others with the exception of their process. XC's process is more open and includes a wider community than other propositions. The result should be a set of community-driven "standards" for creating, maintaining, and providing access to materials in a library catalog. Moreover, since it will be open and standards-based, it ought to be modular and flexible—just the sort of environment necessary when the ultimate goal is to provide sets of enhanced services against library collections such as the ones outlined above.

Collections without services are useless. Services without collections are empty. Search bridges both.

The Charleston Conference is a venue for all types of presentations. This section includes an interesting look at intermediaries and consortia, Google Print and copyright issues, and library advocacy.

Miscellaneous

159

INTERMEDIARIES AND CONSORTIA

John Cox, Principal, John Cox Associates, Rookwood, Bradden, United Kingdom

Transformation of the Supply Chain

In the print world, both booksellers and subscription agents perform an invaluable role in the supply chain from publisher to library:

- They are very good at processing transactions and compiling and providing product and holdings management information for their customers.

- They cater for the very varied administrative and financial requirements of their library customers. If you ask a publisher about fund accounting, or the need for invoices to be set out in a particular format, he would not know what you are talking about. But a subscription agent would!

- They play a vital financial role, both in covering the gap between paying the publisher and being paid by the library, and in managing foreign exchange so that the library paid in its local currency, and the publisher receives payment in its currency of choice.

In short, they have provided an orderly environment for supplying thousands of libraries with a one-stop shop for thousands of books and journals published by thousands of publishers worldwide. They have assumed a function that saves considerable administrative costs in libraries and in publishing houses.

However, the advent of online publishing in the mid-1990s and the formation of library consortia pooling their members' materials budgets in order to increase their clout have both led to a transformation of the journal supply chain. The question is: do intermediaries have a place in dealings between publishers and consortia? If so, are they the traditional booksellers and subscription agents, or are they newcomers?

I am going to concentrate on intermediaries that provide services to libraries. Of course, there are other service companies that provide services to publishers, some of which sell to and negotiate with library consortia, such as Accucoms and Frontline Global Marketing Services, but this is about consortia needs.

Changes in the Online Supply Chain

Printed books and journals are physical products of a manufacturing process. But online publishing is a service business. The two are fundamentally different.

Publishers—not just the large ones—want to deal directly with libraries over online licenses for journals and databases. Originally, publishers wanted to understand this new market, which meant that they had to engage directly with libraries rather than mediating contact through a third party. Indeed, many library consortia wanted to deal directly as well. Negotiations are better handled face-to-face rather than through third parties. In the print world, acquisition was a matrix of individual title selection, ordering and supply. The intermediary provided libraries with the one-stop shop, and publishers with a manageable number of customers with established payment protocols—simple to describe, although very detailed. The online consortium deal is different, and more complex:

- Purchasing online licenses for consortia involves entire publishers' lists, or substantial subject-based collections. They may cover journals, or broader types of content such as reference, databases, e-books, and so on. There are fewer, larger transactions.

- The online product has multiple dimensions, in that the functionality of the service may be of critical importance. Look at the OECD's or Knovel's online products to see that the indexing and tools provided transform "flat" content into information that is truly useful to the reader.

- Pricing is no longer a matter of referring to the publisher's list price. It may be based on a variety of models, but each deal is individually negotiated.

- Online services raise performance, compatibility, technical support, and customer service issues that simply do not apply in the print world.

These issues arise in implementing an online journal license and are best dealt with directly.

Why Have the Traditional Intermediaries Lost Out?

My belief is that they have found it very difficult to make the change from being a library-focused order-processing facility for libraries to that of a service partner in the online environment. My own personal experience at Carfax, where we helped found CatchWord, and made our first online journals available online in 1995, was that the subscription agents did not know how to position themselves to help us market our online journals, even when we asked for help. And we wanted to work with our established trading partners. Only after a decade have the major subscription agents put themselves in a position to be a positive help to publishers, and there are fewer of them than there were.

The Emergence of New Intermediaries

There may be an important role for intermediaries, but it is not the same role in the electronic environment. The traditional vendors are tied to the baggage of their history in a way that new entrants into the online market are not. The following are just a few of the organizations that have developed activities attuned to a new marketplace:

- Content Complete Ltd. is a UK-based company offering procurement and negotiation services to academic library consortia in the United Kingdom, Ireland, Italy and elsewhere, as well as to large multisite corporate users such as pharmaceutical companies. CCL negotiates the deal on behalf of the consortium.

- In China, the Charlesworth Group's subsidiary in Beijing brings the Chinese library community together with publishers serving the rapidly growing Chinese library market.

- The iGroup is a group of companies in the information industry across Asia-Pacific. The iGroup is already the largest provider of information services in the region, with a wide range of client publishers including major names. It operates through a network of regional offices in Australia, China, Hong Kong, India, Korea, Malaysia, the Philippines, Singapore, Taiwan, Thailand, and Vietnam.

Even trade associations are active. Five years ago, the Association of Learned and Professional Society Publishers created a coalition of its nonprofit publisher members to offer collections of their society journals to consortia. The collection now comprises 700 titles, and the process is managed by Swets.

Do Consortia Need Intermediaries?

As I have said, there are plenty of opportunities for intermediaries in the online world. However, traditional vendors such as subscription agents bring great strengths of established library relationships and working relationships with publishers, but they are burdened by the print legacy, and are seen to "get in the way" by some publishers and consortia.

Just as there is an infinite variety of organization among the 304 library consortia actively buying content, there is no single right answer to the question. It all depends on the nature of the consortium, its remit, and the resources available. Whether a consortium employs staff to handle consortium selection, negotiation, and implementation or outsources some or all of those functions can only be answered on a case-by-case basis. I want to conclude with two points:

- Where it is appropriate to outsource, specify exactly what tasks are outsourced and get them priced individually. Do not accept a "percentage of contract value," as this will be inflationary. This is what any purchasing professional would do.

- My management experience, and my recent work on the feasibility of establishing a consortium for Scottish universities leads me to believe that doing it yourself gives you better control and better results.

BUFF BABE THUMBNAILS: HOW FAR CAN GOOGLE GO?

Bruce Strauch, Professor, The Citadel School of Business Administration

The Google Library Project is heavily invested in scanning into its search database books from Harvard, Stanford, Oxford, Michigan, and the New York Public Library. Public domain works may be viewed in full; for books under copyright only a "snippet" is available. For a frequently appearing search term, only three snippets are displayed. This prevents a reader from getting the entire book for free, assuming there was such a person who could be bothered.

In 2005, the Authors Guild and some individual authors sued Google claiming copyright infringement. Then five publishers joined in. The issue as they see it is Google scanning into its database an entire work that is covered by copyright.

Google's defense is Fair Use. Appellate cases with similar facts from the Ninth and Second Federal Circuits are squarely in Google's favor. We'll look at them each in turn. Our first case is a suit against Google itself. And remember that these two circuits are recognized as the nation's leading authorities on copyright law.

Perfect 10, Inc. v. Amazon.com, Inc.; Perfect 10 v. Google, United States Court of Appeals for the Ninth Circuit, 2007 U.S. App. LEXIS 11420 (2007).

Google, like every other computer, is connected to the Internet. *Religious Tech. Ctr. v. Netcom On-Line Commc'n Servs., Inc.,* 923 F. Supp. 1231, 1238 n.1 (N.D. Cal. 1995). Webpages allow computer owners to share information on their computers with others via the Internet. A webpage contains text plus instructions in Hypertext Markup Language (HTML) that lead to an address where images are stored on some other computer.

Google's search engine accesses thousands of Web sites and indexes them in the Google database. A search query by a user then turns up text, images, or videos.

Google Image Search stores reduced, lower-resolution images or "thumbnails" in its server. When the user clicks on the thumbnail, HTML instructions take you to the computer that stores the full-size version.

And now, herein lies the problem. Webpage-X may have HTML instructions leading to a copyright infringing image but then take the instructions down when threatened with litigation by the owner. Now if you went directly to Webpage-X, you couldn't access the image. But Google's cached copy does not update its version of Webpage-X, and the old HTML instructions would still carry a viewer to the image.

Which Led to Our Fight

Perfect 10 markets copyrighted images of naked women, or "nude models" as they call them. You can only view them in the "members area" of the site, for which they charge a fee, which is how they make money.

Some dastardly Web site operators violated Perfect 10's copyright and posted the lustful vixen photos on their webpages. Presumably they paid for access to Perfect 10 and as paying viewers will do, figured they were entitled to use the images.

Google's voracious search engine indexes the webpages and provides thumbnails of the naked gals. And the thumbnails are stored in Google's servers.

In 2001, Perfect 10 got fed up and told Google to stop doing this. In 2004, they sued.

Why is Amazon in the suit? It's not terribly important from our learner's perspective. Amazon partnered up with Google to in-line link with the Google search engine. A buyer of Amazon books would make literary queries and feel that Amazon was giving the result, when in fact it was the masterful Google search engine. And thus Amazon got dragged in.

Anyhow, the district court gave a preliminary injunction against Google displaying thumbnail versions of Perfect 10's buff sirens, but did not enjoin Google linking to third-party Web sites that had full-size images of said sirens. Neither side was happy, and both appealed.

The issue on appeal for a preliminary injunction is the likelihood of succeeding on the merits at trial, which means you have to go through all the law in advance.

Perfect 10 said Google directly infringed two exclusive rights of a copyright owner: display right and distribution right.

Display Right

17 U.S.C. § 106(5) says a copyright holder has the exclusive right to "display the copyrighted work publicly." Display means "to show a copy of it either directly or by means of a film, slide, television image, or any other device or process.. . ." 17 U.S.C. § 101. Copies are "material objects, other than phonorecords, in which a work is fixed by any method now known or later developed, and from which the work can be perceived, reproduced, or otherwise communicated, either directly or with the aid of a machine or device." *Id.*

The image in the computer is the copy. *See MAI Sys. Corp. v. Peak Computer, Inc.,* 991 F.2d 511, 517-18 (9th Cir. 1993). The computer makes a copy when it transfers the image from another computer into its own memory because it is now fixed so it can be perceived, reproduced, or otherwise communicated.

BUT—and this is a big "but"—Google does not display a full-size copy of the infringing photos when it does in-line linkage. Google does not have any "material objects" in which a work is fixed. Rather, Google has the HTML instructions that direct a browser to the full-size image on someone's webpage.

HTML instructions are lines of text, not images. And the instructions in and of themselves do not make the image appear. They direct the browser to where the images lie.

AND, it is of no relevance that Google is directing a browser to images that the third party has taken down from its Web site. It is the Web site computer that is storing and displaying the image.

But what about those thumbnails Google has cached? Well, yes indeed, under the plain language of the statute, those are copies fixed in a manner "sufficiently permanent or stable to permit it to be perceived, reproduced, or otherwise communicated for a period of more than transitory duration." 17 U.S.C. § 101.

So on this issue, Perfect 10 has shown their prima facie case.

Distribution Right

A copyright owner has the exclusive right "to distribute copies or phonorecords of the copyrighted work to the public by sale or other transfer of ownership, or by rental, lease, or lending." 17 U.S.C. §106(3). Copies are "material objects . . . in which a work is fixed." 17 U.S.C. § 101.

Certainly, copies may be distributed electronically. See *N.Y. Times Co. v. Tasini,* 533 U.S. 483,498 (2001). But Google is not distributing copies. The Web site owner is doing it.

Are you asking, what about Napster and that music swapping–type distribution? *A&M Records, Inc. v. Napster, Inc.,* 239 F.3d 1004 (9th Cir. 2001). Napster users had a complete collection of the music. Google does not own a complete collection of Perfect 10's full-size images.

Fair Use

To get an injunction, Perfect 10 still had to show it could overcome Google's affirmative defense of Fair Use. And that meant going through the toilsome four elements.

Purpose and Character of the Use

Is it commercial or for educational purposes? Is it transformative, adding something new, altering the original with new expression or message?

Google's thumbnails are very transformative. True, it's the same picture. But Google is giving us social benefit by improving access to information on the Internet, not providing artistic expression. The original image created for entertainment is now transformed into an electronic reference tool. Even given that the entire image is used, this does not diminish the transformation as long as it serves a different purpose from the original. *Kelly v. Arriba Soft Corp.* 336 F.3d 811, 818-19.

Nature of the Copyrighted Work

Photos of gals in the buff are "creative in nature" and at the core of what copyright is intended to protect. But Perfect 10's images had been previously published, i.e., on the Perfect 10 pay-to-view Web site.

An author has the right to control where a work is first published. *Harper & Row Publishers, Inc. v. Nation Enters.,* 471 U.S. 539, 564 (1985). This right is exhausted of course once it is published. See, e.g., *Batjac Prods. Inc. v. GoodTimes Home Video Corp.,* 160 F.3d 1223, 1235 (9th Cir. 1998) (noting that such a right "does not entail multiple first publication rights in every available medium") .

The end result was creative, but previously published, therefore only slight weight going to Perfect 10 on this element.

Amount and Substantiality of the Portion Used

For purposes of a search engine, the entire amount of the image must be copied. A viewer has to see the entire image to make a decision about pursuing it further.

Effect of Use on the Market

Thumbnails do not hurt the market for full-size images, particularly when the use of the image is transformative.

So the Ninth Circuit found Perfect 10 unlikely to overcome Google's Fair Use defense and vacated the preliminary injunction against use of the thumbnails.

And this, predictably, will be the outcome of the Google Library litigation: no injury to the market for the copyright covered books and big social benefit. But let's go further.

Bill Graham Archives v. Dorling Kindersley and RR Donnelley & Sons, United States Court of Appeals for the Second Circuit, 448 F.3d 605; 2006 U.S. App. LEXIS 11593 (2006).

In 2003, Dorling Kindersley (DK) published *Grateful Dead: The Illustrated Trip (Illustrated Trip),* a cultural history of—you guessed it—The Grateful Dead with a *double entendre* on LSD. Incredibly, this is a 480-page coffee-table book with 2,000 images. A typical page is a collage of images and graphic art with explanatory text.

Bill Graham (né Wolfgang Grajonca) was the acid rock concert promoter who hosted the nonstop 1965–1970 party at the Fillmore Theatres (East and West) and Winterland—the church of rock and roll. And that means all that poster art for the Paul Butterfield Blues Band, Jefferson Airplane, Buffalo Springfield, Big Brother and the Holding Company, *et al.* Bill has now passed on to that psychedelic party in the sky, but Bill Graham Archives (BGArchives), presumably belonging to his heirs, continues to make money off the sale of posters, original concert tickets, and of course, T-shirts.

BGArchives claims copyright in seven of the concert posters in *Illustrated Trip.* DK tried to negotiate a license, but there was no meeting of the minds. DK went forward with publication. Note that the seven posters are significantly reduced in size and have captions describing the concerts in question.

BGArchives made post-publication demands which were rejected and then sued under the Copyright Act of 1976, 17 U.S.C. § 101 et seq. Each side moved for summary judgment on the issue of fair use, that statutory exception to copyright infringement. BGArchives lost in the district court, and hence the appeal. So let's look at those fair use factors.

Fair Use

Purpose and Character of Use

As in *Perfect 10,* the key to this one is whether the new work is "transformative." *See* Pierre N. Leval, *Toward a Fair Use Standard,* 103 Harv. L. Rev. 1105, 1111 (1990). Does it merely supersede the original, or add something new in the way of character, expression, meaning, or message? *Campbell v. Acuff-Rose Music, Inc.,* 510 U.S. 569, 579 (1994).

The district court found the posters were originally . . . well . . . posters. But *Illustrated Trip* is a biographical work. Placing images in chronological order on a thirty-year timeline is transformatively different from tacking them on a telephone pole to advertise a concert.

Curiously, the poster images of this famous era were themselves extremely transformative, using out of copyright images of Franz Stuck, Alphonse Mucha, *L'Assiette au*

Beurre, and the Jugend school for advertising purposes. Which is to say, almost none of them were actually original art other than the lettering announcing the concerts.

BGArchive of course challenged this, arguing that the images were not transformed unless each was accompanied by comment or criticism. See 17 U.S.C. § 107 (stating that fair use of a copyrighted work "for purposes such as criticism, comment . . . [or] scholarship . . . is not an infringement of copyright").

It is established that fair use can protect the use of copyrighted material in biographies and other forms of historic scholarship, criticism, and comment requiring original source material to properly treat their subjects. "Much of our fair use case law has been generated by the use of quotation in biographies. . . ." *Am. Geophysical Union v. Texaco, Inc.,* 60 F.3d 913, 932 (2d Cir. 1994).

And that goes for pop culture—the glory days of the Fillmore—as well as a biography of Millard Fillmore. See *Twin Peaks Prods., Inc. v. Publ'ns Int'l. Ltd.,* 996 F.2d 1366, 1374 (2d Cir. 1993) (noting that a work that comments about "pop culture" is not removed from the scope of Section 107 simply because it is not erudite).

The Second Circuit found that the posters originally had a dual purpose of artistic expression and promotion. In *Illustrated Trip,* the images are historic artifacts marking particular concerts where . . . well, who can remember exactly what went on at a Dead concert. But this is separate and distinct from the original purpose and thus is transformative. See *Elvis Presley Enters., Inc. v. Passport Video,* 349 F.3d 622, 628-29 (9th Cir. 2003) (finds the use of short clips of Elvis performances are transformative when they are short and a voice-over discusses Elvis' career).

This holding is bolstered by the manner of DK's display. The images were reduced in size so that a mere glimpse of their expressive value is discernible. And they were combined with text, timeline, and original artwork to form a blended collage, enriching the presentation of the cultural history and not exploiting the artwork for commercial gain. Plus, in a 480-page book, there are only seven contested images.

Yes, *Illustrated Trip* was published with the aim of making a profit. But the "crux of the profit/nonprofit distinction is not whether the sole motive of the use is monetary gain but whether the user stands to profit from exploitation of the copyrighted material without paying the customary price" (*Harper & Row Publishers, Inc. v. Nation Enters.,* 471 U.S. 539, 562 (1985)). Which is to say they weren't selling posters or a poster book.

So DK won on that one.

Nature of the Copyrighted Work

Poster art is right at the core of protected creative expression. This would weigh in favor of the copyright holder. But when you've got a transformed work, the second factor is not "likely to help much in separating the fair use sheep from the infringing goats." *See Campbell,* 510 U.S. at 586.

Amount and Substantiality of the Portion Used

Interestingly, the reference is to the amount of the copyrighted work taken (*New Era Publ'ns Int'l, ApS v. Carol Publ'g Group,* 904 F.2d 152, 159 (2d Cir. 1990)). So smothering seven posters in 480 pages doesn't help DK. And of course, each of the seven was taken in its entirety.

All the same, it is sometimes necessary to copy the entire work to make a fair use of it (*Kelly v. Arriba Soft Corp.,* 336 F.3d 811, 821 (9th Cir. 2003)); images used for a search engine data base must be copied entirely to be recognized). So factor 3 turns on a reference back to factor 1, purpose and character of the use (*Campbell,* 510 U.S. at 586-87).

And back there, the court concluded the images were historical artifacts and by reducing the size, DK displayed the minimal image necessary to ensure they were recognized as historic artifacts.

Effect of the Use upon the Market for or Value of the Original

As your mom said, what if everyone did it? You look not just at market harm, but harm that could result from widespread use in *Illustrated Trip* fashion. *Harper,* 471 U.S. at 568.

And just to make it more complicated, we balance public benefit from the use with "personal gain the copyright owner will receive if the use denied." *MCA, Inc. v. Wilson,* 677 F.2d 180, 183 (2d Cir. 1981).

There was no effect on poster sales, BGArchives' primary market. But what about a derivative market in licensing the images for use in books?

"[I]t is a given in every fair use case that plaintiff suffers a loss of a potential market if that potential is defined as the theoretical market for licensing the very use at bar." Melville B. Nimmer & David Nimmer, *Nimmer on Copyright* § 13.05[A][4] (2005). But what is to be considered the loss of potential licensing revenues for "traditional, reasonable, or likely to be developed markets." *Am. Geophysical Union v. Texaco, Inc.,* 60 F.3d 913, 930 (2d Cir. 1994).

And then, the Second Circuit again went back to factor 1. and said DK's use is a transformative one. The market is a transformative market (collage-type books) and not a traditional one (poster reproduction). A copyright owner cannot bar others from a fair use market "by developing or licensing a market for parody, news reporting, educational or other transformative uses of its own creative work." *Castle Rock Entm't, Inc. v. Carol Publ'g Group,* 150 F3d 132, 146 (2d Cir. 1998).

So BGArchive did not suffer market harm from the loss of license fees, and DK won.

Andrea Blanch v. Jeff Koons, the Solomon R. Guggenheim Foundation, and Deutsche, **United States Court of Appeals for the Second Circuit, 467 F.3d 244; 2006 U.S. App. LEXIS 26786 (2006).**

Still in the Second Circuit, we find Deutsche Bank AG commissioned a collage by the artist Jeff Koons which was later displayed at the Guggenheim, where it was spotted by the plaintiff Andrea Blanch.

Jeff Koons is an artist known for the celebration of kitsch culture. He is the third most highly paid artist in the world and received $2 million for the work that is the subject of this suit. He incorporates images from pop culture and consumer advertising into his pictures. This is called "neo-Pop art" or, when Jeff is being sued, "appropriation art." This is to say that his sculptures and paintings frequently contain recognizable toys, celebrities, and iconic cartoon figures.

Jeff got whacked in previous litigation for his exhibition "Banality Show" which included three-dimensional reproductions of images from postcards and comic strips. He didn't bother to seek permission and two district courts held it not fair use. *See Rogers v. Koons,* 960 F.2d 301 (2d Cir.), cert. denied, 506 U.S. 934 (1992); *United Feature Syndicate v. Koons,* 817 F. Supp. 370 (S.D.N.Y. 1993).

Undeterred, Jeff Painted On

The Deutsche commissioned work is titled "Easyfun-Ethereal." There are seven billboard-sized canvasses of images culled from advertisements, scanned into a computer, and digitally superimposed over his own photos of pastoral landscapes to then be transposed and painted onto canvas.

"Niagara" has Niagara Falls as a backdrop with four pairs of women's feet and legs dangling over a chocolate fudge brownie topped with ice cream, a tray of donuts and a tray of apple Danish pastries. Jeff calls this a comment on our basic appetites for food, play, and sex "mediated by popular images."

The legs from "Niagara" came from ads and fashion magazines. One was from a photo by big-time photographer Andrea Blanch, whose work can be found in Revlon, Johnny Walker, and Valentino ads.

Andrea's Niagara legs were lifted from *Allure* magazine, an ad titled "Silk Sandals by Gucci." There the legs were resting on a man's lap in first class airplane seats. Koons only used the legs.

Andrea admitted that she has never licensed any of her photos subsequent to the original use, and the market value of "Silk Sandals" did not decrease because of Jeff's money-making shenanigans.

Can Jeff Get By with This?

Andrea sued, and the district court granted summary judgment to the defendants on the theory of fair use. It went up on appeal to the Second Circuit.

The court led off with a Judge Leval quote that the monopoly protection for the individual author is all very well, but "excessively broad protection would stifle, rather than advance, the [law's] objective." Pierre N. Leval, Toward a Fair Use Standard, 103 Harv. L. Rev. 1105, 1108 (1990) (quoting *Harper & Row Publishers, Inc. v. Nation Enters.,* 471 U.S. 539, 545-46 (1985)).

Fair Use was codified in the Copyright Act of 1976 with four nonexclusive factors. The U.S. Supreme Court has warned that fair use determination has no bright-line rules and the four factors "thus provide only general guidance about the sorts of copying that courts and Congress most commonly had found to be fair uses." *Campbell v. Acuff-Rose Music, Inc.,* 510 U.S. 569, 577-78 (1994).

Purpose and Character of the Use

1. First, there's the transformative issue. Does it supersede the original creation or add something new? *Id.* 510 U.S. at 579.

It's not transformative merely because one was a photo and the other a painting or one for a magazine and the other for a museum. See *Castle Rock Entm't Inc. v. Carol Publ'g Group, Inc.,* 150 F.3d 132, 142-43 (2d Cir. 1998) ("Seinfeld Aptitude Test" quiz book not transformative when purpose was "to repackage [the TV show] Seinfeld to entertain Seinfeld viewers") ; *Ringgold v. Black Entm't Television, Inc.,* 126 F.3d 70, 79 (2d Cir. 12997) (copy of plaintiff's painting used as decoration for a TV program's set not transformative because it was used for "the same decorative purpose" as the original).

But Koons's work was indeed transformative. His objective was not to repackage "Silk Sandals" but to employ it. "I want the viewer to think about his/her personal experience with these objects, products, and images and at the same time gain new insight into how these affect our lives." Koons Aff. At P4.

While Blanch "wanted to show some sort of erotic sense . . . to get . . . more of a sexuality to the photographs." Blanch Dep. At 112-13.

Which if you can follow that seems to say that Blanch was creating mass media and Koons was commenting on the aesthetic consequences of said media. Hence, Koons won on the transformative issue.

2. Is it for commerce or for nonprofit education purposes? 17 U.S.C. § 107(1). Well, Jeff is pretty much into commerce, no matter how you dress it up in *ArtSpeak.*

American Geophysical Union v. Texaco, 60 F.3d 913 (2d Cir. 1994) dealt with commercial exploitation via photocopying which was not transformative. But *Campbell* held that commercial use in itself is only a subfactor, and the more transformative, the less commerce will hold weight. *Campbell,* 510 U.S. at 584. Koons's work was not a market replacement for "Silk Sandals." Koon's take-home loot did not exclude the broader public benefits of art.

3. Parody and satire justify copying, which was the whole *Campbell* issue. In satire, "prevalent follies or vices are assailed with ridicule." 14 Oxford English Dictionary, at 500. If Koons is satirizing anything, it's the genre of the photo and not the photo itself.

"By using a fragment of the *Allure* photograph in my painting, I thus comment upon the culture and attitudes promoted and embodied in *Allure Magazine.* By using an existing image, I also ensure a certain authenticity or veracity that enhances my commentary—it is the difference between quoting and paraphrasing—and ensure that viewers will understand what I am referring to." Koons Aff. at p.12.

So where are we? "Niagara" is transformative. It's not truly commercial exploitation, and commerciality is not dispositive anyhow. So Koons won this one.

Nature of the Copyrighted Work

Expressive or creative works are closer to the core of what copyright law intended to protect than factual works. Which isn't to say that nonfiction isn't protected. It's just got a whole bunch of facts between two covers, and only the expressive part is protected.

The district court had called "Silk Sandals" "banal rather than creative." The appeals court disagreed with that, but it doesn't matter when a creative work is transformed into another creative one.

Amount and Substantiality of the Portion Used

Are the quantity, quality and value of the portion used "reasonable in relation to the purpose of copying"? *Campbell,* 510 U.S. 586.

Koons has explained his reasons for using preexisting images vis-à-vis his artistic goals. Did he do it excessively? Did he go beyond his justified purpose?

Of importance to Blanch was the first-class airplane cabin and laying the legs across those of a presumed high-roller alpha-male who paid for the tickets. Koons trimmed all that out, leaving this issue in his favor. But the court said this was not a heavy factor in their final decision.

Market Effects

Does this impact the potential market for "Silk Sandals"? Does this usurp the "Silk Sandals" market? Well, Blanch admitted there was no secondary market for her works, and "Niagara" did not decrease the market for "Silk Sandals." So Koons took round four.

And the holding went to Koons and will doubtless be in favor of Google as well.

Google Library transforms under copyright books into a reference tool such as the world has never seen before giving us huge social benefit. Google is in commerce, but the reference tool has a wide educational use. The snippets of the books take no more than is absolutely necessary for a reference tool and do not supplant the market for the book itself. Indeed, they actually encourage the purchase of the book.

DIRECTING THE SWARM: LIBRARIES, INFORMATION ORGANIZATIONS, AND THE FUTURE OF INFORMATION

Adam Wathen, Interim Head, Collections Services Department, K-State Libraries, Kansas State University, Manhattan, Kansas

Abstract

Libraries are not the only organizations with a stake in the development of new information publishing, distribution, and access models. Other groups have different ideas about the future of information. These ideas push progress in a variety of directions, creating tensions between stakeholders. The way these groups relate and move toward goals is like the way an insect swarm moves chaotically toward its goal. By creating strategic partnerships, libraries can increase their influence over the future of information. I will present:

the swarm as a model of relationships between stakeholders and their chaotic movement toward goals

examples of attempts to direct the swarm (like Google Library Project and Portico)

some tensions between stakeholders and how "coopetition" can sway outcomes

Libraries are only one group of many that have a stake in the future of information policy. We share a core mission with information industry groups as vastly different as movie studios, television networks, music companies, newspapers, news media, search engine companies, cellular telephone companies, advertising agencies, popular and academic publishers, governments, and others. Each of these groups has a similar mission: to connect people with information.

Inherently, these groups have different intentions in their dissemination of information. Some of them, like libraries, try to connect people with the information they seek. Others are intentional about the information they push to their users. As well, in each case, these groups have different biases toward how information policy should be developed in the future. We see the stakes and stakeholders play out in policy battles. For instance,

- The Disney Corporation contributed over $6.3 million in lobbying money in 1997–98 in an effort to influence congress to pass the Copyright Term Extension Act which preserved copyright of Mickey Mouse's image for twenty more years (Sprigman, 2002).

- The Recording Industry Association of America (RIAA) is extremely interested in digital rights management and copyright law. So much so, that it has filed lawsuits against college students who continue to share music files (Valencia, 2008).

- Libraries have mobilized against the federal government's push to see patron checkout records by intentionally not maintaining patron circulation records and finding ways to preserve the right for patrons to check out materials anonymously (Flanders, 2008).

- Concerns are continuously raised about the quality of news information coming out of seemingly politically biased news organizations (Hickey).

- In November 2007, Yahoo.com executive Vice President Michael Callahan apologized for misleading U.S. lawmakers about how Yahoo provided private e-mail information to

China's government to help convict a Chinese reporter to a ten-year sentence for leaking state secrets (Reuters, 2007).

- Finally, Bill Hannay's presentation in this conference about legal mergers in information companies indicated that Thomson-Reuters and Reed-Elsevier understand their stake in developing information policy that favors their situations (Hannay, 2007).

With these kinds of competing interests, the direction of information policy is extraordinarily complex. However, through organization and participation, libraries can have significant influence on information policy.

We Are Part of the Information Industry Swarm

In many ways, the way bees relate to one another in a swarm or fish in their schools is a good metaphor for the relationships between information organizations and their competing interests. Swarm theory can provide a good model for understanding how libraries can position themselves in the chaotic fight for information policy development.

Swarm Theory says that in collective systems (like ant colonies, bird flocks, fish schools, and beehives), individuals don't have to understand the big picture to have an impact on the outcome of decisions for the group. Each member contributes to the direction of the group whether or not that member is intentionally guiding the group toward a goal. Bees follow cues from other bees to know how to act. No master bee is directing the swarm to a new hive or changing the amount of pollen gathered. The individuals, through their actions, create a collective "intelligence" that drives the group toward its destination (Miller, 2007).

In his book *Out of Control: The New Biology of Machines, Social Systems, and the Economic World*, Kevin Kelly describes "swarm systems" as being self-directing, chaotically organized systems in which the members flow along with the swarm to accomplish tasks. He calls these systems "distributed systems" which have no central decision-making body but make decisions as a group in a chaotic way to direct the swarm towards its end. The swarm system is the polar opposite of what we usually strive for in libraries—a linear, controlled workflow.

The relationships between the information organizations identified above are analogous to the relationships between members of a swarm. Kevin Kelly outlines four distinct facets of swarm-like systems:

- "Absence of imposed centralized control"
  - Information organizations are not subject to centralized control. Universally agreed upon standards are few and far between, and are rarely imposed. Even government regulations are limited to specific industries and vary nationally, regionally, and locally. These regulations can be seen as analogous to the environmental restrictions which impact the reactions and direction of swarms (weather conditions, physical landscape, physical laws, etc.). We have the opportunity to influence the regulations which exist and to have intentional impact on the controls to which our "swarm" is subject.

- "Autonomous nature of subunits"

  - Each organization in the information industry swarm has the opportunity to make its own decisions and carve out its own future. These organizations are independent enough from one another that even different libraries in the same library system have a strong amount of autonomy.

- "High connectivity between the subunits"

  - Many influences and trends tie these information organizations together. Information industry groups band together through membership in organizational associations. They informally connect through shared markets and regulations. The interrelationship between media outlets, cultural demand for technology and information, and technological innovation also significantly ties these information organizations together. However, the connectivity that exists in a school of fish or a colony of ants is a much stronger bond than exists between information industry members.

- "Webby nonlinear causality of peers influencing peers"

  - Information organizations exist in an ecosystem of regulations, technology, influence, supply and demand, and choice. Change in one of these organizations impacts other parts of the organization, members of the industry, and other information industries. For example, the development of GIS data systems in the last ten years has changed the way people use technologies. GIS changes married to other technological innovation like Google Maps, cellular phones, and package tracking has created new (and arguably emergent) technologies and marketplace expectations.

Kelly also outlines attributes of swarms which help describe how they function, as follows:

Swarm systems can be extraordinarily **adaptable.** Swarms have the potential to react to any stimulus (and all stimuli) because they have no dedicated, linear procedures. There is very little predictability in the way a swarm might react to any certain stimulus, because the reaction isn't directed by a single bee, the reaction is the reaction of the group.

The swarm is **evolvable.** The "hive mind" learns from its mistakes and changes. Linear systems don't—they work from the assumption that the linear process is a static entity that needs to be insulated from outside stimuli so that it remains stable despite these stimuli. Reaction to outside stimulus in the linear system demands the reevaluation of the process, whereas outside stimulus of the swarm creates the potential for evolution. The swarm does not react the same way to the same stimulus multiple times because of its variety and the changing nature of its members.

The swarm is **resilient.** Swarms are built out of redundancy, so small failures don't result in the failure of the entire process. As in an infantry assault where losses of some troops are expected and anticipated, the swarm doesn't concern itself with the individual but with the collective and how that collective moves toward a destination. Individuals in the swarm are expendable which allows for the swarm itself to move forward.

Swarms are **boundless.** Linear systems contain the potential to carry out the task for which they were designed. A process to make a milk bottle cap only produces a milk bottle cap—there is no room for it to create something else. Swarms, however, have no structure.

Life in the swarm breeds more life. Information breeds more information. Participation creates potential. The more factors that have a chance to impact an outcome, the less predictable the outcome. And, the more participation in swarm systems, the more potential they have (see "emergent" below).

Swarms contain **novelty.** They are made of many unique individuals, and their differences compound the potential of the group. The potential for newness comes from the variety within the swarm. Linear systems force individuals to conform to the guidelines of the system instead of allowing them to have free will or different styles. Allowing chaos within the system allows potential.

Maybe the most important attribute of the swarm is that it is **emergent.** This is the power of the network and of scalability. In the swarm "more is more than more . . . it's different" (Kelly, 1995). Emergent properties can only be developed because of group action. One molecule doesn't provide temperature; it is a result of a population of molecules together which can be precisely measured. One snowflake doesn't cause an avalanche. It is the product of billions of snowflakes together that creates the potential for an avalanche. One drop of water can't create a whirlpool. Often, the more participation in a swarm system the more potential it holds to develop emergent properties.

Emergent properties can be seen in the swarm of the social Internet. The development of millions of tags in Flickr or LibraryThing creates a swarm-like effect. Thousands of people using these tools in concert, bringing their own biases, their own differences, and their own values creates chaos. And, in that chaos, there is no centralized control or decision-making. The users determine the direction in the world of the social Internet.

In this sense, the organization of the social Internet is based on values of trust and participation. The lack of a centralized decision-making body increases the need for users to trust the whole. Users trust the system to produce whether or not the members are individually trustworthy. For example, the value of tagging is in the emergent trends in tags which help describe content. If one user intentionally tags content inappropriately (tagging an image of a baby as "squid") the overall impact is minimized because the group has developed trends in the volume of tags which relegate unusual tags to a place of less prominence. As well, it is in this variety that the potential for the emergent exists—there is no right or wrong in tagging and the direction of the group is developed within the context of that variety.

Directing the Swarm: How Libraries Can Be Intentional about Our Course

With some framing and intentionality libraries can impact the future of information policy. Individuals and organizations can make intentional choices which can guide the swarm. This is illustrated in a scene toward the end of the Disney/Pixar movie *Finding Nemo* (2003). A fishing boat catches a large school of fish, and Nemo, one of the main characters, is also caught up in the net. Nemo rallies the chaotic swarm of fish in the net by organizing them—telling them to "swim down." The chaos of the fish school moves against the pull of the net, and the power of the group working in unison succeeds in breaking the winch arm. Subsequently all the fish are freed.

To use an example from a Disney/Pixar movie where talking fish are organizing chaos to accomplish miracles is, of course, a bit fantastic, but the example is still worth something to us in reality. Libraries can learn to coordinate our efforts to direct our own swarm and change the future of information policy.

The chaos inherent in swarm systems creates an extraordinary amount of unfocused energy. It is in the movement toward the linear where this energy begins to be channeled toward a goal. Unfortunately, the tighter we try to control this energy, the less creativity and potential for emergence exists. The beauty of the Grand Canyon emerged from the relatively loosely channeled waters of the Colorado River. The Alaskan pipeline controls the flow of oil and has no potential to create its own path. In coordination of library efforts we can create enough intentional direction to the chaotic energy to produce results. With too much control, we kill the potential of the swarm.

Libraries have been coordinating efforts in remarkable ways by collaborating with like-minded organizations. We are entering into strategic partnerships and projects like Google Book Search in which Google is digitizing millions of volumes of library content in collaboration with libraries all over the world. This effort is one which is changing the way that libraries serve information, people access information, and how information is organized.

Portico was established as collaboration between JSTOR, Ithaka, the Library of Congress, and the Andrew W. Mellon Foundation to preserve core electronic scholarly literature. By assuming an archival role for this information, Portico has had far-reaching impact on the academic library community. Faculty members have begun to change the way they view the reliability of digital versions of their local academic library collections. Libraries have freed up tens of thousands of linear feet of space in academic libraries previously housed by archived Portico titles. And Portico has indirectly helped the academic library to be allowed to shift its role from storehouse to become more proactive and creative with its space and services.

Libraries also are beginning to play a stronger role in Open Access initiatives. They are collaborating with publishers and faculty to facilitate the creation, access, and dissemination of information in new ways. Libraries are taking on new roles in the information marketplace. They are changing the direction of information dissemination (and the direction of the information swarm) by taking steps to control academic publishing.

Library advocacy groups are helping to organize the future of information by facilitating the ideals of open information every day. Organizations like iBiblio (http://www.ibiblio.org), PLoS (http://www.plos.org), Creative Commons (http://creativecommons.org), Talis (http://www.talis.com), and the Public Knowledge Project (http://pkp.sfu.ca) are shaping policies which further library interests. Libraries should seek out these organizations, support them, and find ways to integrate their missions into our organizations because building these relationships builds momentum in the right direction.

The information swarm isn't just libraries swimming in the midst of information industry sharks who stop at nothing to have information policy swayed in their favor. Things are never so black and white. Many of these organizations are intentionally cooperating with libraries and with each other despite being, at times, in direct competition. Collaboration between directly competing organizations in an attempt to expand the marketplace is termed "coopetition." Examples include Microsoft and Apple sharing resources to develop common software and Toyota and Peugot teaming up to build a city car for Europe in 2005 (Wikipedia, n.d.).

Libraries are in competition with any organization that intentionally seeks to hide or firewall information. Libraries should seek to create as much access as possible for researchers and users, and firewalled information is invisible, inaccessible information. In this sense, I see very little coopetition between libraries and organizations like these.

Peripheral to the library community, the coopetition between publishers and vendors is worth noting. Vendors are participating in collaborative experiments to help push library-publisher-vendor relationships forward. The Colorado Alliance of Research Libraries is testing consortial approval plans with both YBP and Blackwell Book Service. Although YBP and Blackwell are not working directly together, this seems to be a fertile field in which vendors could expand their marketplace and a chance for libraries to influence the way that publishers and vendors think about information dissemination.

WorldCat Selection Service truly has the potential to bring vendors into the same forum to directly compete. And vendors have signed on (although sometimes hesitantly). This looks even more like coopetition between library vendors. But until participation in WorldCat Selection Service reaches critical mass and WorldCat Selection Service effectively integrates vendor workflows into library workflows, the potential of WorldCat Selection Service to create new library relationships around resource acquisitions is constrained.

Directing the Swarm Means Participating

Libraries have the opportunity to make an impact in the information swarm more now than ever. The opportunities created by the social web, new information dissemination technologies, and new roles for libraries in information creation are astounding. We can leverage the power of our new networks and connectivity to channel the chaos and to mobilize our disparate and often disempowered voices.

This call to arms is reminiscent of grassroots movements in which disaffected people rally their voices to change the world—one person at a time. As in grassroots movements, the power of scalability and the ability for one voice to have an impact are meaningful in directing the swarm. Swarm models show that small impacts are impactful all the same and that emergent qualities grow from the compounding of multitudes of small impacts to have an extraordinary amount of power.

So, act! Make a small impact. Draw up local policies. Share them. Join your voice to the cacophony of voices in the swarm. It is not the responsibility of other libraries advocate for the future of libraries and library values; it is the responsibility of each of us to be intentional about adding to the movement of the swarm—to be intentional about directing the swarm.

References

Finding Nemo. (2003). Dir. Andrew Stanton and Lee Unkrich. DVD. Buena Vista.

Flanders, Bruce. (2008, January 17). *Patriot Act and the Lawrence Public Library*. Retrieved from http://www.lawrence.lib.ks.us/policies/patriot.html.

Hannay, Bill (presenter). (2007, November 9). *Media Publishing Giants: Can They Get Even Bigger?* XXVII Annual Charleston Conference: Issues in Book and Serial Acquisition.

Hickey, Neil. (1998). "Is Fox News Fair?" *Columbia Journalism Review* 36, no. 6. Retrieved from http://backissues.cjrarchives.org/year/98/2/fox.asp.

Kelly, Kevin. (1995). *Out of Control: The New Biology of Machines, Social Systems, and the Economic World.* Cambridge, MA: Perseus. http://kk.org/outofcontrol/.

Miller, Peter. (2007, July). "Swarm Theory." *National Geographic.* Retrieved from http://ngm.nationalgeographic.com/ngm/0707/feature5/.

Reuters. (2007, Nov. 2). "Yahoo Exec Apologizes to U.S. Lawmakers on China: report." http://www.reuters.com/articlePrint?articleId=USN0252347720071102

Sprigman, Chris. (2002). *The Mouse That Ate Copyright: Disney, the Copyright Term Extension Act, and* Eldred v. Ashcroft. Retrieved from http://writ.news.findlaw.com/commentary/20020305_sprigman.html

Valencia, Andrew. (2008, January 24). "RIAA Demands Fines from 15 Students." *The Stanford Daily.* Retrieved from http://daily.stanford.edu/article/2008/1/24/riaaDemandsFinesFrom15Students.

Wikipedia. (n.d.). *Coopetition.* Retrieved from http://en.wikipedia.org/wiki/Coopetition.

INDEX